1888

London Murders in the Year of the Ripper

PETER STUBLEY

D1440178

The History Press

~ The Author ~

Peter Stubley is a crime journalist who has spent the last ten years covering murder cases at the Old Bailey. He is also the founder of the London murder map (www.murdermap.co.uk).

First published 2012

The History Press
The Mill, Brimscombe Port
Stroud, Gloucestershire, GL5 2QG
www.thehistorypress.co.uk

British Library Cataloguing in Publication Data.
A catalogue record for this book is available from the British Library.

ISBN 978 0 7524 6543 2

Typesetting and origination by The History Press
Printed in Great Britain

CONTENTS

Prologue

1 JANUARY, 1888

As the church bells rang in the New Year across central London, a woman lay dying. Her left arm had been sawn off and her face was swollen with bruising to her forehead and right eye. Elizabeth Gibbs was slowly succumbing to shock and exhaustion despite the efforts of the medical staff at St George's Hospital in Hyde Park. Outside the temperature was dropping towards - 4° Celsius and the frost lay so thickly on houses, trees and roads that it appeared as if snow had fallen. The capital was in the middle of its coldest winter for thirty years. Later that morning thousands of people would swarm across the frozen ponds and lakes of the city, happy to risk a cold bath when the ice gave way. Life droned on regardless as Elizabeth Gibbs slipped away at 2 p.m. that afternoon, becoming the first homicide victim of 1888. [1]

By the end of the year the police would count a total of 122 cases, of which twenty-eight were classed as murder and ninety-four as manslaughter. More than half of the victims were female, and eight were said to be of the 'unfortunate' class, living on the margins of existence by selling their bodies for a few pennies at a time. Five of those eight are generally accepted to have been the victims of a single serial killer who would never be identified, let alone arrested or put on trial. The newspapers called him Jack the Ripper, and were only too happy to promote the legend to help make them a profit. And it did so, handsomely. But among the acres of newsprint devoted to the unknown murderer, the Victorian public would have read reports of other victims who would not be remembered over 100 years later. Some of these cases would be mentioned in Parliament and in the pages of *The Times*, but they were far less sensational when compared to a knife-wielding maniac loose on the streets with a lust for blood.[2]

Elizabeth Gibbs was one of these other homicide victims, a respectable married woman living in the wealthy area of Belgravia, on a road that was home to Alfred Tennyson, Ian Fleming and Mozart over the years. She was sixty-eight years old and was enjoying a pleasant walk along Grosvenor Place, near Buckingham Palace, when she was knocked down and run over by a horse-driven van carrying bottles of mineral water. Her arm was so seriously injured that it had to be amputated by a surgeon in an unsuccessful attempt to save her life. Following her death, police charged a forty-three-year-old delivery driver from Shoreditch called Alfred Winwood with manslaughter. Winwood was convicted and sentenced to six months' hard labour.

It is just one story among dozens from 1888, and the cast list includes all ranks and classes of society from every corner of the city; from the unnamed newborns dumped on the street to the seventy-one-year-old retired major shot dead at his front door, and the Jewish immigrant working for slave wages in the East End to the Englishwoman living in relative comfort in the West End.

Murder is the ultimate crime, and a particularly shocking one can attract the attention of Queens and prime ministers and help bring about real change. On the other hand, some suspected murders were virtually ignored by the press and public because they were so commonplace in nineteenth-century Britain. But each case can illuminate hidden parts of society and provide colour to those areas well charted in textbooks. Not just by telling the stories of the victims and their killers but also the places that the two met, the cause of death, the action or inaction of the police and the prosecuting authorities, and the reactions of judges and juries. The historian Richard Cobb wrote that 'famous murder trials light up the years and give a more precise sense of period than the reigns of monarchs or the terms of office of presidents'. What might be called 'murderography' has the potential to describe a specific period of time better than any other kind of historical study. This book aims to use the stories of those victims of homicide in one year in late-Victorian London to illustrate the period, and to hopefully give an impression of what it might have been like to live through one of the most exciting eras in our history. [3]

At this time the British Empire was at the height of its influence and power – economically, politically and culturally. London was its capital, and therefore the capital of the world. Its inhabitants included: Florence Nightingale; H.G. Wells; George Bernard Shaw; Arthur Conan Doyle; Oscar Wilde; the American author Henry James; a young student by the name of Gandhi; the Elephant Man, Joseph Merrick; a six-year-old Virginia Woolf; and the fourteen-year-old Winston Churchill. And ruling over all was Queen Victoria, Empress of India, who had celebrated her Golden Jubilee in the summer of 1887 with a vast procession through the streets, and a banquet for kings and princes from across the world. The affection and loyalty of her subjects was obvious. One of the spectators that day summed up the general mood by writing in her diary: 'We are filled with enthusiasm and loyalty. What an Empire! What a City! What an Age! What a Queen!' [4]

Queen Victoria had celebrated the arrival of 1888 by remembering the previous twelve months as being 'so full of the marvellous kindness, loyalty and devotion of so many millions'. She wrote in her journal that there was 'not one mishap or disturbance, not one bad day ... never never can I forget this brilliant year.' But twelve months later her mood was very different. This time she marked 'the last day of this dreadful year, which has brought mourning and sorrow to so many, and such misfortunes, and ruined the happiness of my darling child'.[5] Although the Queen was referring mainly to the death of her son-in-law, the German Emperor Frederick III, there had been little to celebrate in 1888. The economy was still struggling through a depression which began in the 1870s, protestors continued to take to the streets, workers went on strike, and the population was gripped by moral panic over a series of murders without parallel in history. For this was the Year of the Ripper.

1

JOURNEY TO THE
CENTRE OF THE EARTH

The RMS *Ormuz* was the fastest ship in the world. It was 482ft long, 52ft wide, and weighed more than 6,000 tons but its 8,500hp steam engines could propel it halfway round the globe in less than four weeks. Not so many years earlier the same trip would have taken three months. It was equipped with berths for nearly 400 passengers – 106 in first class, 170 in second and 120 in steerage – as well as two saloons, two promenade decks, a library, a drawing room, a coffee room, two smoking rooms and a hospital. No wonder that its proud owners, the Orient Line, had seen fit to boast: 'Were the world a ring of gold, *Ormuz* would be its diamond.' But for John King it was just a means of getting home.[6]

The thirty-nine-year-old chemical engineer was making the voyage from Australia to London with mixed emotions. Just four months earlier, in April 1888, he had arrived in Sydney with high hopes of finding his fortune in the fabled 'workers' paradise'. The auspices had seemed favourable, for that year marked the centenary of the first landing of 1,350 colonists at Sydney Cove. Alas, it had not worked out as he expected and he had decided to return home to his wife,

Mary, and their two young children, eight-year-old John Jr and seven-year-old Alice, in Rutherglen, Lanarkshire, not far from Glasgow and the Govan shipyards where the *Ormuz* was built in 1886.

His journey took nearly seven weeks. After leaving Sydney on 1 August 1888, the *Ormuz* called first at Melbourne and Adelaide before sailing across the Indian Ocean towards Egypt, passing from the Southern Hemisphere to the Northern and leaving the Southern Cross behind. At Suez they took on more coal for the engines before navigating the 86 mile-long canal between the Red Sea and the Mediterranean.[7] After stopping off at Naples the ship rounded Spain, battled through the gales and stormy seas of the Bay of Biscay and gave its passengers their first sight of England through the fog at Plymouth. Two days later it was powering against the flow of the Thames towards the city at the heart of the British Empire. London, a metropolis of more than 5 million inhabitants, was also the symbolic centre of the world, where east meets west at zero degrees longitude.[8]

Finally, on the morning of 11 September 1888, the ship pulled into Tilbury Docks in Essex; it had been built two years earlier at a staggering cost of £2 million.[9] John King stepped on to dry land and began the final leg of his journey by train, first from Tilbury to Fenchurch Street station, and then from St Pancras to Glasgow. It was a far less glamorous arrival than that of a foreign student from Bombay two weeks later. Mohandas Karamchand Gandhi sauntered off the SS *Clyde* in a white flannel suit purchased specially for the purpose. Gandhi wrote in his autobiography: 'I found I was the only person wearing such clothes … the shame of being the only person in white clothes was already too much for me.' Gandhi travelled by train to the luxury Victoria Hotel, and quickly bought a new outfit and a 19s chimney-pot hat at the Army & Navy Stores, determined to appear the quintessential 'English gentleman' during his three-year law course at the University of London.[10]

By the time John King arrived at the impressive red-bricked edifice of St Pancras station he was part of a merry band of twelve fellow passengers from the *Ormuz*. Most of them were already drunk and singing loudly as they crammed on board the 9.15 p.m. night train to Glasgow. Joining King in one of the third-class compartments were three fellow Scotsmen: John Mattison and Charles Lee, who had both worked on board as firemen, and twenty-two-year-old stowaway James McKill, the son of a chemist from Hamilton.[11]

Such was their state of intoxication that nobody could remember what exactly started the argument between King and McKill. 'They seemed as if they were going to take off their coats,' remembered John Mattison, 'I don't know whether they did.' Mattison got out at the next stop and joined his crewmate Charles Lee in the other carriage. From that point everything became a little hazy. He woke up the next morning in the Leicester Royal Infirmary, having accidentally headbutted the window, smashing the glass and cutting his head in the process. Another, more sober, witness believed the argument was between King and Mattison, although McKill had certainly offered to fight anyone who felt they were up to the challenge. King's pockets were bulging with bottles, which he claimed were lemonade. The whisky was in his baggage, he said, but there was no time to retrieve it before the train set off. Whatever the truth, from Kentish Town onwards King and McKill were alone together in the same compartment. When the train reached the next stop at Bedford only McKill remained, lying full length on the seat, dozing. When they reached Glasgow the next morning, nobody noticed that John King had gone missing.

At 6 a.m., about 100 yards from Finchley Road station in north London, a signalman found two shirts and a cap by the side of the tracks. John Cockayne checked there was nothing in them before going on duty. Just over an hour later, three-quarters of a mile down the track towards London, platelayer William Franklin was walking through the Belsize tunnel carrying out an inspection of the line. Near one of the air shafts, half a mile from the London end, he saw a body between the rails and the wall. Its head was missing. Or rather about two-thirds of it had been sheared off and bits of brain and jaw had been scattered over the tracks. Further up the tunnel Franklin also saw a mark on the slimy black brick wall, as if a finger had been drawn along it. The mark began at a height of 7ft 4in and gradually dropped over a distance of about 10ft, at which point it seemed as if the body had collided with the wall, tumbling over and over for another 28ft before coming to rest. Franklin alerted the stationmaster before returning to the scene to move the body to the platform at Haverstock Hill to await the arrival of the police.

Inspector Somers of the Y Division quickly established that the dead man was John King. In a pocket was a ticket to Glasgow, a number of letters, a silver watch and chain, and two purses containing £3 9s 3d, along with papers indicating he had just come from Australia. His clothes and hands were black with muck from the tunnel, but there was no blood on them, and only a small tear to the left sleeve of the coat. Other than the catastrophic damage to the head there were only a few other small scuff marks on the knee and thigh. The doctor who examined him saw no evidence of any struggle. He had certainly not been robbed. Everything pointed to a tragic accident. There was also a suggestion that King had wanted to get two bottles of whisky from the luggage compartment further down the carriage, but did not have time at St Pancras station. Had he made a foolhardy attempt to retrieve his whisky by clambering along the side of the train? The jury at the inquest at St Pancras Coroner's Court seemed to think so, and after commending the police returned a verdict of accidental death.

The twist in the tale came only a few days later when the story appeared in the *Scottish Reader* newspaper. Hugh Mickle, a greengrocer from Kilmarnock, read the report and realised that he had been on that very same train with his friend George Cowan. They had entered a third-class smoking carriage and started a conversation with a young man on his way to Glasgow. This fellow was keen to talk, mentioning how he had just come off the boat from the Colonies. Tall stories, mostly. But one of his yarns was particularly memorable – earlier in the journey he had got in a fight with a stranger and had thrown him out of the train. He then took off his shirts because they were torn and stained with blood and threw them out the window as well. 'I asked him what the gentleman was like,' said Mickle. 'He said he was a gruff sort of man, stouter than himself.' Mickle declined the offer of a swig from the man's bottle and noticed that the passenger had a bruise on his right cheek. There were also small bloodstains on the window next to the platform and on the floor. 'He said he had got a blow on his mouth from the strange man,' Cowan later recalled, 'and that the blood came from a spit out of his mouth.' The two friends from Kilmarnock advised the traveller to try to wash his face and get a shirt before he went home to see his mother. They hadn't taken his boasts at all seriously and parted with him on good terms at St Enoch's station in Glasgow half an hour later. 'He told us a good many yarns,' said Cowan. 'In fact I put it down as a yarn from first to last.' Yet now that they knew of events further down the line in London, it seemed that this was a case of murder.

Thirty-four years earlier the first-ever murder on a British railway had caused uproar in the press – Thomas Briggs had been beaten about the head, robbed and dumped out of a train in Hackney, east London. Due to the subsequent chase of the suspect across the Atlantic, the case had been an international sensation. When the killer Franz Muller was arrested he was carrying Mr Briggs' gold watch and his hat. Muller's own, cheaper, hat had been discarded. By contrast, the case of John King was an altogether more muted affair, particularly after the inquest. But now history seemed to be eerily repeating itself, for John King's soft felt hat was missing. The sailor's cap and shirts found on the railway line must have belonged to the killer.

Inspector Bannister, who had been happy to accept that the death of John King was a tragic accident, now reopened the investigation. He took statements from Mickle and Cowan, and on 21 September went in search of James McKill.

As it happened, McKill had ignored the advice to clean himself up and had proceeded to drink himself into a stupor. He was found lying shirtless in Eglinton Street, Glasgow, and was taken off to the police station to sleep it off. The next day he was brought before the magistrate and fined 5s, but as he only had 1s 10d on him, he was locked up for four days. On his release he had little option but to return home to his parents in Hamilton. It was an unexpected homecoming, but even more unexpected was the visit of Inspector Bannister on 21 September. The detective declared:

> I have come to make inquiry about John King, who is said to have ridden with you from Kentish Town station in a third-class carriage on the night of the 11th, and whose dead body was afterwards found on the line in Haverstock Hill tunnel. You are not called upon to make any statement, and you need answer no questions, but if you do I will write it down, and in the event of any charge being made against you, it may be used against you.

McKill, described as a short man with close-cut hair and sharp, intelligent appearance, was happy to give his side of the story.

He knew John King as a passenger on the *Ormuz*, but after they had got on the train at St Pancras McKill had fallen asleep and had no idea if anyone else had been in the same carriage. He denied making any confession to Mickle and Cowan or throwing his shirts out of the window. He claimed that he had actually sold his shirt in Glasgow for 1*s* so that he could buy a drink. Nonetheless there was enough evidence for him to be charged and returned to London. On the way there Bannister asked where he had got the felt hat found in his home. 'I know that is the dead man's hat,' he replied. 'I had a cap. I don't know what became of mine.' When McKill tried on the cap found on the railway line it appeared to fit him perfectly. 'Yes, that's mine,' he replied.

The justice system was much quicker in the late nineteenth century than it is today. Inquests into suspicious or unexplained deaths were usually held within a few days, and coroners had the power to commit suspects for trial. At the same time, the suspects could also be brought before the magistrates at the local Police Court. Either way, cases of murder or manslaughter were usually heard at the Old Bailey within one or two months. If the charge was approved by a Grand Jury, the suspect would stand trial.

McKill's trial began on 26 October. Under the law of the day, McKill was not allowed to give evidence and had to rely on the skill of his barrister Charles Gill. His defence was that John King's death was an accident and that the victim must have got out of the moving train himself in a state of extreme intoxication. 'The story about there being a fight and the prisoner having thrown the deceased out of the train was too absurd for a moment's belief,' Mr Gill was reported to have told the jury, 'particularly when it is remembered that the deceased was the bigger and stronger man of the two, and besides, the quarrelling and the fighting and the throwing out would all have been done, if the story were true, within three minutes and a half.' If it was true, then one would have expected to see signs of a desperate struggle. Mr Justice Cave advised the jury that if they thought McKill's confession was simply the ravings of a drunken man then they ought to acquit. Even the prosecutor seemed unenthusiastic about the case. The jury did not even bother to leave court and after two minutes of hushed conferring in their box they returned a verdict of not guilty. McKill was a free man.

If this seems an anticlimax, it serves only to demonstrate that not every story has a clean-cut ending. Suspicion and a host of unanswered questions are not enough to convict a man of murder. Neither was the explanation of a tragic accident satisfactory. The victim's family did not recognise John King as the type of man who would recklessly climb out of a moving train to fetch a bottle of whisky. Before his trip to Australia he had been teetotal and an unlikely brawler. Now he was dead, and his wife Mary had to look after his two children alone. She moved back home with her father and brother in Rutherglen and in 1892 got married to a blacksmith. Sadly tragedy had not yet finished with the family. Seven years later, John King's son died at the age of nineteen from appendicitis.

James McKill married a year after his acquittal and had at least three children. His father died in 1893, followed by his mother in 1915. In 1920, at the age of fifty-five, he appears to have emigrated to America and settled down in Cook, Illinois, and found work as a janitor at an oil company. His son Robert got a job on the local electric railway.[12]

2

THE STREETS
OF LONDON

Londoners in 1888 were astounded by the changes that
had taken place since the start of the nineteenth century.
As one observer noted, 'Old London is going, going, indeed,
has well-nigh gone.' It was now an urban giant extending
well into Surrey, Middlesex and Kent, and its centre had
been furnished with new landmarks like Trafalgar Square,
Buckingham Palace, the Royal Courts of Justice, the
National Gallery and the Houses of Parliament. Then there
were the restaurants and theatres, department stores and tea
shops, and hotels boasting elevators, telephones and electric
light in all bedrooms. It was a sightseer's paradise. The
guidebook, *London of To-Day*, summed up the mood in their
1888 edition:

> Since the end of the eighteenth century London has undergone
> a marvellous change. The monster Metropolis, which is still
> swelling every year – to which, indeed, many thousand houses,
> forming several hundred new streets, covering a distance not
> far short of a hundred miles, were added but a year ago –
> which is increasing in a way which makes it bewildering to
> contemplate, not its final limits, but where those limits will
> reach even in the near future: this monster London is really a
> new city.[13]

Of course, not everybody agreed. The writer Ouida argued in an article for *Woman's World* in 1888 that:

> ... for a city which is in some respects the greatest capital of the world, the approaches to London are of singular and painful unsightliness ... The streets are dreary, although so peopled; the sellers of fruit or flowers sit huddled in melancholy over their baskets, the costermonger bawls, the newsboy shrieks, the organ-grinders gloomily exhibit a sad-faced monkey or a still sadder little dog; a laugh is rarely heard; the crossing-sweeper at the roadside smells of whisky; a mangy cat steals timidly through the railings of those area-barriers that give to almost every London house the aspect of a menagerie combined with a madhouse ... To drive through London anywhere is to feel one's eyes literally ache with the cruel ugliness and dullness of all things around.[14]

Nevertheless this new, expanding city required a transport system to match. One by one, the great railway stations were opened: London Bridge (1836), Euston (1837), Paddington (1838), Waterloo (1848), King's Cross (1852), Victoria (1860) and Charing Cross (1864). Sewers were constructed. Bridges were built over the Thames and tunnels were dug under it. People swarmed from one end of the city to another by foot, bicycle, trains and horse-drawn cabs, omnibuses and trams.[15]

All this travelling posed increasing danger to the pedestrian, particularly at the busiest intersections. Piccadilly Circus, which was originally a crossroads, stood at the junction of the two major new thoroughfares, Regent Street and Shaftesbury Avenue, the latter being completed in 1886. The great illuminated advertisements were yet to go up, and the statue of Anteros, the Angel of Christian Charity, would not take its place at the centre of Piccadilly Circus for another five years. What it did have was an endless flow of horses, human beings and goods surging and halting under the direction of dedicated police constables determined to prevent everything from toppling into chaos. It was said that:

> … at the movement of a gloved hand, a stream of cabs, buses, carts, waggons, barrows, drays, traps, carriages – in fact, every variety of conveyance upon four wheels or two suddenly comes to a standstill, just to allow a lady to pass! The lady has as much right to passage-way as the owner of the proudest horseflesh, and it is on this principle that the policeman acts – everybody in turn.[16]

In an age before the combustion engine and exhaust fumes, the interchange was filled with the shouts of drivers, clattering hooves and the snorts of horses, with manure dropping from the back end. Every few minutes another omnibus passed through the vortex on its way to Hammersmith, the Strand, Liverpool Street, London Bridge, and West Kensington. This was the heyday of the buses, 'the most convenient and the cheapest form of travelling from one London street to another'. They ran from early morning to midnight, charging fares of between 1d and 6d depending on distance and time. The first omnibuses, drawn by three horses, travelled between Paddington and Bank and had space for twenty passengers but, in effect, they were little more than a box on wheels with a few windows and a door at the back. By the 1860s the business was dominated by a French-owned outfit, the London General Omnibus Co., but from 1881 they came under increasing pressure the London Road Car Co. The Road Car buses boasted lower fares and more comfortable vehicles, and printed tickets to prevent fraud by conductors. To stand out from the crowd they flew a small Union Jack, a patriotic dig at their rivals. By 1888 the Road Cars were ferrying 22 million passengers a year compared to the London General Omnibus' 95 million. While this competition meant passengers could travel across London for as little as a penny, it occasionally threatened to turn into a hair-raising race.

When the conductor rang his bell the intelligent horses settled into their collars without any word of command, and the passengers took a sporting interest in the driver's efforts to pass the omnibus of the rival company; London General Omnibus Company versus the Road Cars with their little fluttering flags. And everywhere under the horses' noses the nimble orderly boys scuttled about on all fours, with their little scoops and brushes, trying to keep the pavement of our imperial city comparatively clean, and in wet weather failing malodorously.[17]

A similar scene unfolded on the afternoon of Saturday 4 February 1888, as Augustus Maude boarded a road car at Piccadilly Circus to get home to West Kensington. He climbed to the top deck and took his place at the front looking out over the horses as they headed west towards the most fashionable quarters in London. The famous thoroughfare of Piccadilly lay before him – Wren's brick Church of St James, Byron's old rooms in the Albany suites, the Royal Academy at Burlington House, the Arcade, and the Egyptian Hall where Maskelyne conducted his theatrical magic shows. Gathering pace down the slight gradient, the road car settled in a few yards behind a rival London General Omnibus as Green Park opened up on the left-hand side. To the right were the aristocratic windows of the millionaire Angela Burdett-Coutts on the corner of Stratton Street, an ideal viewing platform that, according to Queen Victoria, was 'the only place where I can go to see the traffic without stopping it'.[18] Close to the junction with Half Moon Street, Maude noticed the omnibus in front slow down, as it stopped to allow three ladies get off. The driver of the

Road Car pulled his horses on to the wrong side of the road to overtake, slammed into an elderly man crossing the street and ran right over his legs.

Over at No.94 Piccadilly, in a grand building marked out with a distinctive 'In' and 'Out' on its entrance and exit gates, Lord Charles Beresford was enjoying a leisurely afternoon at the Naval and Military Club. 'Charlie B', as he was known, was the Irish second son of the Marquess of Waterford and an MP who had only three weeks earlier resigned from his post as Junior Sea Lord of the Admiralty in protest at what he saw as Britain's ill-preparedness for war. By contrast, he was admirably prepared for action on this occasion. On hearing the commotion outside the club, he strode to the scene of the accident, put the injured man in a cab and sent him to St George's Hospital on Hyde Park Corner.

The injured man was James Langley, a sixty-eight-year-old widower who had been walking through Green Park and was crossing the road to get home to Shepherd Market in Mayfair. His accident featured in a long list published by a weekly newspaper, which included: a woman run over by a Road Car near Westminster Abbey; a four-year-old boy who knocked a kettle of boiling water over himself; a man who fell into a tub of boiling water at work; a boy whose hand was crushed at a printing machine; the suicide of a young watchmaker's wife using cyanide; and a dock worker whose legs were crushed by a heavy case. Sadly, James Langley would not recover. Surgeons amputated one of his broken legs but the shock to his body was too great and he died two days later. It had been a successful life. He had been born and married in Berkshire but in his twenties had moved to London to make his way in the world. By 1881 he was a master carpenter employing five men. On his death, he left a personal estate of £650 to his eldest son, Isaac.

Every year nearly 150 people were run over and killed in London, and more than 4,500 were injured.[19]

The overwhelming majority of deaths did not result in criminal proceedings, the modern charge of causing death by dangerous or reckless driving being unavailable until 1956. It was murder, manslaughter or nothing. In the case of James Langley the inquest jury returned a verdict of accidental death, but at the Police Court the prosecution argued that the omnibuses were racing down the hill at up to 10mph in an attempt to be the first to pick up passengers. The magistrate sent the driver of the Road Car omnibus to trial for manslaughter at the Old Bailey. On 2 March 1888, Walter Prescott, twenty-eight, was acquitted after a number of witnesses, including passenger Augustus Maude, testified that the buses were not racing and that the driver had done all he could to avoid an accident after the vehicle in front pulled up suddenly without warning. He may have been guilty of negligence, the judge remarked, but it was not gross criminal negligence.[20]

The competition for fares between rival drivers was so fierce that it occasionally erupted into physical violence. Frederick Sheward, forty-three, was well known among other Hansom cab drivers for constantly complaining that they had been 'rubbing up' against his vehicle. On Saturday 22 September he returned to the busy stand in Charing Cross Road at 10 p.m. to find his paintwork had been scratched. This time he picked on fifty-year-old James Williamson, a 'rigger' who looked after the cabs on the rank.

'Look at my cab, it is disgraceful, it is always the same every night as I come back,' Sheward ranted.

'I have not done it, I have to look after my living,' replied Williamson. 'It must have been done elsewhere.'

'You ought to be ashamed,' continued Sheward.

The argument went back and forth for several minutes until another cab driver, Henry Matthews, decided to intervene and shouted, 'Leave the old man alone.'

Sheward replied, 'Mind your own business, what has that to do with you?'

Matthews then got off his own vehicle, walked up to Sheward and punched him in the face, giving him a bloody nose. This delighted Williamson, who began cheering and taunting Sheward, 'You've got what you deserve you bloody monkey.'

As Matthews left in his cab, Williamson and Sheward continued to argue. Williamson was threatening to hit the other man with his walking stick. 'I'll knock your bloody head off.'

At this, Sheward hit Williamson in the face, knocking him to the ground near the junction with Great Newport Street. 'Take that,' he added, before walking off.

Williamson, who was unconscious and bleeding from a head wound, was placed into a cab and taken to Charing Cross Hospital at around 11.15 p.m. An hour later he suffered two epileptic fits. Williamson died that morning and a post-mortem revealed he had suffered a fracture at the base of his skull and brain damage from hitting his head on the ground as he fell.

Sheward was arrested at his home in south Lambeth at 6.40 a.m. on 23 September by Detective Sergeant Henry Scott.

'I have come to see you with respect to a man who was knocked down last night,' said Detective Scott.

'Yes, he was messing about my horse's head,' replied Sheward. 'He struck me first, and I struck him.'

Sheward was put on trial for manslaughter at the Old Bailey the following month but was acquitted after several witnesses admitted that Williamson was a 'quarrelsome man'. Another cab driver, William Andrews, also told the court that Williamson struck out at Sheward with his walking stick before being knocked down. By contrast Sheward was said to have an 'excellent character as an honest, sober and peaceful man'.[21]

While most of the busiest roads were to be found in the centre of London, crossing the street in an era before traffic lights and zebra crossings posed dangers to the pedestrian all over the city. One guidebook for tourists noted that:

> Crossing, although a matter that has been lately much facilitated by the judicious erection of what may be called 'refuges', and by the stationing of police constables at many of the more dangerous points, still requires care and circumspection … One of the most fatal errors is to attempt the crossing in an undecided frame of mind, while hesitation or a change of plan midway is ruinous.

However, it added that, 'to the wayfarer London is the safest promenade in the world'.[22]

On the evening of Saturday 28 July, Ann Rowley, a seventy-four-year-old widow, was on her way to Peckham after visiting her grandson near Charing Cross. She walked to Westminster and paid 2*d* to board the tram heading to New Cross. As it reached the High Street opposite Rye Lane the passengers could hear a band playing loudly outside a butcher's shop, celebrating its first day of business. Ann Rowley stepped off the back of the tram and then went to cross the road behind it. She barely had chance to respond to the rough cry of, 'Get out of the way', before a Hansom cab coming the other way slammed into her at 9mph. She was flung 10 yards along the road before the wheel of the cab ran over her right leg. If the driver knew what had happened, he appeared not to care and continued driving.

'I cried out to the cabman to stop, and ran after him, holloaing as loud as I could,' recalled one witness, the plumber William Graham. 'I said to him "Mate, stop! You have run over that woman".'

The driver had turned round and replied, 'Go to buggery', before setting off again with a slash of the reins. Others now joined in the chase and it was only through the force of an outraged mob that the cab was brought to a halt. The driver seemed more concerned about losing his two existing fares than the condition of Ann Rowley.

'He came back with a great crowd of people,' remembered another witness. 'They were all holloaing at him, and there was a great deal of confusion and excitement – he refused to turn the fare out and assist the lady into the cab, and this put the people out.'

Twenty-five-year-old George Ernest Holden was a butcher by trade. Although he was licensed to drive a cab, he had no vehicle of his own and had taken one without permission from the rank in Peckham High Street.[23] Most people who saw him that day took the opinion he was 'silly' drunk, the kind of condition brought on by two or three glasses of beer. He still hadn't sobered up by the time he arrived at the shop owned by Ann Rowley's grandson, Robert Portwine, off St Martin's Lane. As the lady was taken out of the cab, Holden kept repeating, 'It was not my fault, missus', and, perhaps excited to find that Mr Portwine was also a butcher, went around everybody in the premises trying to shake their hand. When he was arrested a few hours later, he was back in the Greyhound pub in Peckham.

Ann Rowley ended up at Charing Cross Hospital with a broken right leg. It was put in splints but two weeks later had to be cut off because the wound wasn't healing and had begun to rot. She died on 25 August, nearly a month after the accident. The inquest jury returned a verdict of manslaughter against Holden, but following his trial at the Old Bailey, he was found not guilty. Perhaps the jury were swayed by his claim that Mrs Rowley had assured him that it was not his fault. His barrister also made the point that the doctor who first attended the injured lady had not been called to prove that Holden was under the influence of drink. As the Hansom had been driving at a 'perfectly proper rate of speed', there was no negligence proved.

Then, as now, the elderly were at particular risk from London traffic. A similar fate met Maria Rider, sixty-seven, on the night of Thursday 19 January 1888, as she tried to cross the busy Borough end of Great Dover Street at the junction with Long Lane. She had made it to the middle of the road, near a traffic island equipped with a urinal, when a van being driven by one horse struck her at around 8mph. She was taken into a nearby shop by a passing ship's steward and then to hospital where she died on 13 February from head injuries and a subsequent bacterial infection. The driver, Edward Dye, a biscuit dealer en route from London Bridge to the Swan pub 30 yards down the road, had the grace to instantly apologise when stopped by witnesses. He also appeared 'perfectly sober' and was driving on the correct side of the road. Dye was acquitted of manslaughter on the evidence that the victim had suddenly stepped into his path.

Children were just as vulnerable to death on the roads. David Cavalier was only a toddler, twenty-two months old, when he was run over in Bethnal Green, east London. It was 8.30 p.m. on Sunday 8 July and he was playing on the pavement outside his home in Warner Place. Further down the road two plain-clothes policemen were patrolling. There was no traffic and all seemed quiet until a horse and cart carrying a woman and child galloped round the corner from Old Bethnal Green Road at around 10mph. Eliza Cavalier, no doubt keeping one eye on her son and one eye on the housework, noticed the boy run into the road just as she heard the clatter of the approaching vehicle. 'I ran into the road to protect him,' she recalled. 'My hand just touched his clothes when I was thrown away by the horse and knocked down and the cart went over me. I was so frightened.' While Eliza suffered only minor injuries, the wheel of the cart had passed right over her son's head, fracturing his skull, and he died not long after being taken to the Children's Hospital in Hackney Road. According to newspaper reports the driver of the cart, fish porter Thomas Tarplett, twenty-five, had been drinking, although he was sober when taken down to the police station. A month later he was cleared of both manslaughter of the child and causing bodily injury to the mother, after witnesses testified that he was a 'peaceable, steady and well-behaved young man'.[24]

The only case that resulted in a guilty verdict was that of Elizabeth Gibbs, who was run over on Tuesday 27 December 1887, but who died on 1 January, 1888. Perhaps the driver, Alfred Winwood, was convicted because of the status of his victim – the respectable wife of John Gibbs, a wealthy estate agent who had served as a land steward on the grounds of Bayfordbury Mansion in Hertfordshire, the seat of the wealthy merchants, the Baker family. But it was clear from the evidence that Winwood had also cut the corner of Halkin Street and Grosvenor Place, and was on the wrong side of the road. He also narrowly avoided killing John Gibbs and another pedestrian. As Mr Gibbs explained:

> I was just a trifle in front of my wife, and immediately I [had] left the pavement and gone perhaps two or three steps, I suddenly became aware of a two-horse van coming down upon me, so close that I had neither time to think or act … I was knocked down towards the middle of the street … the moment I touched the ground I had presence of mind to swing myself round, and by that means I escaped the wheels.

He got up and found his wife lying in the road, her left arm crushed by the wheel.

When Winwood was flagged down by a postman who had witnessed the accident and told that he had run a woman over, he replied, 'What the bloody hell has that got to do with me?' and drove off. It appeared as if he had been drinking. Winwood was also late attending the inquest, and was arrested on a warrant issued by the coroner. He was forty-three, and employed by Messrs Batey's Mineral Water and Ginger Beer Co. as a delivery driver for the Fulham district. At trial, his defence involved accusing John Gibbs and his wife of 'contributory negligence' by not taking more care crossing the road. His punishment for the crime of manslaughter was six months' hard labour, which in 1888 might still have involved 'picking oakum', a walk on the treadmill, lifting cannon balls, or sewing. It might have been a longer sentence had the jury not recommended him to the mercy of the court. After his release he returned home to his wife Sarah at a small house in Shoreditch they shared with a family of four, giving his occupation in the 1891 census as 'traveller'.

As for John Gibbs, widowed so soon into the new year, he placed a death notice in *The Times* in tribute to his 'dearly-loved wife' and spent the rest of his life living with two of his daughters, first at Ebury Street in Belgravia and then in Hampstead. He died in 1905 at the age of eighty-five.[25]

One final case of interest did not involve horse-drawn transport but the bicycle. By the 1880s the awkward penny farthing had been refined to something similar to the modern bike, with lower seats and a chain connecting the pedals to the wheel. This new 'safety bicycle' would grow in popularity during the rest of the century, and there were cheers in the House of Commons in July 1888 when it was announced that bicycles and tricycles would be allowed on all roads in Hyde Park and St James' Park. The design would be further improved with the pneumatic rubber tyre, invented by John Boyd Dunlop and patented in 1888. But, as with any method of transport, there would be reports of fatal accidents. One night in February that year a hotel landlord, forty-two-year-old John Watney Green, was knocked over by a cyclist in Kenley, Surrey, and died the next day – although the doctor suggested death was actually due to exhaustion and delirium tremens.[26]

Looking back from the twenty-first century it seems incredible that there was no real ambulance service in 1888. Dedicated horse-drawn carriages had been provided by the Metropolitan Board of Works for carrying fever and smallpox cases to hospital for twenty years, and it was possible to summon them by telegram for a small fee. The medical magazine The *Lancet* had recommended a centralised service in 1865 but the state of the nineteenth-century communication system (telegram, word of mouth and only a few primitive telephones) meant that it was quicker and easier to commandeer a carriage at the scene. The matter was left to local organisations like the Middlesex Hospital Board, who had a 'chair and horse' to transfer the injured from 1877, and the London Hospital who had one from 1881. The St John Ambulance provided carriages during the 1887 Jubilee celebrations, although early paramedics were often branded 'body snatchers'. London would have to wait for the development of the motor engine before the first centralised ambulance service began in 1907.[27]

3

LIFE IN THE SUBURBS

The growth of transport both echoed and spurred on the growth of London itself. It was now expanding as fast as the suburban railway could lay down its tracks. More and more people were finding it convenient to commute to the City from what had once been open country. Areas like Leyton, Tottenham, West Ham, Southgate and Willesden doubled, tripled or even quadrupled in population between 1871 and 1891, as the middle class pursued respectability and the workers seized on the cheap fares to move out in search of a better quality of life. In 1888 young couples from the lower middle class were advised to choose houses 'some little way out of London. Rents are less; smuts and blacks are conspicuous by their absence; a small garden, or even a tiny conservatory is not an impossibility'. Out in the suburbs there was fresh air, fewer shop windows to tempt the wife into extravagant spending, and less opportunity for the mother-in-law to interfere. The recommended areas were Sydenham, Forest Hill and Bromley in the south, and Finchley and Enfield in the north.[28]

Moving out of the city centre did not guarantee a peaceful existence, however. As the population expanded to the outer regions, so did the conflicts that decorate everyday life. While incidents were fewer, and less serious, murder still occasionally crept out to the suburbs.

~ South ~

Surbiton was only fifty years old, and a true creation of the railways (the station's original name was 'Kingston-on-Railway'). Although it did not become an urban district until 1894, it was a typical commuter town consisting of Victorian townhouses and churches on the dividing line between Greater London and the Surrey countryside. And while it was well within the boundary of the Metropolitan Police District's V Division, it was an unlikely setting for a murder.

Seventy-one-year-old Major Thomas Hare had been living in a four-storey semi-detached house at No.13 St James Road for fourteen years following his retirement from the army. It was set away from the road and visitors had to climb the steps to knock on the door and await the attendance of the housemaid. The major, who had served in the 27th (Inniskilling) Regiment of Foot and the Cape Mounted Rifles in South Africa, had relatively few problems to occupy his twilight years other than the disability of his wife of nearly forty years, Frances. They owned another property in Surbiton Hill and were supported by their two youngest sons, both employed responsibly by the local council and a bank respectively. The oldest was serving with the army in India.[29]

Their second eldest, Gordon, was most definitely a concern. If he had a role model it might have been Cecil Rhodes, who went to South Africa in 1871 and within twelve years was president and founder of the De Beers diamond mining company, earning £50,000 a year. Or perhaps it was Rimbaud, who in 1888 was involved in arms dealing and spying in Ethiopia, the only country to retain its independence during the Scramble for Africa between 1881 and 1914. Both were in their mid-thirties and making their mark on the world.[30] Gordon was at a similar age but had achieved almost nothing. He had been to America to tend cattle, and Australia, but wherever he travelled in search of his fortune he would inevitably return every one or two years to ask his father for maintenance. By 1885, having paid out several thousand pounds, Major Hare told his son that he had to find his own way. Gordon's requests for maintenance then turned to demands, threats and even violence. A warrant was issued. Two days before he was due to appear before the magistrates, Gordon went to the family home and threatened to blow out his father's brains unless he was found employment. As a result he spent three months in prison, but the effect was only to deepen his resentment.

Gordon went abroad again, reportedly to join a travelling circus in Mexico. By the summer of 1888 he was back at his parents' front door, but his father firmly told him he was trespassing and that he should leave. The following day, Saturday 25 August, his youngest brother Maynard, twenty-one, spotted him in the City. Gordon walked up to him and said, 'You may as well speak to me. No one will speak to me, and it's a matter of life and death.' Over a lunch and lemonade, Gordon explained that he was taking medication because he was unable to sleep at night. He took out a handful of revolver cartridges, but Maynard thought he was only suggesting suicide. Maynard later recalled:

My brother has always been a source of great trouble. When I was quite a boy he was sent to America and there was employed tending cattle … It was always a grievance that they [his parents] would not keep him as he liked. He thought everyone should go out of their way to supply his wants.

It did not matter how much my mother suffered, he thought he should be supplied with money ... My brother had an allowance of one guinea a week and he took it with scorn. My father got him an office in the City, but his behaviour was such that he could not keep the situation.

That evening Gordon checked into the Kingston Hotel and the following morning a maid noticed that all the pictures in the smoking room had been turned to face the wall. At 5 p.m. that Sunday he left the hotel and set off for St James Road. His father was at a service in St Mark's Church and the housemaid, Martha Hodsell, refused to let him in, having direct instructions from Mr and Mrs Hare. Gordon tried the back door before returning to the front to sit on the top step and wait. At 7.50 p.m. his father returned from church. 'Major Hare!' shouted Gordon angrily. Moments later a gunshot rang out, followed shortly afterwards by a second.

A friend of the family, Dr Matthew Coleman, ran to the gate to see Major Hare lying on the steps, gasping, with a bullet wound to his neck. In the porch Gordon fell to the floor, dead. Having shot his father he had placed the barrel of a revolver into his mouth and discharged a bullet into his brain. 'The lips were blackened but his moustache was not singed,' reported *The Times*. In his pocket were begging letters to friends for money and work.

The inquest was presided over by coroner Athelstan Braxton Hicks, the son of the obstetrician who gave his name to phantom pregnancy contractions. After allowing the jury to examine the body of father and son, he summed up the case by saying that, 'the only gleam of satisfaction to be obtained from this awful tragedy was the fact that by committing suicide Gordon had spared his mother and other relatives the painful ordeal of appearing against him on a charge of murder, for which crime he would undoubtedly have hanged'. As it was, Gordon and his father were buried in the same grave in Kingston the following day, 29 August 1888.[31]

～ North ～

Thirty miles or more north, on the edge of the Metropolitan Police District, lay the village of Shenley in Hertfordshire. It was beyond the reach of the Midland & Great Northern Railways and remained a parish of farms and countryside, the home of craftsmen, labourers and those who wished to live away from the smoke and fog of London.[32] Even now, Green Street in Shenley remains bounded by ploughed earth, hedgerows and trees, with the occasional cottage set back from the road. In 1888 No.91 was part of a long brick building made up of four 'cottages' and the Green Willows pub. It was occupied by Edward Cullum, a gamekeeper turned agricultural labourer born and bred in Suffolk. Once married, and with two sons in tow, he moved first to Hemel Hempstead and then to Shenley. He was now in his sixties and his eldest had left home having trained as a blacksmith. The youngest, twenty-four-year-old Henry, had returned home the previous year after leaving his employment as a porter for the Midland Railway in Normanton, Yorkshire. Since his return he had done little but fall in love with a young woman living next door but one.

Emily Bignall was twenty-three and had two children from two different men. She was fond of Henry and her mother Sarah had never seen them quarrel. Although, there was one time around Christmas that Emily had come home with a revolver she had taken away from Henry for safekeeping. And at the end of February, Emily appeared to have been crying while Henry was visiting the cottage. But they seemed quite friendly when they started chatting over the palings in the backyard at around 11.30 a.m. on the morning of 7 March.

One or two minutes later the neighbours heard a man cry out, 'You Beast!' Then two shots were fired and Emily fell to the ground. Emily's mother, Sarah Bignall, recalled:

> My child fell into my arms and said 'Oh Mother!' She was bleeding from the neck and holding her apron up to her neck on both sides. I dragged her towards my door and she fell to the ground. I put my fingers to try and stop the blood and then I saw it rush out the other side. I ran to the door and shouted 'Murder'. I remember no more and believe I fainted.

George Atkins, a baker who had been having lunch at the Green Willows pub, rushed out at the sound of gunfire and saw Henry Cullum flinging the revolver into the garden. Atkins asked him, 'What have you done it for?'

Henry replied, 'I'd some strange impulse upon me. I love the girl more than I love my life.' Atkins noticed that Cullum was bleeding from the hand, having somehow shot himself after shooting Emily.

'You've killed her Harry!' Atkins exclaimed.

'I've killed another one besides her,' replied Cullum, 'my father. I expect he'll die broken-hearted.' Cullum then collapsed.

The murder fell to be investigated by Inspector Robert Butt from the S Division based at Barnet, although the case did not offer much of a puzzle. The press called it a 'love tragedy', an outrage caused by jealousy over her previous relationships. Below one report of the case, the *Reynolds's Weekly Newspaper* inserted an advertisement for an 'Electropathic Belt' to aid men and women suffering from 'any form of nervous derangement, loss of power, debility, or functional disorder'. Henry Cullum would not rely on a defence of insanity at trial, although he had been examined by a doctor at the request of his father three months earlier.

Dr Ross Smyth found there was no reason to put him in an asylum, albeit he was fond of an activity that many believed was a disease of the mind – masturbation.

Five months later Henry Cullum pleaded guilty at the Hertfordshire Assizes and was sentenced to death. 'The prisoner appeared quite unconcerned,' reported *The Times*. The execution was fixed for 21 August but five days beforehand he was reprieved and sent to Broadmoor Asylum in Berkshire. He was still a patient there three years later, his occupation being listed as 'garden labourer'.

For some observers, the case wasn't so much about mental illness, or jealousy, but the law on firearms. Anybody could buy a gun, and anybody could carry a gun around in public provided they had a licence. Licences could be purchased for 10*s* from the Post Office. The penalty for not having a licence was £10, or up to a month of hard labour. The jury at the inquest into the death of Emily Bignall clearly found this situation worrying, as they added to their verdict the statement that they: 'desire to represent to the government authorities the necessity which exists for the adoption of some measures limiting the use of revolvers, whether by heavy tax or otherwise; especially that the sale or delivery of them to persons of immature age should be restricted.'[33]

It would be another fifteen years before restrictions were placed on the sale of firearms to under-eighteens, drunkards and the insane. And it was not until 1920 that firearms certificates would be universally required.

⟶ West ⟵

Isleworth was a small town in Middlesex known for its aristocratic mansions and fruit gardens. In 1888 it was also home to a large soap factory run by Pears Soap, one of a new breed of businesses in late Victorian Britain. Pears were an international giant, selling to customers from New York to Australia, and they poured £100,000 a year into promoting their products. Their full-page adverts promised to leave users with: 'fair white hands, bright clear complexion, and soft healthful skin'. Their flagship store in Oxford Street boasted a vision of ancient Pompeii, complete with floor mosaic, veined marble columns and a fountain.[34]

On 15 April two women arrived in Isleworth from the town of Netherton, near Dudley, in the Midlands, hoping to find seasonal work in the orchards. Charlotte Whale, a twenty-six-year-old chain maker, and Sarah Procter, a thirty-six-year-old nail maker, had lived together on and off over the last few years. It was a troubled relationship, for Charlotte had previously given birth to a child fathered by Sarah's brother and Sarah was so upset that she threatened to kill her brother if they married. During the train journey to Brentford, Sarah seemed anxious and perhaps a little paranoid. She was heard to say, 'I don't think you will behave true to me.'

Charlotte replied, 'I will – you shall go to the same place with me to live and we will sleep together, and if we can get work we will work, together.' But if Sarah and Charlotte were lovers, it was not said openly and the newspapers remarked only that they were: 'on the most friendly terms'.

The pair did find a place together, at Mitchell's Cottages off Wharton Place, and it was arranged that they should sleep in the same bed. On Monday 16th, Sarah felt too ill to go out looking for work and complained of a pain in her lower back. Charlotte tended to her friend, took her meals and applied a mustard poultice. The following morning they were taken a cup of tea before they were due to start work at 8.45 a.m. A few minutes later the landlady, Mrs Callow, went upstairs and heard groaning. Through the open door she saw Charlotte lying on the bed in her nightdress; her face covered with blood. She had been repeatedly battered with a water jug until the side of her head caved in to expose the brain. She was dead by the time the doctor arrived.

Sarah Procter seemed proud of her accomplishment, and claimed that she had borne a grudge ever since Charlotte had pushed her over three or four years earlier. She also insisted that Charlotte had not spoken to her for eighteen months before they came to London, and had ripped up and burnt a letter that she was due to send to her brother and sister. 'I done it, and I meant to do it, and I know I will have to swing for it,' Sarah said, drinking calmly from a cup of tea.

The supposedly destroyed letter was later recovered intact. In it, Sarah Procter complained that she had been ill since she arrived in London, 'for the air is too strong for me'. She asked for 8s 6d so she could come home again, as there was no work for her, and even if there was she would not be able to stand it. It was becoming plain that Sarah Procter was suffering from delusions. There was also a history of epilepsy in her family as her father, her brother and one of her sisters had all suffered fits.

Her state of mind would feature largely in her defence to the charge of murder. At the inquest it was on plain view as she accused Mrs Callow of sleeping with her and Charlotte on the night before the murder instead of her husband. A month later at the Old Bailey, the jury were told that Sarah had started to show odd behaviour after being knocked down by her brother, Charles, for insulting their mother in October 1883. Ever since she had complained about a pain in her head, occasionally treating it with an herbal brew made from plants. 'My head is very bad,' she would say. 'My head will kill me.'

Surgeon Thomas Standish theorised that a burst eardrum might have caused inflammation of the internal ear and then the brain, leading to delusions and ultimately insanity. 'A person seized suddenly in that manner might act almost automatically, and I think would not be able to reflect on the nature of what they were doing, in such a manner as [to] withhold an ordinary person from committing a crime,' he told the court. Another doctor who examined her in custody also believed she had suffered chronic inflammation of the membranes of the brain, and possibly a 'modified epileptic fit' at the time of the murder.

'She professed not to know or recollect what had occurred after she had taken the cup of tea, but she volunteered that she had no reason for doing it, she did not know why she could have done it,' said Dr Henry Bastian. Apart from her strange behaviour, she had been a hard-working woman, having spent twenty-five years at Lewis & Co. nail manufacturers up until her journey to London. The judge remarked that the jury could not treat Procter as a rational being and accordingly that she be found insane at the time of the killing. Sarah Procter was sent to Broadmoor Lunatic Asylum.[35]

⏤ East ⏤

Beyond the East End, on the other side of the River Lea, lay the parish of West Ham and the industrial suburb of Stratford. Here were mills, porcelain factories and chemical works. Perhaps most importantly for the area it was home to the works of the Great Eastern Railway (GER). For forty years its assembly line had turned metal plates into fully functional locomotives that would carry passengers from London to Cambridge, Great Yarmouth, Ipswich and Southend. In 1891, they set a new world record time of nine hours forty-seven minutes to build a six-wheeled steam engine. Many of the workers lived in the Stratford New Town houses built by the 'Railway King' George Hudson to the north-east of the station. For them, the life of hard labour at the workshops from Monday to Friday was relieved only by the pub at the weekend.

On Saturday 28 April, three colleagues at the GER boilermaker's yard – Robert Marjoram, a forty-two-year-old blacksmith; Edward Lock, a boilermaker; and Charles Coote, a thirty-three-year-old hammer man – were enjoying a drink at the Boar's Head public house in Queen Street. At around 2 p.m. there was a dispute about half a sovereign, although who exactly was owed it was not clear. Either way, it ended with Marjoram and Lock going outside to settle it. A fair number of other drinkers followed to watch the entertainment. Marjoram was a heavily built man and appeared intoxicated; he did not even put up his fists. Lock took advantage by knocking Marjoram to the ground with his first blow. When Marjoram got back up Coote left his position by the door of the pub and knocked him down again. This time Marjoram's head smashed into the kerb with a sickening thud, knocking him out cold.

'His mouth was open and full of blood, he was insensible,' said James Regan, a local man who helped carry Marjoram home to nearby Henniker Road. Marjoram remained unconscious the rest of the day but the doctor was only called in the next morning. He died at 8.30 p.m. that Sunday evening from a brain haemorrhage. There was a 5in fracture to the rear of his skull where his head had hit the pavement.

Who was responsible for Robert Marjoram's death? In common with other killings in or outside pubs, the alcohol consumed by many of those present may have had something to do with the conflicting witness accounts. Henry Buck, who had tried to pick Marjoram up after the first blow, was punched in the eye for his trouble and did not see the end of the fight. Mary Lancaster, Walter Bland and Thomas Serle saw Coote floor Marjoram with a punch to the mouth, while William Lye believed it was more of a hit to the chest. The doctor saw no sign of any injury to the lips or the teeth.

When arrested by the detectives of the K Division, Lock denied striking Marjoram down while Coote appeared to show some remorse. 'I did not strike him, I only pushed him,' he said. 'I am very sorry I went away, but I was so upset I did not know what I was doing.' Both were charged with manslaughter and both were acquitted by the jury at the Old Bailey after a trial.[36]

4

LIFE IN THE CITY

While significant numbers of Londoners were moving out of the centre in search of a better life, many more remained in the working-class districts at the heart of London: Greenwich, Deptford, Battersea, Rotherhithe and the legendary East End. The railways were not only encouraging the daily commute from the suburbs, they were also bringing in poorer people unable to make a living in the Home Counties. In the capital they would seek employment among the sprawling, overcrowded mass of markets, pubs, shops, docks and factories.

~ Markets ~

London has a rich history of markets, with many dating back to the Middle Ages. Even now, Billingsgate, Smithfield, Spitalfields and Covent Garden cling on in the face of competition, while others have fallen by the wayside. Watney Street market at the heart of the East End once had more than 100 shops selling cheese, meat, fruit, shoes and clothing.

One of them was distinguished by a cast-iron sign reading – 'J Sainsbury Ltd' – part of a growing enterprise which would become the largest grocery retailer in Britain by the 1920s. There were also dozens of stalls and wandering hawkers catering for the relatively poor population living between Commercial Road and the London Docks. This lent a disreputable air to the district in the eyes of the more well-to-do inhabitants. 'It is well known [that] for many years past Watney Street has been the happy hunting ground of every class of street hawker, and the sights to be witnessed in the neighbourhood during every Sunday was disgraceful in the extreme,' read one newspaper report. 'Persons attempting to pass to Christ Church to public worship were subjected to every conceivable annoyance and insult.' Following a series of complaints from the local ratepayers about this 'nuisance', the parish vestry ordered that from 29 September 1888, there would be a ban on 'any stall, costers' barrows, goods for sale, or any other matter' on the street between 12 midnight and 7 a.m. Monday to Saturday and all day Sunday. The headline in the *East London Advertiser* of 6 October conjured up images of the clearing away of rampant criminality with the headline: 'A Raid on the Watney Street Market'.[37]

Although the report did not mention it, the image of the market had hardly been helped by a fatal stabbing three months earlier. Henry Talbot, aged twenty, was a master butcher who ran a stall with the help of his sixteen-year-old brother John. Both lived with their father in nearby Sheridan Street. On Thursday 12 July, John was sent away for lunch but was told not to be long. The boy returned nearly two hours later at around 4 p.m.

'I thought I told you to make haste,' said Henry, with some annoyance.

'I have been to dinner and had to wait in the coffee shop,' John replied.

The fraternal bickering continued until John finally told his brother, 'Hold your tongue.' At this, Henry lost his temper and attempted to headbutt the boy. Both men were holding butcher's knives in their hands, and the brief clash ended with a blade buried in Henry's left breast a few inches below the nipple. 'Now I've got it,' Henry moaned. As blood poured from the wound he began to walk towards the London Hospital but only got to the top of Watney Street before collapsing. His last words to his brother, as he was put into a cab, were: 'It was not your fault – go back and look after the stall.' Half an hour later he was dead, the blade having pierced his heart.

John gave himself up to police the next morning. He told detectives: 'We had some words, which I thought was a lark. He butted me with his head and hit me with his fist. He ran on my knife which I was holding. It was all an accident.' Daniel Day, who was sitting in the next stall, agreed; he testified that Henry had run on to the knife trying to 'buck' his brother in the face. After the inquest jury returned a verdict of death by misadventure, the charge of manslaughter was thrown out by the magistrate and John was discharged.[38]

Watney Street is now much changed – the market steadily declined through the mid-twentieth century, Sainsbury's moved out and a large proportion of stalls packed up never to return. The street is now lined with ugly blocks of flats, although there are plans to 'regenerate' the area and restore some of its lost character.

Butchers were also a major feature of Clare market, which was sited between Lincoln's Inn Fields and the Strand to the west of the new Royal Courts of Justice, which were officially opened by Queen Victoria in 1882. The market had thrived

since the seventeenth century but by the late nineteenth had
been reduced to a grim collection of:

> … streets and lanes, where the shops are tenanted by butchers,
> greengrocers, etc. and where the roadways are crowded with
> costermongers' carts, and the kerbs and kennels with stalls
> where nearly everything is vended. Here herrings or mackerel,
> as the season may be, are sold at marvellously low prices; while
> the vegetables equally cheap, are fresh and excellent in quality.
> The din and bustle lasts till midnight and it is a strange phase of
> life to study the faces and listen to the conversation of people
> bargain-hunting in this market.

Twenty years later it was barely hanging on to existence and
was replaced by the London School of Economics.[39]

George Best was a sixty-year-old waiter living in Stanhope
Street, one of those narrow thoroughfares which formed Clare
Market. Having finished work on the evening of Thursday
27 September, and already inflamed by drink, he began hurling
'vulgar and filthy language' at his neighbour's wife, Alice
Dowden, who was standing at the window of No.6 with her
two children. She called her husband William, a twenty-four-
year-old market porter, to defend her honour with the result
that the two men were soon at each other's throats. The fight
ended with Best falling backwards and cracking his head on
the kerbstone. He was put on a barrow but was already dead
from a brain haemorrhage by the time that he arrived at the
nearby King's College Hospital. Dowden was charged with
causing the death but the witness evidence was contradictory –
some alleged he punched Best in the face, others said he threw
up his arm in self-defence and that the death was an accident.
Again the verdict of the inquest jury was crucial: death by
misadventure, and the case was dismissed by Bow Street
magistrates the following week. 'The language and action of

the deceased quite justified the prisoner in pushing him on one side,' reported one newspaper. 'The decision was received with applause, which was quickly suppressed by the usher.'[40]

~ Pubs ~

London in 1888 was a city of more than 10,000 public houses, each one an oasis of light and warmth amidst the fog, smog and darkness. The pub was an extra living room, a community meeting place or just somewhere to escape from the wife, work or cold. 'This form of amusement seems to be the favourite one with families,' wrote one journalist, 'for in house after house there are little groups comprising a grey-haired old lady with a glass of neat gin, a buxom young woman with a baby and ditto, and a burly young fellow with a big pewter.' The pub, open for business between 5 a.m. and midnight, was an 'Elysian field for the tired toiler' and 'the centre of attraction for the masses'. It was not a place for the distinguished lady or gentleman, who believed that combining the masses and alcohol led inevitably to 'ruffianism'. There were more than 7,000 arrests for drunkenness and more than 16,500 arrests of 'drunk and disorderly characters' in London in 1888.[41] Occasionally, as in the case of Robert Marjoram in Stratford, these petty rows and scuffles ended in death.

On Christmas Eve, 1888, a large group of friends were drinking at the Queen's Head in Tanner Street, Bermondsey. As the name of the road suggests, the leather trade was important for the parish. Bermondsey was a working-class area, populated by casual labourers, dockers and street sellers, for whom a drink at the end of the week was just reward. But what was a man to do when money was tight? One solution was to join his friends for a 'Yorkshire Round'. Everybody would put what money they had into a hat and the total would be used to pay for all the drinks. It was Christmas, after all, and good will to all men. The job of collecting the coins fell to John Kellar, a thirty-three-year-old labourer, but Alexander McKie disputed how much was in the hat and Kellar claimed that he had not paid his fair share. Despite the best efforts of the landlady to calm the situation down by offering Kellar a free drink, he pulled off his coat and demanded to fight McKie for 5s.

'You could not hit me or give me a black eye in a twelvemonth,' taunted Kellar.

'You seem to have a spite against me but for what I don't know,' replied McKie. 'I don't want a black eye and I don't want to fight.'

Kellar walked out into the passage, turned and shouted, 'If you are a man, come out and don't act like a cur.' That was it for McKie, and he followed Kellar outside.

The fight was to last two rounds. After taking off their upper clothing, they shook hands and squared up for the duel. The first round ended with both men grappling each other and falling to the floor. The second ended abruptly when Kellar fell over trying to land a punch. His head hit the pavement and he was knocked unconscious. He was taken to hospital in a cab but died four days later on Friday 28 December from a fractured skull.

McKie, aged twenty-three, was committed for trial for manslaughter at the Old Bailey on the basis that in trying to ward off the blow he had caused Kellar to fall. But the prosecution openly admitted that Kellar was the aggressor throughout and the judge, Mr Justice Denman, said he thought 'it would be a pity to brand the prisoner as a felon for the rest of his life'. The jury quickly found him not guilty.[42]

In another case, the fatal fight was to be over just one shilling rather than five. On the night of Saturday 30 June, William Walker, a twenty-four-year-old labourer, and

Robert Hodges, a thirty-seven-year-old 'hawker' or street seller, were having a drink together at the Cooper's Arms in Sun Street, Finsbury. Walker owed Hodges money and it was decided they should settle their argument with a 'fair stand up fight' outside the pub. This one went three rounds before Hodges threw Walker to the ground by grabbing his legs, lifting him off his feet and throwing him backwards as if he was tossing a caber. Hodges then flung himself on top of his rival as if it were an exhibition wrestling match. Walker had to be carried home to Alexander Chambers, the lodging house-cum-beer shop in Horse Shoe Lane where both he and Hodges were staying. Despite its location not far from Finsbury Square, lodging houses were generally miserable places that catered for those who had just enough money to avoid sleeping rough. The noble-sounding name was a common feature of these properties, although the illusion could hardly have lasted long once a man passed through the front door. Walker spent the next three days in bed, his occasional vomiting the sign of a serious head injury. He died shortly after being taken to the infirmary on Tuesday 3 July. The post-mortem revealed a fractured skull.

Hodges stood trial at the Old Bailey for manslaughter and hardly helped his case by confessing that he could not remember the fight because he was so drunk. While two witnesses testified that Walker's death was caused by the fall, rather than any direct blow, others said that hugging a man and throwing him to the ground was not the stuff of a fair fight. Hodges was convicted and sentenced to three months' hard labour.[43]

Coincidentally, Sun Street would have a minor part in the police investigation into the Whitechapel murders. On 9 September 1889, a Mr E. Callaghan, formerly resident at No.27, made a statement about one of his lodgers named Mr G. Wentworth Bell Smith. This gentleman, who claimed to have been raising money for a Canadian society, stayed out late most nights and wore a pair of rubber boots which dampened the sound of his footsteps. In August 1888, at around the time of the murder of the prostitute Martha Tabram, he returned home at 4 a.m. with some story about having his watch stolen in Bishopsgate Street. Marks of blood were found on his bed and a few days later he left the house, claiming that he was returning to Toronto. However, there were reports that he had been seen getting into a tramcar in September. Mr Callaghan added: 'We all regarded him as a lunatic and with delusions regarding "women of the streets" who he frequently said ought to be all drowned ... the writing of Bell Smith is in every way similar to that sent to the police and signed Jack the Ripper.' This theory, like many, many others, was investigated and discarded.[44]

While the consumption of alcohol had declined slightly since the height of the 1870s, in 1888 the English were still guzzling down an average of 1 gallon of spirits, 40 gallons of wine and 30 gallons of beer per year.[45] Perhaps the type of people most notorious for heavy drinking in London were sailors, who saw fit to celebrate their brief stay on dry land by dousing themselves with hard liquor. On 28 May, John Shorting, a forty-two-year-old seaman from Jarrow in the north-east of England, was in Greenwich with the steamship *James Joicy*. His first port of call was the Hatcliffe Arms, where he made the acquaintance of two women keen to be bought a drink. Next was the Ship & Billet a few yards down Woolwich Road. About an hour before closing, the barman refused to serve him any more alcohol, as he was plainly drunk enough already. Shorting was staggering towards the exit when a local boy, nineteen-year-old Jeremiah Duggan, took objection to something Shorting said to his female acquaintances and punched him in the face. When Shorting got up he was again punched to the ground, whereupon one of the women poured a pot of ale over his head. Shorting was dead by the time he arrived at the infirmary.

Although committed for trial on a murder charge, Duggan ended up on trial for the lesser offence of manslaughter. It was said that there was no quarrel between the two men and that the blow was unprovoked. But while a number of witnesses described one or two blows to the head, another described it as 'a quick shove'. The doctor admitted the fatal brain haemorrhage could in fact have been caused by excessive drinking alone. A not guilty verdict was the inevitable result.[46]

It was not just men involved in petty life and death struggles in the pubs and taverns of London. Women too were at the mercy of the devil's nectar because of its quality as a powerful eraser of memories, whether of the drudgery and violence of domestic circumstances or the degradations of life on the streets. Brawls between women were not that uncommon and provided an entertainment of a kind for the male observers. The socialite Margot Tennant (who later married future Prime Minister Herbert Asquith) became directly involved in one such 'catfight' at the Peggy Bedford pub in Whitechapel during one of her philanthropic visits to the East End in the late 1880s. Noting that it was 'hot, smelly and draughty' and 'crowded with sullen and sad-looking people', she had only to wait a few minutes before a row broke out. A merry cad tried to pluck the flower from the hat of her new-found acquaintance Phoebe, an employee at the nearby packing factory. The situation quickly deteriorated:

> Provoked by this, a younger man began jostling him, at which all the others pressed forward. The barman shouted ineffectually to them to stop; they merely cursed him and said that they were backing Phoebe. A woman, more drunk than the others, swore at being disturbed and said that Phoebe was a blasted something that I could not understand. Suddenly I saw

her hitting out like a prize-fighter, and the men formed a ring around them.

Rather than abandon her friend, the young Miss Tennant surged into the middle of the scrum to break it up, only to find herself caught between two women slinging their fists wildly at each other. 'Women fight very awkwardly and I was battered about between the two. I turned and cursed the men standing round for laughing and doing nothing and, before I could separate the combatants, I had given and received heavy blows.'[47]

A similar scene in Bow, east London, in 1888, had more disastrous consequences for those involved. On the night of 21 April the coal merchant William Cook was driving down Fairfield Road when he saw a crowd of people outside the Caledonian Arms pub. At the centre of it were two women fighting. One of them clearly had the upper hand, landing several blows to the face of the other before dragging her by the hair down on to the flagstones. The impact left a savage cut to the centre of the victim's forehead, prompting one of the onlookers to shout, 'My God! The woman is killed.' Mr Cook, seeing that others were attending to the injured lady, followed the attacker in his trap as she calmly walked off. For half an hour or more he shadowed her without seeing a single police officer to raise the alarm, until she finally ran into a house. Fortunately he was able to get her name from a few boys hanging around in the street. Sarah Ann Ward was a seventeen-year-old factory worker and described as tall but slightly built – although according to one report she was known as the 'champion woman fighter of Old Ford'.

Ward had gone to the Caledonian Arms with four young men that evening. They had seemed a happy group, and offered a drink to shoemaker William Astell and his friend Arthur Wood, a plumber. This seemed to rile Mr Astell's wife

Annie, who had an old quarrel with Ward and clearly did not approve of her and her companions. 'If you've not got enough to pay for a glass then I'll buy one,' she told her husband. 'We don't want to drink with them, have you not had enough of them?' At this the atmosphere turned sour and abuse was hurled back and forth until Ward started trying to goad Astell into a fight. In an attempt to keep the peace, landlord Thomas Gillett ordered Ward to leave and then advised Mrs Astell to go home via the back door. Her husband drained his drink and followed a few seconds later.

'When I got out I found that my wife had been struck,' he recalled. 'I accused Ward of striking her. She turned round and said, "Yes you bugger, and I will strike you", which she did on my left eye. I made a blow at her in retaliation, and as I did so someone knocked me senseless to the ground. When I recovered I found my wife standing up against the window.'

Mr Astell was too groggy to note his wife's injuries that night but saw her the next day in hospital. She was conscious, but her skull was fractured and the damage to her brain would lead to her death three days later on 25 April.

The inquest returned a verdict of manslaughter and Ward went on trial a month later at the Old Bailey. As in the previous cases, the evidence was contradictory. Richard Wilson, a plasterer, claimed Mrs Astell was actually willing to fight and had left the pub rolling up her sleeves for battle. Two witnesses said Mrs Astell fell over her husband's legs during the fight of her own accord. The jury didn't find it an easy decision but after two and a half hours' deliberation in their room they found Ward not guilty.[48]

Fairfield Road would feature in newspaper reports for different reasons three months later when 1,400 'matchgirls' went on strike at the Bryant & May factory. It had begun on 2 July in response to the sacking of at least one worker for refusing to follow instructions, and continued until

18 July when the company agreed to their demands. These included the abolition of all fines and deductions from wages, the provision of a breakfast room, the formation of an official union and the taking back of the ringleaders. This resounding victory was achieved with the support of the press, a sympathetic public and socialists like Annie Besant, who had published an article condemning the way the company paid out dividends at 20 per cent while its workers earned from as little as 4s 6d a week. The success of the matchgirls demonstrated what could be achieved by organised protest and set the mood for the Great Dock Strike of 1889, which inspired the spread of trade unions throughout the country.[49]

5

IN DARKEST LONDON

It was 19 February 1888, and the world's greatest living explorer, Henry Morton Stanley, was laid up like an invalid in a hut in the middle of darkest Africa. His expedition to rescue the Governor of Equatoria, Emin Pasha, was in ruins. Half of his expeditionary force had deserted or died. The remainder were scattered across hundreds of miles. They had been waylaid by pygmies armed with poison arrows, flesh-eating ants, diarrhoea and starvation. They had bartered their guns, ammunition and even their clothing for food. Their specially designed 25ft boat and dozens of boxes of ammunition had been abandoned in the forest. A journey that had been expected to take seven months had now lasted more than a year and the end was not yet in sight.

Stanley would spend twenty-three days drifting in and out of consciousness, his mind muddled with morphine, until his fever passed. When he finally met with Emin Pasha at Lake Albert on 29 April 1888, his band of weary stragglers looked like they were the ones in need of deliverance. Stanley did his best to keep up the pretence, producing three bottles of champagne that had been carefully preserved all the way up the Congo, but his mission had been a resounding failure.

This did not prevent Stanley receiving a hero's welcome on his return to London, or publishing a one-sided account of his adventure, *In Darkest Africa*, in 1890. His tale of half-naked savages, slave traders and cannibals was a sensational success, a triumph of civilisation over savagery. But for some readers, it served as a reminder of the darkness at the very heart of the British Empire: the East End.[50]

Even before Jack the Ripper, that stretch of city beyond the Tower of London already had its own mythology. That area encompassing Whitechapel, Spitalfields, Ratcliffe and the docks resembled some black hole sucking in every beggar, whore and crook, corrupting all it touched and threatening the destruction of respectable society. For those of comfortable means, born and bred to succeed, it seemed that even the third-world savages were 'not half so savage, so unclean, so irreclaimable, as the tenant of a tenement in an east London slum'. It was this reputation that fuelled the fashion for 'slum tourism', inspired by the journalistic accounts of social commentators like Charles Dickens, Henry Mayhew and James Greenwood. Scores of curious young men and women sought to complete their education by observing the poor in their native habitat. One fifteen-year-old girl, said to be the daughter of a Lord, was so enthused by Walter Besant's book *All Sorts and Conditions of Men* that she decided to investigate the life of a flower seller for herself and spent the night with a Jewish family in Mile End. At around the same time, the Princess of Wales ventured into Whitechapel to see another kind of 'freak show', Joseph Merrick, the Elephant Man, at his small flat at the rear of the London Hospital.[51]

In the 1880s, newspapers began competing with their own first-hand accounts full of florid descriptions of the blood and filth found in an area dominated by slaughterhouses, cellar workshops and drinking dens. This was the 'New Journalism' that would wring every drop of drama and sensation from the Ripper murders. George Sims told of the families 'packed like herrings in a barrel, neglected and despised, and left to endure wrongs and hardships [as] if they were related of a far-off savage tribe'. Howard Goldsmid, a nineteen-year-old undercover journalist and ex-grammar school boy, covered his face with dirt, donned a soiled shirt and coat, tattered boots and a deerstalker hat, stuck a clay pipe between his lips and ventured into the worst lodging houses he could find. Paying 4*d* for a bed, he slept in festering rooms jammed full of hags too old and hideous to sell their bodies, abandoned wives, destitute widows, the crippled and infirm, the homeless, the unemployed, loafers, cadgers and thieves – not to mention the fleas and bugs rampaging over every inch of skin. Eleanor Marx, the thirty-three-year-old daughter of the late revolutionary socialist Karl Marx, began exploring the East End herself in 1888.

> Sometimes I am inclined to wonder how one can go on living with all this suffering around one. One room especially haunts me. Room! – cellar, dark, underground – In it a woman lying on some sacking and a little straw, her breast half eaten away with cancer. She is naked but for an old red handkerchief over her breast and a bit of old sail over her legs. By her side a baby of three and other children – four of them. The oldest just nine years old. The husband tries to 'pick up' a few pence at the docks – that last refuge of the desperate – and the children are howling for bread. What has become of those children heaven knows. – But that's only one out of thousands and thousands.[52]

This 'furore for social facts' also attracted professional men like Charles Booth, who set out to map economic conditions in the East End in a bid to disprove some of the wilder assertions being flung around. And while his colour-coded view of the city revealed a healthy middle and upper-working class lining the main streets, he estimated that a third of the population was on or below the poverty line of 21*s* a week for a medium-sized family. What was to be done? In an age without state benefits, the task of relieving the distress of the poor was left to the church, charities and rich philanthropists like the banker Nathan Rothschild, the first Jewish member of the House of Lords.[53]

The characterisation of the East End as a 'plague spot' only became more exaggerated when Jack the Ripper started murdering prostitutes in the autumn of 1888. There were, however, some journalists who felt the stereotyping unfair. The *Illustrated London News* reported that: 'Those who are well acquainted with the East End of London will not assent to the unfavourable notion of its general character and condition which is often ignorantly expressed in conversation among persons in society remote from that part of the metropolis.' In its view, Whitechapel, Stepney and Bow were similar to the manufacturing districts of Manchester and Leeds. 'The wide and airy thoroughfares, frequented by decent, orderly, and cheerful people, most of whom are in pretty constant and regular employment at various factories; the neatness and comfort of their habitations, and their orderly domestic and social life, may be an agreeable surprise to visitors.' The *East London Observer* also attempted to inject some balance by claiming that Whitechapel was safer than any other part of the country due to increased police patrols.[54]

Two major reasons for the focus on the East End, and Whitechapel in particular, were concerns about 'sweated labour' and unchecked immigration. To some, they were two sides of the same coin. The East End was overcrowded, and the lack of work encouraged the exploitation of men, women, girls and boys. People were so desperate for a few pennies to buy food, drink and a bed for the night that they would work for a penny an hour, sixteen hours a day, six days a week, in hot cellars churning out cheap goods like trousers, boots and jackets for the department stores. The blame for this situation was put not only on the unscrupulous 'sweaters', but also on the thousands of Jews flooding the streets of Whitechapel and Spitalfields. It was claimed that the Jews were driving down wages, pushing out English workers, forcing the respectable middle classes out of their homes and setting up illicit gambling dens. It mattered little that many of these newcomers were fleeing from persecution in Eastern Europe following the assassination of Tsar Alexander III in Russia.[55]

In the summer of 1888 both issues were examined in parallel by the House of Lords select committee on the sweating system, and the House of Commons select committee on Emigration and Immigration. Often the evidence overlapped – the Lords heard that 'foreigners were much more steady than Englishmen', while the Commons investigated claims that sweaters were offering money to Polish and Russian Jews to come to England.

One of the major contributors to the immigration committee was Arnold White, who had in 1886 attempted to finance a 'society for the suppression of the immigration of destitute aliens', and wrote that 'England will cease to be England if our rulers do not show that they love the English more than the frugal, unlovable foreigner'.[56] The committee was told that hundreds of 'aliens' were arriving every week at Tilbury Docks alone. Some ports, such as Dover, did not even count the number of immigrants. The figures showed that at least 9,000 had arrived from Hamburg and other European ports in the year up to 30 June 1888. For all the government knew there were thousands pouring unchecked into the country.

But why England? Henry Dejonge, a Jewish cigar maker, told the committee: 'In many instances they are sent for by their friends and relatives, and the great attraction I should think from what I have heard from them, is the freedom there is in this country as compared to the despotic country they are leaving.' The suspicion was that they were being encouraged to leave; Samuel Hoare MP noted that: 'It was stated a short time ago that there was some Polish newspaper which stated that the streets of London were paved with gold and advising poor people to come over here.' Their ultimate destination was the East End, and Whitechapel, which Charles Booth described as 'the great centre of the foreign population of London'.[57]

It was estimated that there were at least 60,000 Jews in east London, half of them foreign born. Two out of the multitude living in Whitechapel in 1888 were twenty-five-year-old Abraham Potzdamer and his wife Hannah, aged twenty. It was said they had arrived from Russia in September (although their surname hinted at a connection with Germany) and that she had formerly worked at a 'house of ill fame'. At first they stayed with a family of Jews running a cookshop – the Victorian equivalent of a greasy spoon – in Brick Lane. Abraham took a job there but apparently he gave it up after eight days because the work was too hard. It seems this did not endear him to his young wife and she moved in with one of his friends, Louis Cohen, at No.147 Backchurch Lane. It was a road 'inhabited mostly by a low type of foreigners and small shopkeepers', including the whisky wholesaler Kinloch & Co. and a chandler by the name of Gallowitz. Behind the houses on the western side of the lane ran the railway line that the Potzdamers most likely arrived on from Tilbury Docks.

Now homeless and wifeless, Abraham Potzdamer tried to support himself by taking work as a boot finisher, like many immigrant Jews in the East End. Skilled finishers could earn as much as 45s a week, but it was now a trade under intense pressure from large-scale manufacturers. Many were casual workers required only to polish and tidy boots, the last stage of a production line. Prices had been cut by nearly half over the previous thirty years, and wages had followed suit. Small-scale workshops thrived by 'sweating' their employees for sixteen or eighteen hours a day, and fining them if they were late or produced shoddy goods. Foreigners were happier to do the back-breaking work than the English, most likely because they had little choice – it was either work or starve. Still, even at the rate of 3s a week for new recruits, they were better off than in Poland or Russia.

Without a job, Potzdamer would have had to walk to the soup kitchen on Fashion Street operated by the Board of Guardians. There he would join the throng of foreign Jews, described in one contemporary novel as:

> ... strange stunted swarthy hairy creatures with muddy complexions illumined by black twinkling eyes. A few were of imposing stature, wearing coarse, dusty felt hats or peaked caps, with shaggy beards of faded scarfs around their throats. Here and there, too, was a woman of comely face and figure, but for the most part it was a collection of crones, prematurely aged, with weird, wan, old-world features, slipshod and draggle-tailed, their heads bare, or covered with dingy shawls in lieu of bonnets, red shawls, grey shawls, brick-dust shawls, mud-coloured shawls. Yet there was an indefinable touch of romance and pathos about the tawdriness and witch-like ugliness, and an underlying identity about the crowd of Polish, Russian, German, Dutch Jewesses, mutually apathetic, and pressing forwards. Some of them had infants at their bare breasts, who drowsed quietly with intervals of ululation.[58]

At first Potzdamer kept away from his wife, not even revealing his new address. This might have indicated that he had accepted her decision and moved on, but in reality he was sinking into a deep depression. He confided in his brother that he felt life without her was not worth living.

On the morning of Wednesday, 1 February, he was spotted hanging around in the street outside Louis Cohen's house. Cohen thought little of it, and at around 1 p.m. sent Hannah Potzdamer out to buy some provisions. Moments later he heard a terrible scream, and the cry of 'Murder!'. He rushed downstairs and followed a trail of blood leading out the front door. Outside he found Hannah lying in the middle of the road, with crimson gushing from her neck. She was able to lift her hand and gesture weakly at her escaping attacker before slumping unconscious. Cohen and a group of neighbours set off in pursuit.

Potzdamer crossed Commercial Road and ducked into Greenfield Street with his bloody shoemaker's knife in hand, only to see PC Collinson coming in the opposite direction. Turning his back upon the officer, he drew the blade across his own throat. As the policeman grabbed him, Potzdamer plunged his fingers into the wound to widen it and finish the job even quicker. Both he and his estranged wife died on the way to the London Hospital a few hundred yards away. One newspaper illustrated its report by depicting Hannah Potzdamer being wheeled past a shocked gaggle of neighbours in a barrow. Brief reports were filed under headlines such as 'Terrible Tragedy in London' and 'Murder and Suicide at the East End'. But if this episode shed any light on the terrible conditions in which people were living in Whitechapel, the full picture would not emerge until later in the year.[59]

While reports of East End poverty filled the pages of books, newspapers and Parliamentary reports, other areas of the capital suffered the same problems in relative silence. Before Whitechapel, probably the most notorious district was the 'Mint' in Borough, a few minutes' walk from London Bridge.

In the early to mid-nineteenth century it was said that there was 'no spot that looks so murderous, so melancholy and so miserable'. Mint Street, a maze of stinking alleys and dilapidated lodging houses, had been a notorious hideout for villains and a rich hunting ground for diseases like cholera. Between 1881 and 1886 much of it was demolished, and the new Marshalsea Road opened in 1888 to take traffic from Borough to the Southwark Bridge. 'Formerly the borough was one of the nastiest districts in the Metropolis,' wrote one observer in 1886, 'now however … the borough is comparatively respectable.' Slum clearing wasn't a total solution, as the evicted were simply pushed into surrounding areas. Part of the Old Mint remained standing, along with a large number of common lodging houses catering for prostitutes, pickpockets and the poor at 4*d* for a stinking, dirty room crammed full of vermin-infested beds. The police officer Tom Divall, who served with the Met from 1882 to 1913, later wrote that, 'I think I can truthfully say that no other known place could equal it for vice.'[60]

Just to the east of the Mint lay the General Post Office on the part of Borough High Street then known as Blackman Lane. The postal service was in the middle of a boom period that only levelled off after 1910, and was making more than £3 million a year net profit. The late nineteenth century was a time when there were six deliveries a day and letters posted before 6 p.m. could be delivered the same evening. Stamps cost ½*d* for postcards and 1*d* for letters under an ounce in weight. More than 100,000 people worked for the Post Office, collecting, sorting and delivering seventy items of mail per person per year.[61] Two of them were William Hall, aged thirty-two, and George Figes, both sorters at the headquarters in St Martin's-le-Grand. At 1 a.m. on 7 December 1888, they left work and started making their way home along the Marshalsea Road towards New Cross. A man and a woman came towards them, and the woman tearfully complained that she had been insulted by her companion. At that moment a third stranger suddenly appeared and knocked the hat off the companion before walking away. This strange series of events led Hall and Figes to follow the woman to the Borough to seek out a police constable. While Hall stopped and had a smoke outside St George the Martyr Church, the hat-tipping stranger reappeared and, without a word of warning, punched him on the side of the head, knocking him to the floor. Hall was able to walk to the Stone's End police station and identify his attacker as William James, a thirty-three-year-old street hawker, before being taken to Guy's Hospital. He died a few hours later of a fractured skull and brain haemorrhage.

The inquest returned a verdict of wilful murder against James after witnesses testified that the fatal blow had been entirely unprovoked. During the hearing, Constable Sutherland recalled how James had walked up to the group at the corner of Marshalsea Road shortly before the attack and declared himself to be Jack the Ripper. It had only been three weeks since the murder of Mary Kelly but these kinds of boasts were becoming so familiar that those in court burst into laughter.

The following month James stood trial for manslaughter before Mr Justice Denman at the Old Bailey, the murder charge being replaced with the lesser alternative by the Grand Jury. James claimed that he had only pushed Hall away because he was 'interfering improperly with the woman', but eventually changed his plea to guilty and was sentenced to twelve months' hard labour. It was not his first brush with the law – he already had a criminal record for assaulting the police.[62]

The West End was often held up as a direct contrast to East End poverty; Kensington, Knightsbridge and Mayfair were where the rich dwelt in opulent luxury when they weren't enjoying the clean air of their countryside retreats. But while

Booth's poverty map showed Hyde Park surrounded by the golden yellow colour denoting the 'upper classes', it also revealed scattered pockets of the black 'semi-criminal' and dark-grey 'poor'. In the alleyways behind Paddington railway station, in the homes along Horseferry Road and Peter Street in Westminster, the streets off King's Road, Chelsea, in Soho, and Lincoln's Inn Fields, the poor lived yards away from people spending more in one day than they would in a year, despite the best efforts of the landowners to cleanse their districts.

Notting Hill and Notting Dale epitomised these contradictions. In the sweeping crescents, gardens and walks along Ladbroke Grove down to Campden Hill and Holland Park stood row upon row of terraced Victorian townhouses. They had replaced the failed Hippodrome Racecourse, an 1830s' attempt to bring the glamour of Ascot and Epsom to the city; in the late nineteenth century its inhabitants included the writers G.K. Chesterton and Arthur Machen, and the spiritualist Helena Blavatsky. That these grand properties failed to attract the wealthy upper classes away from Mayfair and Belgravia was mainly due to the proximity of an area known as the 'Potteries and Piggeries' to the west along Pottery Lane. Forty years earlier it had been condemned as 'a plague spot, scarcely equalled for insalubrity by any other in London' and as being worse than famine-stricken Ireland.

It comprises some seven or eight acres, with about 260 houses (if the term can be applied to such hovels), and a population of 900 or 1,000. The occupation of the inhabitants is principally pig-fattening; many hundreds of pigs, ducks and fowls are kept in an incredible state of filth. Dogs abound for the purpose of guarding the swine … There are foul ditches, open sewers and defective drains, smelling most offensively and generating large quantities of poisonous gases; stagnant water is found at every turn … Nearly all the inhabitants look unhealthy, the women especially complain of sickness, and want of appetite; their eyes are shrunken and their skin shrivelled.

It was said that in 1860 a woman stumbled into a bog near Latymer Road and drowned. Gradually the pigs and kilns disappeared but even in 1888 the area around St Ann's Road and Bangor Street was a notorious slum populated by beggars, gypsies, Irish immigrants and drunks.[63]

At 10.30 p.m. on Saturday 20 October 1888, George Quinney was still serving cooked fish at his shop in Bangor Street when a quarrel broke out. Michael Patten, a well-known local drunk going by the nickname of 'Brummie', had made an unsolicited remark to the wife of nineteen-year-old labourer James Marshall, known as Scottie. Tempers flared, and Quinney ordered them outside. The ensuing brawl attracted a small crowd, who shouted and jeered as the pair tussled on the pavement. 'Patten fell in the gutter, and when he was there Marshall kicked him on the back of the head and punched him,' recalled William Bond, a shopkeeper's son. 'Before they began to fight I heard Marshall say "Come on, I will fight you now I have got you".' Within minutes a uniformed policeman arrived and ordered them to break it up, before ushering Marshall and his wife into the fish shop to finish their supper. Patten tried to get another drink at the Red Lion pub, but was quickly told to leave and walked back to the common lodging house where he was staying, at No.27 Crescent Street. Conveniently the lodging house also contained a beer shop.

At 11.30 p.m., Patten was standing in front of the fire in the kitchen when he was told that Joseph Lay, one of Marshall's friends, wanted to have a word. Patten wiped a little blood from the back of his head and put on his hard hat before going outside in his bare feet. It would be Patten's second fight of the night and the last of his life. It was witnessed by the wife of a coal porter, Agnes Cooling:

I saw Lay punching Patten about the body, just outside the archway, and I heard Patten fall. I heard his head go against the wall. Lay went back and said 'Get up, what's the matter with you?' Patten made no reply then Lay dragged him out by his coat collar and then Marshall rushed up and punched him in the chest and kicked him in the head. I said, 'Oh you have killed the man, I will fetch a policeman.' I went for one but could not find one and when I returned the place was all clear.

In fact, Lay and another man had carried Patten inside the lodging house. The next morning he was found dead in his bed.

Lay was arrested the same day. 'He insulted Scottie and his wife at the fish shop and was turned out,' he said in a statement. 'I was standing outside the Shamrock, in Crescent Street. He came up; he was drunk and wanted to fight. We had a struggle and he fell on the kerb.'

Two days later, Marshall was arrested but denied being involved in the second fight in Crescent Street. 'I had never spoken to the man before in my life,' he told magistrates. 'I am innocent of touching the man after the fight with him at St Ann's road. It is all lies.'

Both men stood trial for manslaughter at the Old Bailey and both were found not guilty. The case hinged on the medical evidence – the lack of certainty about the cause of the wound at the back of Patten's head and the bleeding on his brain were crucial. Dr James Miller, a surgeon living in Notting Dale, testified that death could have resulted from either the fall at the fish shop or the one outside the lodging house. The jury probably had little sympathy for a man who, according to Lay, 'was well known about the neighbourhood to be drunk, and he would have three or four fights a night before he came home'. For some, it was a way of life.

6

POLICING THE METROPOLIS

Just as the city expanded and evolved, so did the group of men dedicated to maintaining law and order. At its formation in 1829, the Metropolitan Police began with 144 police constables patrolling five divisions. Eight months later there were 3,200. By the end of 1888 the figure was 12,025 over twenty-one divisions covering an area of 688 sq. miles. Gone were the top hat and rattle, replaced by the helmet (1864) and whistle (1884). But they were not just uniforms patrolling the streets any more – the force now took on the investigation of crime, the protection of public buildings and public figures, and the surveillance of criminal gangs and terrorists. The policeman could just as well wear plain clothes, and walk his beat disguised as an ordinary member of the public. He could also be stuck behind a desk.

There were still large numbers of officers out on the streets twenty-four hours a day, seven days a week. Just over 9,000 were available, of which roughly 60 per cent were used for night duty between 10 p.m. and 6 a.m. During daylight hours there were 1,561 men on ordinary beat duty, 522 at 'fixed points', and eighty-eight watching over the hackney carriage stands.[64]

So who were these police officers? Many were from poor and working-class families, men in their teens and early twenties who either felt a sense of duty or saw the chance of a steady job where there was little real alternative. Fortunately, because of a public enthusiasm for police stories and the Ripper murders, a number of policemen went on to describe their experiences – albeit occasionally with exaggerated nostalgia – in print in the late nineteenth and early twentieth centuries. Walter Dew, the detective who later became famous for the capture of Dr Crippen, joined the Met in 1882 on a wage of 15s a week. He had left school at thirteen and was sacked from his job as a clerk for deserting his desk to watch the Old Bailey being ravaged by fire. Benjamin Leeson was the son of a country policeman but worked as a cricket groundsman from the age of twelve before joining the force in 1890. Frederick Wensley came to London to join the police at twenty-two in January 1888. After a few weeks of drills, he was given a brand new uniform and sent off to patrol the streets of Lambeth, only to be drafted over to help in Whitechapel at the height of the Ripper scare. John Sweeney, the son of an Irish farmer, worked as a gardener before taking up a clerical job in the Hammersmith T Division in the late 1870s. Tom Divall was born on a farm in Sussex; he started work at eight years old and spent his teens as a car-man for a railway company before joining the force in 1882. Frances Carlin was another policeman's son but started work in the commercial office of a coal company at fifteen before being recruited to the Limehouse Division in 1890. Arthur Neil was born in Lewisham; he left school at fifteen and worked as a footman until he was accepted by the Met in May 1888, having been rejected by the City of London police.

Each had their own opinion of the worst areas of London, although most chose Whitechapel because of the notoriety of the Ripper murders and their effect on the police force.

Dew believed H Division had 'a reputation for vice and villainy unequalled in the British Isles' even before Jack the Ripper. Leeson also recounted how he had first encountered the area when he wandered by mistake into 'the notorious Shovel Alley itself, a dirty, ill-lit court of about twenty houses, or rather, I should say, hovels'. When he asked for directions the children hurled abuse: 'Copper lost his way!', 'Do him in!' and 'We kill all coppers who come down this street'. Wensley, who spent six months off work after being beaten up while on duty in the New Cut, believed Lambeth was 'a model of propriety and decorum compared with Whitechapel'. It wasn't just common criminality, prostitution and gruesome murder, but also 'organised gangs of desperate men and lads, armed with lethal weapons, terrorising whole areas, blackmailing tradesmen, holding up wayfarers, and carrying out more or less open robbery in any direction that offered'. That didn't mean other areas made for an easy life – Sweeney recalled the Hammersmith of 1880 as being:

> … plagued by numerous gangs of roughs who … indulged in
> a large amount of petty larceny, amused themselves by having
> faction fights in the streets, wrenching off door-knockers,
> breaking windows, shutters and facias, pushing people about
> and assaulting them if they remonstrated. Several houses were
> broken into while the occupants were at divine service.

Charles Arrow, a police inspector in the 1880s and '90s, said that he had heard Tottenham Court Road was 'the most wicked road in London', while Divall insisted that there was 'no doubt Deptford was the rowdiest district in London' thanks to the docks. 'Their great object was to attack the police,' he remembered, 'and I have often seen our charge room at the station more like a slaughterhouse than a place for human beings.' When he was transferred to Southwark M Division, he found it 'inundated with criminals of all descriptions from all parts of the world'. Writing in 1893, the former Chief Inspector Cavanagh remembered a mass brawl outside a pub near Union Street as: '... men and women skull-dragging each other all over the place, pokers, flat-irons, bellows etc. in free use everywhere. Shrieks of murder, police, fire, robbery filled the air.' Detective Robert Fuller, working there in the 1880s, told of 'hundreds of thieves and loafers lounging about the street corners in gangs that would not be allowed anywhere but in such a place as this'. In Fuller's memory, Borough saw 'no end of murders' and Rotherhithe was prowled by 'gangs of ruffians' robbing men and women at will. Even in the City of Westminster officers would have to chase thieves through the 'labyrinth of streets and a network of low "doss houses" into which the person who committed a crime could dive and be lost'. Patrolling the streets was not a job for the fainthearted – in 1888 there were more than 2,200 assaults on officers of the Metropolitan Police.[65]

PC Michael Lewis had the more comfortable beat of Chelsea, known as B Division. He had been born in Cork in Ireland, and had served in the Royal Irish Constabulary before getting married to a local girl and coming to London. By 31 May 1888, he was forty-eight years old and had given twenty years to the Metropolitan Police. That night he was on duty patrolling the King's Road, so-called because it was originally Charles II's private highway to Hampton Court. Now open to the masses, it was seen as a shabbier version of Oxford Street, 'with its straggling, dirty, stucco mid-century houses and shops' which were easily outshone by the grander residences along nearby Cheyne Walk. There was, however, one section which attracted the artistic minds of London. The Vale, on the north side of King's Road, just a few hundred yards past the Town Hall, was a land of quaint little cottages and 'wild gardens and houses hidden behind trees'. The painter James

McNeill Whistler lived at No.2, known as 'The Pink Palace', and in later years Walter Sickert would occupy No.1. Oscar Wilde was an occasional visitor.[66]

No doubt PC Lewis and his colleague Robert Feek were less concerned about the beauty of their surroundings than the human activity on the streets that night. For one, there were two men hanging about suspiciously on the pavement; PC Feek, who was new to the beat, ordered them to stop obstructing the footway and move along. There was some grumbling from one of them about how they couldn't even stop and chat for five minutes after getting off work, but they moved away and the officers continued down to the junction at Beaufort Street. It was on the way back towards the Vale at around 7.10 p.m. that they saw the same two men walking out some gates with zinc flower boxes on their shoulders. 'Where did you get that from?' Feek asked.

The first man, Edward Warne, made no reply but the second man gave the game away by saying, 'We might as well have gone home at first as be copped like this.' Feek grabbed hold of them and called Lewis over to help him escort them down to the station. Warne, aged thirty-five, and his accomplice Frederick Wood, aged twenty-four, worked as car-men – a delivery driver of sorts – and it turned out that Warne had done a bit of work in the Vale a few days earlier. He had obviously spotted the zinc boxes in one of the gardens and had decided that they were an opportunity he could not refuse.

The four men had barely left the Vale on the way to the station when Warne grabbed PC Feek by the testicles and threw him to the ground. Ignoring his pain, Feek held on to his man, despite suffering a kick in the stomach for his efforts. Meanwhile Wood was also wrestling to get free from Lewis, and at the same time trying to kick PC Feek. The next few minutes were a tangle of arms and legs as the policemen battled to get their prisoners under control. As Feek recalled:

A struggle ensued between Lewis and Wood, and Wood caught hold of his throat and hold of his waist. Wood was trying to get at me to release Warne. Lewis fell to the ground in the struggle, Wood on the top of him. I got up from the ground, and asked Warne to go to the station quietly. He said 'Let me go' then kicked me in the bottom part of the stomach and knocked me under a bus wheel. I got up and struck him a blow with my fist; he made another kick at me, and got me down on the ground; I had to call for assistance, as he got hold of my testicles a second time.

Help was at hand, although not from the crowd of eighteen to twenty people who had gathered to watch. PC Thomas Wilson, who had run to the scene from the station further down King's Road, helped Lewis take Wood back to the station. Meanwhile, a local pub landlord and a parish surveyor on his way home from work went to the aid of Feek. Eventually, Warne saw sense and gave up the fight. Both men were taken into custody at the station and charged with assault and resisting arrest. The two constables then began cleaning themselves up so they could get back on duty. By 8.50 p.m. they were ready. But as they entered the yard, PC Lewis grabbed Feek's arm and said: 'Chummy, I feel so faint', before slumping to the ground. Blood oozed from his eyes, nose and mouth. Five minutes later he was dead.

The post-mortem revealed that Lewis, a slight but otherwise healthy man, had suffered a rupture to the right ventricle of the heart. Police surgeon Richard Daniel believed the direct cause was excitement or violent exertion, most likely as a result of the struggle in King's Road. But Lewis had told his inspector that Wood had not assaulted him – in Lewis' words, 'We had an "up and downer"' and I think I must have ricked my chest.' The jury at the inquest returned a verdict of wilful murder against Wood. Both he and Warne were then charged before the magistrate, 'as it is alleged by the prosecution that they had a common felonious purpose, and that when taken into custody they offered a common resistance to their lawful apprehension'.

It was a weak case but bolstered mainly by the fact that the victims were police officers. When it came before Mr Justice Hawkins at the Old Bailey he ruled that the evidence did not amount to murder or manslaughter, and the charge was dismissed. Warne was instead sentenced to five years for grievous bodily harm on PC Feek, while Wood received three months' hard labour after pleading guilty to stealing the zinc and resisting arrest.

Michael Lewis was one of sixty-eight Met Police officers who died in 1888, although his was the only death linked to violence. For others it was typhoid fever, pneumonia, bronchitis, diphtheria and other common diseases. One drowned accidentally, while another hanged himself. At that time there was no automatic right to a pension, either for a retired officer or their widow. PC Lewis' wife, Mary, was given a £49 lump sum from the Constables' Death Fund, but otherwise relied on the 17s a week earned by her two youngest sons, who were aged fourteen and sixteen and lived at home with her in Lots Road, Chelsea. Her second eldest son had died two years earlier and the eldest, aged nineteen, was serving as a soldier in India. When her plight was raised at court, the magistrate expressed his hope that she would receive a compassionate allowance and in the meantime 'to relieve her necessities temporarily' gave her a sovereign out of the poor box.[67]

In 1890 there was a mass strike in support of the Police Pensions Bill. Whether or not the threat of industrial action played any part, the Act was passed allowing retirement on 60 per cent of pay after twenty-five years' service. But pensions were just one of a series of crises threatening the force at that time.

In 1888, they not only had the Whitechapel murderer and a feral press to deal with, but also public dissent in the streets, a divided leadership, a troubled relationship with the Home Office and the stirrings of mutiny within the ranks. Much of the unrest could be traced back two years earlier to 8 February 1886.

On that day, a crowd of 5,000 unemployed and casual labourers ran riot through the West End after leaving two mass meetings held by the London United Workmen's Committee and the Social Democratic Federation in Trafalgar Square. Windows were smashed first in Pall Mall and St James' on the way to Hyde Park before the group returned to target shops along Oxford Street. But the damage caused during the rampage wasn't so much to property; it was the fear created that the West End was at risk from the marauding mobs of the East. The American journalist George Smalley wrote that the multitude was, for three hours, 'in absolute possession and unchecked control of the West End of London'. Panic quickly took over and for the next three days shopkeepers closed and boarded up their businesses as rumours spread of mobs arriving from Deptford and other wild areas of London to join the uprising. Once the hysteria had subsided, the blame landed squarely on the Metropolitan Police, and Commissioner Edmund Henderson felt compelled to resign after seventeen years in the job. He would be replaced by Sir Charles Warren, an officer in the British Army who was called back from Sudan to bring some discipline to the police and the capital.[68]

But the West End riots hinted at more trouble to come. The behaviour of the mob could not be explained just by wanton criminality. As the journalist Howard Goldsmid wrote later that year:

Most of the men who took part in the riots of that day came from the low lodging houses, and though the majority perhaps

were actuated solely by cupidity and greed, there was many a
stern, determined man there who believed that in plundering
and destroying he was merely executing the righteous wrath
of starved oppressed and discontented labour against harsh,
bloated and unsympathetic capital.

Goldsmid warned, a little melodramatically, that without
reform there might instead be revolution.[69]

This hardly seemed likely when the Golden Jubilee was
triumphantly celebrated the following year. If anything the
people of London seemed more enthusiastic than ever for
the monarchy and the society it represented. When Henry
Mayhew, the great investigator of the Victorian poor, died
the same month it was said that 'no one cared very greatly'.
But the mask soon slipped once the pomp and ceremony
died away. It was estimated that in 1887 there were 20,000
men out of work and that 27 out of every 100 workers in
east London, Battersea and Deptford were unemployed. The
homeless continued to gather in Trafalgar Square during the
summer, and by August and September it was effectively a
campsite 'occupation'. There they were entertained, educated
and agitated by socialists against the Conservative government
of Lord Salisbury. With the Liberal Party weakened and split,
it was the 'Classes against the Masses' – working-class politics
were on the rise.[70]

Warren's response to this continuing blight on a London
landmark, as well as the problem of having to monitor
repeated processions through the West End, was to ban them
from the square. His proclamation of 8 November 1887 read:

In consequence of the disorderly scenes which have recently
occurred in Trafalgar Square, and of the danger to the peace
of the Metropolis from meetings held there and with a view
to prevent such disorderly proceedings, and to preserve the

peace, I, Charles Warren, the Commissioner of Police of the Metropolis, do hereby give Notice, with the sanction of the Secretary of State and the concurrence of the Commissioners of Her Majesty's Works and Public Buildings, that until further intimation no Public Meetings will be allowed to assemble in Trafalgar Square, nor will speeches be allowed to be delivered therein; and all well-disposed persons are hereby cautioned and requested to abstain from joining or attending any such meeting or assemblage; and Notice is further given that all necessary measures will be adopted to prevent any such meeting or assemblage, or the delivery of any speech, and effectually to preserve the public peace, and to suppress any attempt at the disturbance thereof.[71]

The challenge was quickly taken up by the left-wing press and a demonstration was called for Sunday, 13 November. This meeting would embrace a number of different grievances, including the poor and the unemployed, casual workers, dock workers and radicals, and protestors against coercion in Ireland and the imprisonment of William O'Brien MP. Joining the marchers were the socialists Robert Cunninghame-Graham MP and John Burns, who had been acquitted of inciting the West End riots, Annie Besant and the playwright George Bernard Shaw. Press reports put the numbers between 10,000 and 150,000 people. Opposing them were 2,000 constables and 400 soldiers equipped with bayonets and rifles.[72] In the end the army was not called into action, but forceful attempts to disperse the protestors left 200 injured. Besant remembered how 'peaceable law-abiding workmen, who had never dreamed of rioting, were left with broken legs, broken arms, and wounds of every description'. Shaw, who had gone home for a cup of tea at 5.15 p.m. after failing to get to the square, later condemned Sir Charles Warren for turning 'an ordinary political meeting ... into a formidable riot' and further claimed that 'the terrible edged tools with which he is at present playing so wildly must be taken out of his hands at once'. Burns and Cunninghame-Graham were arrested, convicted of unlawful assembly, and were sentenced to six weeks' hard labour at the Old Bailey.[73]

William Bate Curner, a forty-one-year-old stonemason and member of the Deptford Liberal Club, was in the crowd that day, on what was to become known as 'Bloody Sunday'. During the riot he suffered a blow to the head and following his arrest was sentenced to fourteen days' imprisonment. When he died suddenly on 3 January 1888, more than a month after his release from prison, his widow was convinced that he had effectively been killed by the police. She told the inquest that her husband had complained that 'the policemen that took him were most barbarous and cruel'. Two days later his body was carried through the streets in an open hearse bearing the banner 'Killed for Trafalgar Square'. The secular funeral became a small demonstration involving members of radical, socialist and Irish National organisations and was attended by Annie Besant and W.T. Stead, the editor of the *Pall Mall Gazette*. Once the body had been lowered into the grave, a socialist choir sang William Morris' 'Death Song', composed following the riot. It began:

> What cometh here from west to east awending?
> And who are these, the marchers stern and slow?
> We bear the message that the rich are sending
> Aback to those who bade them wake and know.
> Not one, not one, nor thousands must they slay,
> But one and all if they would dusk the day.

The *Reynolds's Weekly Newspaper* linked his death to that of Alfred Linnell, who had died after suffering a broken leg at another demonstration on 20 November. It proclaimed:

Another victim to the Queen and the classes has fallen, and it is impossible to say how many more deaths may result from the Queen's Jubilee truncheoning of the citizens of London … The blood of Linnell and Curwin [*sic*] calls to the fellow citizens of these unhappy murdered men for vengeance.

But just as the inquest on Linnell's death failed to ascribe any blame to the police, Curner was found to have died from heart disease and natural causes 'and not from the effects of violence from any person or persons whoever'. The *Morning Post* used the Curner verdict to attack the liberal press and the demonstrators. They wrote:

The champions of lawlessness were sorely in need of a martyr or two, whose deaths might be effectively [used] as advertisements of their cause. The result of the inquiry is eminently satisfactory in so far as it may lead some well-meaning but injudicious persons to look with more suspicion upon the other stories of massacre and brutality and the like, which are dressed up in such specious garb to harrow their feelings.

While many accounts of Bloody Sunday state that three men died as a result of police brutality, the *Morning Post* was adamant that 'no proof that would convince any reasonable man has yet been brought forward to show that any single person was fatally injured by the police in suppressing the riot of the 13th of November'.[74]

Demonstrations continued throughout 1888. The release of Burns and Cunninghame-Graham from prison was celebrated with a public meeting on 20 February. On 4 March, Robert Harding from Poplar was arrested trying to padlock himself to a seat in Trafalgar Square while wearing a board reading: 'This is a protest against the forcible exclusion of the people.'

On the back was the question and answer: 'What is the main business of the government? To steal from the people to feed vast numbers of professional murderers.'

In May, Cunninghame-Graham was still persisting in his attempt to defy Warren and hold a meeting in the square. He partially succeeded on 14 July and by then the *Morning Post* was wearily describing the event as 'the customary demonstration of agitators'. In early November, the Revd Stewart Headlam told a crowd of unemployed workers that 'if Jesus Christ came into Trafalgar Square he would very soon get arrested.' But it was not just in Trafalgar Square – in July a radical 'anti-sweating' demonstration took place in Hyde Park, and a socialist league demonstration was held at Victoria Park on 18 November. The anniversary of Bloody Sunday was marked by a crowd of 4,000 at Hyde Park and calls for Sir Charles Warren to resign.[75]

Warren had in fact already handed in his resignation a few days earlier on 8 November, although his decision appears to have had more to do with internal politics than external events. His arrogant, commanding manner led him into conflict with both the Home Secretary Henry Matthews and his Assistant Commissioner James Monro, the head of the Criminal Investigation Department. Warren believed Matthews was meddling in police affairs and Monro was trying to bypass him by dealing directly with the Home Office. In August 1888, Warren demanded that either he or Monro would have to resign, and Monro walked. If Warren thought that would make his life easier, he was mistaken, because Monro was simply transferred to the Home Office and retained much of his influence over the CID.[76]

Monro's replacement, Sir Robert Anderson, an Irish lawyer who had worked for the Home Office, did not do much to relieve the burden. Anderson took up his post just hours after the prostitute Mary Ann Nichols was murdered in Whitechapel on the morning of 31 August. The following week Anderson left for Switzerland, having been advised by his doctor that he was 'physically unfit' and needed two months' rest. A few hours after his departure another prostitute, Annie Chapman, was murdered. 'The newspapers soon began to comment on my absence,' Anderson later recalled in his memoirs.

> Letters from Whitehall decided me to spend the last week of my holiday in Paris, that I might be in touch with my office. On the night of my arrival in the French capital two more victims fell to the knife of the murder-fiend; and next day's post brought me an urgent appeal from Mr Matthews to return to London; and of course I complied.[77]

That double murder in the early hours of 30 September also added complications by involving the City of London police. After Catherine Eddowes was murdered on their patch, the City offered a reward of £500, something that the Met had deliberately not done following the previous attacks. Warren and Matthews had previously agreed that rewards had been shown to have little effect but Warren, perhaps trying to improve his standing with the press, went on to suggest that £5,000 should be offered. He also enthusiastically adopted a suggestion that bloodhounds could be used to track down the killer. On 9 October he played the part of the hunted man in a test of two dogs called Barnaby and Burgho in Hyde Park. Although *The Times* had called for just such an experiment a week earlier, the general opinion was that Warren was opening up the police to ridicule. There were suggestions that the CID was not up to the job, and that better candidates for the job of catching criminals might be found outside the police force. Warren felt it necessary to circulate a statement defending the system of recruiting candidates younger than twenty-seven and of at least 5ft 9in in height, adding that 'as a general rule it has been ascertained by the Criminal Investigation branch that the candidates who have applied to be appointed direct to detective duties have not possessed any special qualifications which would justify their being so appointed'. The feminist Frances Power Cobbe responded with her own letter to *The Times* asking why there should not be female detectives. 'She would pass unsuspected where a man would be instantly noticed, she could extract gossip from other women much more freely ... a keen-eyed woman might do as well in her way as those keen-nosed bloodhounds.' The flood of suggestions, comments, theories and criticisms was endless, and Warren was beginning to crack under the pressure.[78]

The commissioner hit back with an article in the November edition of *Murray's Magazine*. His main gripe was that he was the victim of a sensationalist press and public which praised the police when things went well, only to condemn them as soon as the chance presented itself. 'Year by year the metropolis of our Empire has become more and more prone to dangerous panics, which if permitted to increase in intensity must certainly lead to disastrous consequences.' In his opinion, his handling of the Trafalgar Square riots had ensured that for 'almost the first time during this century the mob failed in ascendancy over London and in coercing the government'. The police had also successfully dealt with the threat from Fenian terrorists and disrupted a plot to bomb the Golden Jubilee. Yet now that he had restored peace, he was facing an 'insidious' attack on the system of policing itself. Such behaviour would lead to more officers on the streets, higher taxes, and the adoption of the 'elaborate detective operations practiced on the continent', where government espionage was rampant. He wrote:

> This violently fickle conduct of the public is very dangerous to the preservation of peace ... it is straining the administration

of the police, it is endangering the discipline of the force, it is encouraging the mob to disorder and rapine, and it very much increases the police rate.[79]

The article not only astounded the government and the press, it also upset the ranks. In a direct reply to the commissioner, an anonymous 'PC' lambasted Warren's 'exultant egotism in each page' and his fondness for the word 'mob'. According to the author, the force was demoralised under his command and officers were regretful rather than boastful about the clearing of Trafalgar Square. 'The friendly feeling that had previously existed between the great majority of the poorer portion of the public and the police received a rebuff, not yet got over.' Warren had also snubbed the detective department, brought in harsh punishments for drinking on duty and introduced a new squad drill more suited to the armed forces. The radical liberal MP Charles Conybeare supported the pamphlet with a letter calling for 'the freeing of London from the incompetent and arrogant administration of Charles Warren'.[80]

Matthews responded to the article by sending Warren a copy of an 1879 Home Office circular asserting its power over the Metropolitan Police by banning anyone in the force, including the commissioner, from publishing anything relating to the department unless approved by the Secretary of State. Warren replied, 'Had I been informed that such a circular was to be in force, I should not have accepted the post of commissioner' and handed in his resignation for the second time on 8 November. The following day, the mutilated body of the prostitute Mary Kelly was discovered in Whitechapel. It was clear that the stalemate could not continue, and Matthews accepted Warren had to go on 10 November, although he would not formally leave the job until 1 December. Warren's defeat was completed when it was announced that James Monro would be his replacement.[81] Monro would make no mention of Warren in his report to Parliament for the year 1888, but noted that:

> ... crime during the year has shown a decided tendency to increase. This fact may be accounted for, to a certain extent, by circumstances which affected the administration of the Force in a peculiar manner at different periods of the year. The agitation which centred at Trafalgar Square, and the murders in Whitechapel, necessitated the concentration in particular localities of large bodies of police ... diminishing the number of men ordinarily employed in other divisions.[82]

Coincidentally, the so-called Ripper also appears to have resigned, never to be identified. But the Whitechapel murders were not unique in baffling the detectives of the metropolis. Newspapers began retelling other unsolved, undiscovered or unavenged cases going back to the beginning of the nineteenth century. One 1888 murder in particular would haunt the Metropolitan Police and its detectives.[83]

7

THE CURSE OF
SCOTLAND YARD

At 6 a.m. on of 1 October 1888, a carpenter employed by
the firm J. Grover & Sons was working on the foundations
of a new building in Whitehall. Frederick Windborn walked
down the ramp into the basement and passed through the
30ft-long vault to a recess where he kept his tools. Groping in
the darkness, he felt something strange, which on inspection
with a lighted match appeared to be a neatly wrapped parcel
measuring roughly 2ft by 2.5ft. If he also noticed the maggots
crawling about the place, his curiosity was not aroused
sufficiently to investigate. It was only on the following day, after
chatting about it with a colleague on his lunch break, that it
was decided to take a closer look. It was not, as Windborn had
thought, a lump of old bacon, but the decomposed body of a
woman enclosed in a piece of black petticoat and tied up with
string. The head, arms and legs were missing, and the spine
had been sawn through above the pelvis. *The Times* described
it as a 'horrible spectacle' but went on to say that the victim
appeared to be 'a remarkably fine young woman'. All the
circumstances pointed to murder. But why leave the body on a
busy construction site? Although there were no guards at night,

the area was surrounded by an 8ft-tall hoarding and was closed to the public. Was the reason connected to the building itself? This new edifice was to become known as New Scotland Yard, the home of the Metropolitan Police.

The decision to move from the old headquarters at No.4 Whitehall Place had been taken in 1885 when it became clear that more space was needed. They chose a site which encompassed 70,000 sq. ft of land on the Victoria Embankment; it had been sold by the Metropolitan Board of Works for the building of a National Opera House. Work had begun to designs by the architect Norman Shaw, but when that scheme ran into trouble the police raised a £200,000 loan to take over the project and asked Shaw to adapt his plans. The result was a striking building of red brick dressed with 2,500 tons of white Portland stone hewn by the convicts at Dartmoor. The circular turrets at the corners and thick square chimneys on the roof gave it the appearance of a castle crossed with a Victorian mansion. When it finally opened in 1890, the legend of 'The Whitehall Mystery' only added to its Gothic stylings.

Other workers at the site testified that they had not seen the parcel on 28/29 September, yet the presence of maggots indicated that it had lain there for weeks. The medical evidence suggested that death could have taken place earlier that month, but a piece of newspaper used to wrap the body was dated 24 August 1888. Detectives searched the vaults for further body parts on 3 October. They found nothing, but they were lucky to escape with their lives when a 4-ton steam crane at the site toppled from its 150ft-high platform through the first floor to the very spot where the remains had been discovered the previous day. As one newspaper reported:

> The detectives in the vault, hearing the crashing overhead and loud cries of warning, rushed out into the open, just in time to see the engine bury itself in the ground upon which but an

instant before they had been standing. The heavy machinery fell within 2ft of a constable who did not manage to escape so quickly, and then the boiler burst with a loud report, flooding the surrounding ground with hot water.

Further pieces of the puzzle emerged when the torso was matched to a right arm found three weeks earlier. On 11 September, shortly before 1 p.m., a group of labourers came across a pale object wrapped in string on the north shore of the Thames near the railway bridge off Grosvenor Road and Ebury Bridge Road. The police were called and the arm was passed on to Dr Thomas Bond, who would later play a part in the Whitechapel murder investigation. He concluded it had been removed after death and had belonged to a Caucasian woman of around twenty years of age.

On 6 October it was reported that a woman's leg had been found in Guildford, but two days later this was discounted as belonging to a bear. A more startling discovery was made on 17 October when a news agency journalist visited the building site with a dog. If the police detectives from A Division had made a thorough examination of the scene, it was shown to be inadequate in spectacular fashion when the Russian terrier indicated a 7ft-wide recess on the opposite side from the location of the torso. Digging into the ground by candlelight, they found first a left leg and then, a few inches deeper, the left arm. Dr Bond believed the leg had been there for weeks, perhaps six, and had been cut from the body after death. As to how the woman died, he was unable to offer up an explanation. The jury returned a verdict of found dead rather than wilful murder, preferring to leave the mystery to the police. As *The Times* reported:

The jury had before them the surmise that no one would so mutilate a body except for the purpose of concealing an identity, which once established might lead to the detection of a terrible murder. The body, it was clear, was a woman above twenty-five years of age, who had not died of a disease … but beyond that fact they could not go except by supposition.

The dismemberment of the Whitehall victim suggested some knowledge of anatomy, while the finding of the separate parts at different locations and times suggested a deliberate attempt to conceal a crime. The killer's methods were similar to those used in another case the previous year, in Rainham, Essex. On 11 May 1887, a lighter-man spotted part of a human torso floating in the water. The head, arms, upper chest and legs were missing. By 1 July, the police had recovered eleven separate body parts from stretches of the Thames in Temple and Battersea, and in the Regent's Park Canal near St Pancras. As in the Whitehall case, the head was never recovered. When pieced together they formed a dark-haired Caucasian woman aged between twenty-five and forty and around 5ft 3in tall. There was no obvious cause of death and the inquest jury returned a verdict of found dead.

Links have been drawn from both cases to the 'Thames Mysteries' of September 1873 and June 1874. In the first case, parts of a woman's body were recovered at Battersea, Nine Elms and Woolwich. While the head was again missing, the face and scalp washed up on the shore at Limehouse. In the second case, a headless body with one leg and no arms was recovered from the riverbank at Putney. And the headless torsos did not stop at Whitehall. In June 1889, a riverside labourer pulled in a female torso wrapped in an apron at Horsleydown in Southwark. Other parts – but not the head – were found in the river at Battersea, Nine Elms and Limehouse. A section of the torso was left in Battersea Park and the right thigh was spotted in the garden of the Shelley estate, which may have been the killer's deliberate nod to Frankenstein's monster, or entirely coincidental. Unlike the other mysteries, the victim in this case was identified as Elizabeth Jackson, a suspected prostitute whose family were living in Chelsea. Three months later another torso, complete with both arms, was found by a police officer under a railway arch in Pinchin Street, off Backchurch Lane in Whitechapel. The head and legs were never recovered. While the murder was at first feared to be the work of the Ripper, it had more similarities with the Thames cases due to the severing of the head and legs by knife and saw. In 1894, Chief Constable Sir Melville MacNaghten grouped together the Pinchin Street discovery with Rainham, Whitehall and Elizabeth Jackson.[84]

It was not unusual to find a dead body floating in the Thames in the 1880s. In 1888 there were several reports of 'mysterious deaths' connected to the river. In May a five-year-old boy was found drowned off the Shadwell Basin. He had last been seen going for a walk with his mother, but they never returned. The mother was never traced. In August, a number of witnesses saw twenty-four-year-old Alfred Cooper dive off London Bridge for a 10s bet. He never surfaced and the jury returned a verdict of accidental death.[85]

Statistics for 1882 show 544 corpses were recovered from the Thames and open verdicts were returned in 277 of those cases. Without obvious signs of injury, it was difficult to reach a firm conclusion about the cause of death and many of the deceased were never identified. The discovery of a severed arm might suggest a 'revolting murder' or 'a grim joke by some medical student'. In 1888, *The Times* noted that:

… a remarkable feature in the case of the discovery of the mutilated body at Whitehall is the number of missing women brought to the notice of the authorities by persons making inquiries respecting the remains. It is thus shown that very many women leave their friends without communicating with them and pass out of sight of those nearest to them.

It also reported that there were 'an average number of mysterious disappearances of women' that year. In 1887, there were 18,004 reported missing persons, of whom 9,203 were restored to their friends and eighty-five were suicides. That left a total of 8,716 people unaccounted for in London. Often the job of tracking them down was left to private detectives, who widely advertised in books, magazines and newspapers of the day.[86]

There were also many other reports of women being dismembered and their body parts being dumped around the capital in the nineteenth century. The head of Hannah Brown was found at the Regent's Canal near Edgware Road in 1836, and the torso and legs of Julia Martha Thomas were recovered from a box washed up on the shore at Barnes in 1879 (the skull remained missing until it was dug up in Richmond in 2010). A woman's head was found in a mews off Tottenham Court Road in 1884. However, the victims were not just women – in 1857 a carpetbag full of male body parts was found at Waterloo Bridge. He was never identified.

But if there was a second serial killer in operation in London in 1888, their crimes were completely overshadowed by events in Whitechapel and Spitalfields. The discovery of the torso at the new police building was relegated to twelfth in *The Times* contents page on 3 October, first place going to 'The East End Murders' and the identifications of the victims Elizabeth Stride and Catherine Eddowes. In between, there were reports on the Paris theatres, the Church Congress and the new German Emperor Wilhelm II. There were few similarities between the Ripper murders and the Whitehall mystery, but that did not stop the newspapers suggesting a connection. The speculation was enough to prompt somebody to send a letter to the Central News Agency on 5 October:

Dear Friend, In the name of God hear me I swear I did not kill the female whose body was found at Whitehall. If she was an honest woman I will hunt down and destroy her murderer. If she was a whore God will bless the hand that slew her, for the women of Moab and Midian shall die and their blood shall mingle with the dust. I never harm any others or the Divine power that protects and helps me in my grand work would quit for ever. Do as I do and the light of glory shall shine upon you. I must get to work tomorrow treble event this time yes yes three must be ripped. Will send you a bit of face by post I promise this dear old Boss. The police now reckon my work a practical joke well well Jack's a very practical joker ha ha Keep this back till three are wiped out and you can show the cold meat. Yours truly Jack the Ripper.

If there was a 'Thames Torso' murderer killing women, cutting them up and disposing of the parts separately, it is possible that they claimed a second victim in 1888. On the morning of 28 September, a boy walking past the Blind School on Lambeth Road in Southwark noticed a parcel on the grass behind the railings. It contained the decomposed arm of a woman. No other body parts appear to have been recovered and while it was initially thought to belong to the torso at Whitehall, the finding of both arms for that woman suggested this third limb belonged to yet another victim. Or it may have been an impudent act of body disposal rather than a murderr. Likewise, the placing of a woman's torso, arm and leg in the vaults of New Scotland Yard may just have been a morbid joke at the expense of the police. 'It seems a strange fatality that the site of the future home of the Metropolitan Police should have been tainted with undiscovered crime,' wrote the authors of an 1889 book on the history of the force. 'Let us hope that this is not a bad augury.'[87]

8

TWO MYSTERIES

A new kind of detective had arrived on the scene in London 1888. His name was Sherlock Holmes. The fictional sleuth was described by his creator, the novelist Arthur Conan Doyle, as a 'walking calendar of crime' who 'appears to know every detail of every horror perpetrated in the country'. Holmes, appropriately for the period, was also a social investigator with a taste for 'long walks, which appeared to take him into the lowest portions of the city'. His first case appeared in print in *Beeton's Christmas Annual* of November 1887, and was then repackaged in book form in July 1888. Holmes went on to appear in three more novels and fifty-six short stories, one of which – *A Scandal in Bohemia* – was set on 20 March 1888. There was no murder to solve, but the episode was notable for the fact that Holmes was outwitted by a woman while endeavouring to save the King of Bohemia from blackmail. It was a rare defeat, but his powers were as sharp as ever despite his addiction to cocaine. Within seconds of Watson's visit to No.221B Baker Street, Holmes deduced that the doctor had put on 7½lb, had returned to practice, had got very wet recently and had a clumsy servant girl. 'You see but you do not observe,' the detective declared.

Sherlock Holmes also tapped into another theme – the apparent incompetence of Scotland Yard. The former Chief Inspector Francis Carlin, writing in 1919, felt aggrieved that the public were left with the impression that the police were a 'crowd of inept blunderers', adding that Holmes was allowed 350 pages to catch his man whereas the Yard detective 'has to get his man quickly or not at all'. In some of these real-life cases the investigation only uncovered more and more loose ends. What may at first have looked like clear-cut murder ended up as a genuine mystery or a collection of suspicious circumstances with no real evidence.[88]

➤ A Nagging Toothache ➤

Fifteen-year-old Frederick Playle had an errand to run. His master William Barber, the manager of a chemist's shop in Walthamstow, east London, had written a note and wanted it delivered to a customer a few hundred yards away. It was only to be delivered to a Mrs French, mind, nobody else. So, when Frank got to No.208 Boundary Road a few minutes later and Mrs French's husband answered, he quickly made his excuses and left. Later that afternoon he went back again with the note and on this occasion he was able to hand the young woman the message. Mrs French replied with a simple, 'Tell him yes.' His errand complete, Frank returned with the reply to Mr Barber, ready for his next task, which was to fetch a shilling's worth of brandy from the local public house. Shortly after his return at 4 p.m., Mrs French arrived and was shown into the back parlour where the chemist occasionally performed tooth extractions. Mr Barber, who seemed a little strange or 'dull' in demeanour, told Frank he could go home for a few hours. Being an obedient fellow, young Master Playle did as he was told.

When the boy returned to chemist's at 6 p.m. he found it closed and the lights switched off. Rather than shrug his shoulders and wander off, he walked round the back along a footpath and scaled the wall into the garden. Once inside the premises he knocked at the parlour door. There was no answer. Frank opened the door and let his eyes adjust to the darkness of the room. There on a sofa near the window sat Mrs French; she looked unnaturally pale and motionless, almost like a showroom mannequin. Frank decided to get help from the butcher and the grocer next door, and they in turn fetched a doctor.

Having taken the woman's pulse, Dr George Thorpe at first thought Mrs French had fainted. Her pulse was slow and he could barely detect her breathing. Her dress had been undone four or five buttons from the top, but her clothing was otherwise in order. While examining her closely he detected a sickly sweet smell coming from her mouth: the distinctive odour of chloroform. There was a bottle of it on the shelf nearby, as well as several other jars containing smelling salts, carbolic lotion, carbolic acid and soda water, some toothache tincture, brandy, cotton wool, a handkerchief and a hand bowl containing water. Mrs French's gloves, brooch, umbrella and bonnet were on the table next to one of Barber's hats.

The police were called, but it was past midnight when they discovered that the till had been plundered. Perhaps as much as £15 was missing. There was also no sign of Mr Barber. A description was issued:

William Barber, aged thirty-five, chemist's assistant, height 5ft 8.5in, fair complexion, hair and moustache, near-sighted, dressed in grey jacket, dark trousers and a hard felt hat. He is splay footed.

Annie Mary French died at 11.45 p.m. the next day, Sunday 22 July 1888. She was twenty-two years old and had been married to Arthur George French, a grocer's assistant, since the summer of 1886. By all accounts they had lived happily together. Mr French said that he had last seen her that Saturday at 2 p.m. when she told him her toothache was coming on again. Two weeks earlier she had bought a bottle of Chlorodyne – a mixture of morphine, cannabis and chloroform – from Hamilton's for the same problem and he assumed she had gone out for some more. Annie was otherwise in good spirits and when she failed to return to the house at 7 p.m. he assumed she had gone to visit her mother. Questioned about William Barber, he said the chemist used to come round to his house every other day and dined there on Sundays by arrangement. The two men were friends and went on morning walks together.

At the first inquest hearing on 25 July, Mr French was questioned about whether he suspected there was anything going on between his wife and Barber. 'Never,' he replied. 'She told me she utterly disliked him and wished he would keep away from the house.' Mr French had behaved more coolly towards the chemist as a result, and it was noticeable that the previous Sunday, Barber was very quiet during dinner and complained of feeling miserable. 'He said it was very lonely being in the house alone. He was a man who drank freely. Lately he had taken to drinking spirits, but I never saw him the worse for drink.' As far as he knew, Barber's mood had nothing to do with his wife. So the evidence of Frederick Playle came as a shock. The teenager confirmed that Annie French had called at the chemist's shop every morning for the last nine months at around 11 a.m. That was the cue for Barber to send him away on an errand, and when he returned he nearly always found Mrs French with Barber in the back parlour. Even so, he had never seen Barber acting improperly towards her or even seen him put his arm round the woman's waist. The husband couldn't believe that there had been so many visits – he had always got the impression that Barber disliked the company of women. Nevertheless, there was now a possible motive – had Barber poisoned Mrs French when she called off their affair?

The next day, Annie French was buried in Bow cemetery whilst the police continued to search for the missing chemist. Then, on Saturday 28 July, an unshaven and downtrodden Barber was arrested in Brentford. He had taken a room above a coffee shop in the high street, but he had attracted attention due to his 'superior dress' and the curious way he read the daily paper, scanning the news while pretending to be absorbed by the advertisements. After being apprehended by a local constable, he admitted that he was the wanted man, but insisted that Mrs French must have accidentally poisoned herself in an attempt to soothe her toothache. 'We were great friends but there was nothing improper between us. I tried to restore her but failed and I ran away in the excitement of the moment. I did not know exactly what I was doing.' He had taken the money from the shop but most of it had been stolen from him by a woman while he was drunk. Barber had pawned his waistcoat but had kept a bottle of prussic acid in his pocket with a note which insisted that he was not to blame for 'The Walthamstow Mystery'. It appeared he had been planning to kill himself.

On his appearance before the magistrates he sobbed as the clerk read the charge of 'causing the death of Annie French by administering to her a noxious drug'. The evidence included the statement he gave to police after his arrest:

> Mrs French had complained of having suffered from toothache for some few weeks, and I had on several occasions rubbed on chloroform or camphorated chloroform. I had told her at any

time when the toothache came to come down immediately and then I would give her a draught to take, and would rub her gums with chloroform and would afterwards apply some strong caustic such as carbolic or nitric acid to destroy or wither the nerve. Just as I was about to prepare the draught some customers came into the shop and Mrs French said to me in a rather pettish way 'go and attend to your customers'. I left her in the room with the preparations and on my return I found she had taken the whole of the contents of the strong solution of morphia.

He said that he had tried to revive her with some brandy and the smelling salts, and undid her dress round the neck and bathed her forehead with cold water. 'Immediately after doing this she fell from my arms on to the couch and said "I am dying". I looked at her and saw she was changing fast and could not recover. In my fright I rushed away, not knowing what to do with myself.' Barber vehemently denied that sexual assault was on his mind, or that he was planning to perform an operation. As for the note he had sent to Mrs French, he claimed that it only referred to some cigarettes that he had asked her to make.

His account was not entirely convincing but his reference to morphine, both in his statement and in the suspected suicide note, tallied with the latest medical opinion on the cause of death. Chloroform poisoning was thought to be unlikely due to the lack of any irritation in the throat. At the conclusion of the inquest in August, the coroner declared that the case was even 'more mysterious than ever' and left it to the jury to decide whether they needed to hear any more evidence. If Barber had given Mrs French the drugs then he was guilty of murder, but if Mrs French had taken them it was either an accident or suicide. 'So far as he could see, there was no evidence to lead them to any conclusion,' reported the *Standard* newspaper. 'It was, however, in his opinion a very strange thing that she should have taken it herself.' It was unfair to call Barber to give his account at the inquest as he had already been charged by the police, the coroner added. The inquest jury returned an open verdict, unable to be sure exactly how Mrs French had met her death.

The prosecution continued, however, and Barber was committed to the Old Bailey for trial. On 18 September, the case was considered by the Grand Jury and was thrown out. Barber was a free man.[89]

~ At the Pleasure Grounds ~

On Wednesday 25 April 1888, a Mrs Ann Smith, aged fifty-one, of Hemsworth Street, Hoxton, stood before the magistrate at Worship Street Police Court to make a desperate plea for help. Her twenty-five-year-old daughter Elizabeth – known as Annie – had left the family home that Saturday to attend a dance. She had never come back. Mrs Smith checked with all the local police stations and asked questions in the neighbourhood. Annie had simply disappeared. She was 'a good steady girl' with a regular job as a machinist for a local firm in Kingsland Road. Her father, Albert, was a respectable carpenter and shop fitter. But the police were reluctant to investigate without evidence of foul play, and Mrs Smith could only hope that by appealing to the magistrate they would get some publicity. The following day, after a report was carried by *The Times*, the police swung into action.

Twenty-four hours later Mrs Smith learned the dreadful truth. Their daughter was dead. Annie's body had been found by police officers dragging the backwaters of the River Lea near Millfields. Two local men had been arrested and it was suggested that there was evidence of a sexual assault.

'There seems little reason to doubt that a shocking outrage and murder have been committed at the East End of London,' began the report in *The Times*. Further details emerged bit by bit over the coming days. Annie Smith, a 'passionate' girl fond of a drink, had gone to the 'Pleasure Gardens' at the back of the Greyhound pub on Lea Bridge Road on 21 April 1888. She was a regular visitor to the Saturday open-air dances, at which couples paraded on a covered platform to the accompaniment of a quadrille band. She had met with her fiancé, William Henry Stead, a well-dressed man described by locals as a 'toff', but as the evening wore on she had become increasingly drunk and upset. At around 9 p.m. she collapsed on the doorstep of the Carman's Rest coffee shop and began vomiting. It seemed she had been at the brandy. 'I am sick of it,' she groaned, 'I wish I was settled [married].' When told she would give herself a headache with all the alcohol, she replied, 'My heart aches, not my head.' Annie then returned to the pleasure grounds and rejoined her fiancé, but he was clearly unhappy that she had been off by herself. After a quarrel, Stead slapped her face and left. Annie wandered off and asked a group of costermongers to carry her to the Ship Aground pub in their barrow because she felt faint. After a drink she accused one of them of stealing her purse, although he insisted that he was just pinning up her dress. Annie was next spotted walking across the Millfields in the company of a small group of men.

The two suspects arrested by police were George Anthony, a twenty-three-year-old bargeman, and Charles Cantor, a thirty-year-old labourer. Anthony claimed that on the night of the dance he, Cantor and a few of their friends had heard about the suspected theft and had chased two men towards Clapton. He had fought with one of them in a ditch, but the purse was never recovered. 'I asked the woman if I should go up the road with her,' he said. 'She and me then went up Lea Bridge together as far as Chatsworth Road. I left her there and

I don't know where she went.' He later added that they had gone across the marshes, across Strong's Bridge and along the towpath to the waterworks gate. 'I then saw Charlie Cantor coming along the path and I went away. I left her standing against the wall and I went along the path over Pond Lane Bridge across the fields and down home. Charlie Cantor was talking to her when I left.'

As for Cantor, he told the police, 'I can't tell you anything about her, sir, except that I saw her standing against a post.' He refused to answer questions at the inquest, on the advice of his solicitor.

Further investigation revealed that the wall referred to by Anthony was a third of a mile from where Annie had been found dead at 5.20 a.m. on Friday 27 April. Although rats had gnawed away her left cheek and part of her right arm, there was no evidence of any violence or struggle. Her dress was muddy and wet but intact. The broken umbrella found on a nearby path was unconnected to the case. The surgeon, Dr Charles Aveling, concluded that the relatively small amount of water in the stomach of Annie Smith showed that she had not struggled when she entered the river, either because of weakness or some other reason. The evidence was slim, to say the least, but the case was intriguing enough to be given the tag 'The Lea Mystery', and an illustration of the Greyhound 'Pleasure Gardens' featured on the front page of the *Penny Illustrated Paper* for 5 May. Three days later the jury returned an open verdict, unable to say what had caused the young woman to drown.

At Dalston Police Court, the two suspects returned to hear that the prosecutor had effectively given up the case. The only evidence against Cantor was the statement of Anthony and that would be inadmissible. Anthony had scratches on his face, but they could have come from the fight with the costermonger. As to his being the last person seen with Annie

Smith, there was the statement of one witness that she was alone at 1.30 a.m., by which time Anthony was at home. There was no evidence that the girl had been robbed or sexually assaulted. The magistrate had heard enough, and allowed the charges to be dropped.[90]

Six months later there was an even bigger sensation at the Greyhound 'Pleasure Gardens'. Before an estimated crowd of 60,000 people in the grounds and the surrounding Hackney marshes, an aeronaut styling himself as 'Professor Higgins' ascended in a balloon. At 2,000ft, he set himself free and plunged to the earth. Above his head a homemade parachute fluttered and then finally caught in the flow of air, allowing the professor to descend slowly to the ground about a mile away from where he had begun. 'The people seemed almost mad with excitement and seizing the Englishman who had successfully accomplished the feat, carried him shoulder high in triumph to the hotel where a fresh ovation was accorded him,' reported the *Birmingham Daily Post*. By day, Higgins was a Clapton omnibus driver and amateur gymnast, but he had turned to ballooning after the American aeronaut and self-proclaimed 'inventor of the parachute', Professor Baldwin, made a descent at Alexandra Palace in July. In fact, the modern parachute had been invented in the late eighteenth century, but the public did not seem to care. It was in the grip of a new balloon craze that would continue into the mid-1890s. Professor Higgins survived a series of accidents while touring the country before eventually dying in a performance at Leeds in August 1891.[91]

9

HOME SWEET HOME

In twenty-first-century London, the majority of homicide victims are male. The ratio is usually between 2:1 and 4:1. But while 1888 was perhaps a freak year for murder in comparison to surrounding years, the late nineteenth century does reveal a different pattern. The returns of the Registrar General reveal that usually more than half of homicide victims in London were female (*see* Appendix). Why were women more at risk? Was it because violence against women, particularly in the home, was more acceptable at this time? In the Victorian era, eight out of ten murdered women were killed by a husband, lover or suitor; and while 26 per cent of convicted murderers were men who killed their wives, only 1 per cent were women who killed their husbands.[92]

Two female murder victims in 1888 stand out from the rest. They were both middle class and living in comfort. They took no obvious risks – in fact both their lives centred round their homes and nothing within those houses suggested that they might meet violent ends. Yet it was their very wealth and comfort that would attract the attention of their killers. Burglaries, break-ins and robberies were not that common according to the police returns – there were 499 burglaries, 1,408 cases of housebreaking, 590 cases of business break-ins, 107 robberies and twenty-six assaults with intent to rob (at present there are 60,000 reported cases of residential burglary every year in a city which has almost doubled in population). However, these two victims were in all likelihood not chosen at random.

‑ The Lady's Maid ‑

The home of Lucy Clark was decorated with all the trappings of an illustrious career – Dresden china, antiques, fine clothing and jewellery. Pride of place on the mantelpiece was a signed portrait of Lady Lonsdale, Gladys Lowther, the daughter of Sidney Herbert, the late Conservative MP and supporter of Florence Nightingale. Lucy Clark had once been her maid and the picture was just one of the many presents she had been given during her employment. That was some time ago now – Lady Lonsdale was now Marchioness of Ripon, the husband of Earl de Grey (who was himself the grandson of a prime minister) – and Lucy Clark had set up her own dressmaking business in the West End catering for the tastes of the aristocracy. She took premises in Marylebone and advertised her trade with a brass plate on the front door reading 'Modes et Robes'. Lucy Clark was very much a 'respectable' woman. 'She was described as a tall and remarkably fine person, of pleasing manners, but very reserved in disposition,' reported the *Penny Illustrated Paper*. 'She was in the habit of wearing several rings, and her watch chain and pendants were generally to be found conspicuously displayed on the outside of her dress.'

At the beginning of 1888, Miss Clark was forty-nine years old and living alone, except for her cat, on the first floor above a shop at No.86 George Street, Portman Square.

Home Sweet Home

She was a religious woman and was last seen by her neighbours attending the evening service at Portman Chapel before visiting a nearby coffee house on Sunday 15 January. A week went by, and neither the milkman next door, nor the owner of the general store could remember seeing her. It was on Monday 23 January that an estate agent visited the house to show two ladies the unoccupied floors above Miss Clark's residence. William J. Betts left the prospective clients in the shop while he picked up the post and quickly checked everything was suitable for a viewing. In the gloom he could just make out the form of a woman slumped at the bottom of the staircase. Lighting a match and peering closer, he noticed that she was lying in a large pool of blood. He immediately fetched the police and a local doctor.

Lucy Clark was cold and stiff, and appeared to have been dead several days. But this was no accidental tumble down the stairs – her skull had been fractured into five pieces by heavy blows from a blunt object. Turning the body, Dr Henry Timms saw the throat had been cut from ear to ear, the blade slicing through the blood vessels and windpipe to the spine. So severely, in fact, that it had left a notch upon the bone. There was blood on the floor of the passage between the body and the front door, and blood going up to Miss Clark's rooms. Detective Inspector George Robson followed the trail upstairs and found the place ransacked. The bedroom was in total disorder; drawers had been pulled out and rifled through and their contents scattered across the floor. There was some food in the kitchen and three empty bottles of stout. In the front room he found an empty jewel case and an empty watch case and two gold rings lying on the carpet. If the murder had been carried out by burglars or robbers, they were not experts. The next day detectives discovered gold, silver and banknotes amounting to more than £11, and a bank book indicating £97 in savings and £250 in stocks and shares.

Inspector Robson also found a letter in Miss Clark's handwriting dated 'Saturday, January 13' [Saturday was actually the 14th]:

Harry, I am waiting an answer from you to know what is your intention – to pay for the damage you did to my gold chain, and make good the other things you have stolen from me. I have taken my chain to a jeweller. But you have broken and twisted it so badly, and one piece you have broken off, he cannot mend it for less than 7s 6d, and the double ring, of the same quality, would be 10s I think the action you did was that of a villain. You know I had it in my power to make you pay one way or another, so you had better let me know if you wish to do so of your own free will.

The letter was addressed to 'Mr Henry Chadwick, 78, Gloucester Street, South Belgravia'.

Inspector Robson took the clue to Miss Clark's brother Francis, a stonemason living in Walworth Road, south London. Francis had last seen her alive in early January and knew she kept various items of jewellery, including a gold watch and chain, at the house. There had been some family disagreement after her nephews, Harry and Walter Chadwick, checked on the cat while their aunt was ill at their mother's house over the New Year. When she returned home to Marylebone on 4 January she had found some of her jewellery missing. It was a possible motive and the detective's next visit was to twenty-one-year-old Henry Chadwick at his family home in Gloucester Street.

Henry, who worked as a surveyor at an architect's office, denied any quarrel. What about the jewellery? 'Surely she had not told you anything about that?' he replied, before finally admitting that he and his brother had opened a jewel case using some keys they had found in a tin box under the table.

They were drunk and had taken two gold stoppers and broken a chain. His brother Walter had pawned the gold stoppers for 10s. Henry had visited his aunt again on Monday 16 January to ask for her forgiveness and to promise to repair a neck-chain which he had broken. Inspector Robson also questioned nineteen-year-old Walter, who was unemployed and had no allowance to speak of. He had not been to his aunt's house since the theft, and on Tuesday 17 January he had travelled to Stratford by train to see the manager of the radical club on the high street and had spent the evening at a pub. How did he pay the return fare? He must have had money off his brother or from a friend, he said.

There was suspicion but no real evidence. Could the nephews really be responsible for such a brutal murder? The medical evidence was that Miss Clark had been beaten about the head with a blunt object such as a mallet, and the bruises to her arms suggested that she had tried to fend off the attack. She was still alive when the knife was drawn across her throat. The police surgeon believed this fatal wound was inflicted by someone standing in front of Miss Clark. Two different types of attack – did this suggest two killers? Yet Inspector Robson found neither murder weapon at the house. It was still unclear exactly when the murder took place. Inspector Robson favoured the night of Tuesday the 17th, although a business letter found at the victim's home appeared to have been opened on the 18th. The detective had also established that Walter Chadwick had gone to Stratford on Wednesday the 18th, rather than the previous night. There were other intriguing but unconfirmed newspaper reports. A coachman came forward to say that he had seen two men leave the house and drive off in a Hansom cab at 11 p.m. on Friday the 20th. The driver was tracked down and he told police that he had taken two men to Cannon Street station. It was also said that Miss Clark's gold watch had been pawned in Fleet Street for

£3 under the name of Gill and a fictitious address, St George's Road, on the 18th. This watch was identified by the victim's relatives, but the manager of the shop failed to identify the man who attended his premises. He was said to be under thirty years of age, pale, wearing a dark overcoat and a tall silk hat, and spoke with 'a little bit of bombast'.

The Chadwicks were arrested, detained at Marylebone police station while their rooms were searched, and then released. For the next few days, until the inquest on 27 January, the brothers were kept under surveillance. Their movements were read out to the court but revealed little more than a few meetings with the other members of Lucy Clark's family. Henry Chadwick told the court that he had gone round to apologise to his aunt after work on the evening of Monday 16 January and had spoken to her on the front step.

> She said she had written me a letter, but finding the language a little stronger than she intended she had not posted it. She asked after my mother, and then kissed me and bid me goodnight. She asked me up but I felt ashamed and declined to go.

Henry said that he then went home, calling in at the local Warwick pub to have a drink with his brother until around 10 p.m. The following day he was at home all evening, apart from spending a half hour at the Warwick. He also spent Wednesday and Thursday evening at the same pub, whereas Friday evening he had played chess with his brother at home.

Walter Chadwick thought he had gone to Stratford on Tuesday 17 January, but if that was Wednesday then he must have stayed at home. The coroner was later to remark that the younger Chadwick 'had not given a satisfactory account of himself', and that the suspicion resting upon them resulted from their own behaviour. Suspicion, however, was not enough to bring charges and the inquest jury returned a verdict of 'wilful murder against some person or persons at present unknown'.

The police investigation continued as Lucy Clark was laid to rest at Brompton cemetery on Monday 30 January. Officers were still attempting to trace items of jewellery believed to have been stolen: a gold watch, a gold chain, a gold necklace, three gold rings, three pairs of gold earrings, a gold brooch and two pairs of bracelets. They pulled up the flooring and flushed the drains looking for a weapon. They examined the brothers' clothing under a microscope and questioned the laundrywomen, but nothing of interest was found.

Journalists also made their own enquiries and interviewed the mother of the Chadwick brothers. Mrs Chadwick 'was very lady-like and courteous in her demeanour, but showed traces of deep mental anguish', reported *Lloyd's Weekly Newspaper*. The family had clearly been torn apart by events, and one relative had openly accused the brothers of the murder. 'I felt in all my heart that they were innocent and that all would come right,' said Mrs Chadwick.

> The young men I knew did wrong in taking some of her valuables, but they had too much affection for their aunt ever to think of murdering her. No! The murderer or murderers must be sought for somewhere else. But this untimely end, I am sorry to say, is no more than what all of us have feared and expected, and I can prove it.

Mrs Chadwick claimed that her sister had been worried about her home being broken into and that her family had repeatedly tried to persuade Miss Clark not to live alone in George Street. 'Whether you believe in presentiment or not, she at all times was depressed, and sometimes said she had had such an unpleasant dream that she thought something was going to happen to her.'

The investigation was gradually wound down before becoming overshadowed by other, blacker crimes. As the *Penny Illustrated Paper* reported:

> Sedulously active and vigilant though the Metropolitan Police are under the leadership of Sir Charles Warren, it is mournful to recall the number of criminals who have not been found out, and who may be yet in our midst. Where are the perpetrators of the fiendish murder of poor Mrs Samuels, the wife of the milk-shop keeper in Bartholomew Road, Kentish Town? Where lurk the Great Coram Street, Burton Crescent, and Euston Square murderers? It is earnestly to be hoped that to the black list of murderers at large will not be added the men – or women – concerned in THE BRUTAL ASSASSINATION OF MISS LUCY CLARKE. [*sic*]

The 'Marylebone Murder' was indeed added to the list. Four months later another woman was killed during a suspected robbery at her home in another respectable area of London.[93]

~ The Banker's Wife ~

Canonbury, north of Islington, seemed an ideal place for a sixty-nine-year-old bank clerk like Charles Cole Wright to live. It was close to the city, but green enough to satisfy any yearnings for the clean air of the countryside. Once a land of open fields, grazing cows, a fourteenth-century manor house and a tranquil pond, it attracted visitors to the historic Canonbury Tower and the tea gardens of the Canonbury Tavern opposite. By the nineteenth century, it was a well-to-do suburb of London comprising villas, terraces and cottage-style houses. Mr Wright's home at No. 19 Canonbury Terrace, on the west side of the road now known as Alwyne Villas, boasted a healthy six rooms, including two kitchens. It was a comfortable life, although not without troubles – his Irish-born wife Frances, then seventy-one, was suffering from bronchitis and they had been having trouble finding a decent servant girl who would stick at the job. By Wednesday 16 May 1888, they had not had a regular maid for nine months.

That day Mr Wright left the house at just before 2 p.m. as usual, having said goodbye to his wife who was sitting in the front room. 'I returned according to custom at half past five in the evening, and noticed a crowd about the house. I was then informed my wife was dead,' he recalled. He went upstairs to the bedroom and was allowed in to see the body. The only injury that he could see was a slight mark over her left eye, which had not been there earlier in the afternoon. Had she fallen? The gossip of the crowd was that it was a robbery. Mr Wright remembered that his wife had complained that morning about a man visiting the house to ask about the water supply. He had advised her to keep the chain on the door and had ensured the door was closed when he was out. Mr Wright quickly made a tour of the house but there didn't appear to be anything missing. Most of their valuables had been stolen some five years earlier whilst they were on holiday at the seaside.

The alarm had been raised by two French ladies living opposite. Madame Bertha Prevotal had been observing the street from her first-floor window at around 2.30 p.m. when she saw two men climb the steps of No. 19 and knock on the front door. One of them was carrying a bag on his left shoulder. The door was opened and moments later she heard three cries as the men pushed inside. She shouted out to her friend, Selina Chefdeville, and told her what had happened.

Madame Chefdeville put on her hat and shawl and went to investigate:

> I crossed the road and knocked at the door, but no one opened it. I could hear them moving about inside. I went to the door three times, but could get no reply. There was no policeman or any person to be seen anywhere. The neighbour suggested a policeman should be sent for, and he went to fetch one. While he was gone the men came out of the house. I cried 'Burglars' but they dashed past.

Madame Chefdeville valiantly gave chase as the men split up and ran in different directions. Setting her sights on the man carrying the bag – described as being in his early twenties and dressed in a long overcoat and a round hat – she pursued him for several hundred yards across Canonbury Road and down Astey's Road along the New River, shouting and hollering in half-French and half-English. Along the way she passed a delivery driver and a milkman, who might have gone to her aid if only they could have understood what she was saying. Slowly the word got out and by the time the suspect made it to River Street, Madame Chefdeville had recruited a small crowd of young men and boys, all crying 'Stop thief'. Unfortunately the man had built up too much of a lead and was last seen dumping his bag between two Pickford's furniture vans before crossing Essex Road into Norfolk Street.

Back at No. 19 Canonbury Terrace, a police officer had arrived and had entered the house via the back kitchen. Inside he found Mrs Wright in the hallway at the foot of the stairs, slumped against the wall in a half-sitting position with her arms stretched out. She was dead although her body was still warm to the touch, indicating that she had passed away only a few minutes earlier. Under her dress, a police inspector found two pockets tied round the waist with a piece of tape. In one was £17 10s in gold, cleverly concealed from view by the use of several pins. The second contained a little over 12s and some keys. If it was a robbery it had likely been interrupted by Mrs Wright's collapse. This theory was borne out by the post-mortem findings that she had died of shock. The stress of the robbery had overwhelmed her diseased heart and she had collapsed before the intruders had the chance to ransack the house. The inquest jury agreed and returned a verdict of wilful murder. It was now up to the police to catch the two men responsible.

Three days after Mrs Wright's death, *The Times* ran an editorial offering up its theories on the case. Was it a 'commonplace story of household robbery' tainted by the sudden death of the elderly resident?

In that case the only lesson to be drawn is that London dwellings, especially in lonely and out of the way districts, are singularly insecure, even when they seem to offer little attraction to the burglar or the criminal idler ... a man who lives alone with his wife without even a single servant would seem to offer as little temptation to the robber as the *vacuus viator* who sings along the highway ... nevertheless it must be acknowledged that if a novelist of the type of Gaboriau or Du Boisgobey were in search of materials for a story of mystery, crime and detection, he could find no more effective opening than this plain narrative of the crime of Canonbury Terrace. In fiction of this character the reader knows very well that the more commonplace the original circumstances and the more obvious the *prima facie* explanation, the more certain it is that a deep and terrible mystery will be found to be involved in them before the tale is ended.

The Times called for 'the most attentive and searching investigation', adding:

> It is not enough to search at large among the criminal
> classes of London for two men who would be likely to
> rob an ill-guarded and poverty-stricken house in a lonely
> neighbourhood. It is necessary to discover an intelligible and
> adequate motive for the crime, and to prosecute an inquiry
> concerning those persons on whom such a motive would be
> likely to operate.

The police issued descriptions of the wanted men based on the witness accounts. The first was 5ft 6in tall and dressed in black trousers, a vest and a dark cutaway coat. The second was shorter, at 5ft 1in, and 'of military appearance' with tweed trousers and vest. The round-up of known criminals began immediately with seven arrests in Westminster, Hackney, Holloway and the City. None of the witnesses could make a firm identification, although Madame Chefdeville indicated that one of the twenty-five men in the line-up was of similar height and build to the suspects. A further ten were arrested as enquiries continued over the following days, but they were all released.

Then another lead emerged. Shortly before the murder, three men and a woman had been drinking at a pub not far from Canonbury Terrace. They looked as though they were planning something and one man had a bag. The landlord overheard snatches of their conversation – 'We must have more than that', 'Well I wish I was down in Spitalfields again' and 'Great Eastern'. The group then drank up and walked off in the direction of Mrs Wright's house.

Yet all the police had were descriptions, and no hard suspects. Perhaps the strongest evidence they did have was the carpetbag dumped by the robber during his escape, which suggested a skilled labourer or engineer of some kind. According to reports, detectives first concentrated their attention on the East End, in the neighbourhood of Spitalfields, before turning to scour Clerkenwell with an equal lack of success.

One elderly resident of Islington saw the case as proof of the inadequacy of the police in that area, despite the police rates paid by its respectable inhabitants. In his opinion, the estates of the Marquis of Northampton surrounding Canonbury Tower had 'always formed the happy hunting ground of burglars, though neglected by the higher class of their profession, the murderers'. The police appeared to believe that quiet areas required less protection and as a result ruffians were free to 'assail ladies in broad daylight in Canonbury Lane', and homes were left at the mercy of vandals and housebreakers.

A week went by and the police were no nearer to tracking down the killers. On 22 May an estimated crowd of 2,000 people gathered in Canonbury to see Mrs Wright's funeral cortege set off on the long journey to Nunhead cemetery. In a way they were returning to a place that held happier memories – the Wrights had married in Newington in 1843 and had set up home in Maze Pond, Southwark. It had seen the birth of their daughter Frances, who had died tragically at the age of seventeen following their move to Islington. Now the mother was dead too, her body enclosed in an elm coffin inside a polished oak case with a brass plate reading: 'Frances Maria Wright, died 16th May 1888, age 71.' The procession southwards was a grand one – a newspaper report described how:

> ... a closed hearse, two funeral coaches and a private carriage, left No.19 Canonbury Terrace at ten minutes past one and was followed by the crowd, whose expression of sympathy with the relatives of the deceased was general. An escort was formed of officers of the Metropolitan Police force, who walked on either side of the cortege to the boundary of their division, Islington Green.

Slowly the investigation stagnated and resources were moved elsewhere. The newspapers turned their focus to other

London crimes. If the Canonbury murder was going to be solved it would require a flicker of detective genius, or more likely a stroke of luck.

The breakthrough came on 27 August. At 3 a.m. Sergeant Michael Walsh was patrolling the neighbourhood of Old Street when a drunken woman, aged about eighteen or nineteen, approached him to complain that she had been assaulted. Once they had reached the station, Phoebe Field explained that her partner had hit her because he thought she was still seeing a man by the name of Henry Glennie. This man Glennie had committed the Canonbury murder, she claimed. Sergeant Walsh, ears pricked, pressed her for more details.

They had met several weeks earlier at her neighbour's house in King's Cross Road. Glennie had been away from London, he said, and was starving. Virtually all he'd had for the previous seven weeks was hop tea. They liked the look of each other and went back to her place for the night. He promised that he would look after her and asked her to go and live with him in a room off the Caledonian Road. The next day her partner, a diamond fitter called Alfred Edwards, found out and came round to confront them in the street outside.

'I'm not going to have her going with men who are stealing and burgling and breaking into houses,' Edwards said.

'I've not got her for that at all,' Glennie replied. 'You meet me tonight and I will have it out with you. I might as well be killed for six or seven as for one.'

A few nights later she was in bed with Glennie when he started tossing and turning and calling out for his mother. He moaned something about a murder and then, 'Never mind, mother, it will soon be all right.' Phoebe asked him about it but he wouldn't say anything until the next night when he told her, 'It was me that done the Canonbury murder.'

'No, never,' Phoebe replied.

'Yes I did, me and Long Bob and the eldest Parsons.'

'How did you know how to go there?'

'A girl that worked there told me. I won't tell you which one of them it was.'

Glennie said that he had gone up to the door and asked the lady to let them in by saying he was there about the gas fittings. When she opened the door he told her, 'Mother, don't scream and I won't hurt you.' When she cried out he hit her on the side of the head and she fell down. Long Bob was searching her pockets when Glennie exclaimed, 'I think I have killed her.'

Long Bob said, 'Now you have killed her I can't touch it', and they both ran off without the money.

After the confession came a warning, 'Whoever tells of it will be sure to be killed.' If Glennie couldn't kill the snitch, then his parents and his friends would. A few days later Phoebe Field left him and went back to Alfred Edwards.

The details of this alleged confession did not match perfectly but it was clear that the police had to track down this new suspect. Henry Glennie was twenty-four years old, and up until February 1888 he had worked for the Eagle Range Co. making coal and gas stoves. Former colleagues confirmed that he used a bag for the tools and two of them identified the red carpetbag dumped in Canonbury. When Glennie was finally traced, he was not arrested immediately but instead placed under surveillance. They hoped that he might lead them to the man known only as 'Long Bob' or give some clue as to who had tipped him off about the Wright house. The 'eldest Parsons' he referred to was said to be Charles Parsons, who had been tried for a watch robbery in March. Phoebe Field heard that he had been sentenced to five years in prison, but the records show that he was actually acquitted.

Finally, on the night of 19 September, the police arrested Glennie in the Caledonian Road. 'I shan't say anything,' he replied. 'I can prove what I am and what I do.' At the station in Upper Street, he claimed that he had been with his sister at her confectionary shop in Neasden on the day of the Canonbury murder. Then Sergeant Stephen Maroney produced the key piece of evidence, the red carpetbag. 'I have obtained information that this bag belongs to you.'

As Glennie took hold of the bag and began examining it nervously, his face grew pale. After a pause, he gathered himself together and said, 'Well, I admit it is my bag, or rather, it was mine. I sold it with some tools to a man in the Star and Garter public house in Caledonian Road.' Glennie couldn't say who the man was, or how much he had received, but he claimed that the transaction took place the week after he left the employ of the Eagle Range Co. No matter, the police charged him with murder and asked the magistrate for more time to prepare their case.

Four days later the police found another witness. Mary 'Polly' Dominey was a twenty-one-year-old charlady who had worked at the Wright house on and off for the previous two or three years. She had left about six weeks before the murder took place to look after her baby. On the night of her arrest, 23 September, she was held in the library at Upper Street police station but refused to say a word. Eventually, she was persuaded to admit that she knew Henry Glennie and that she suspected his involvement in the crime. A few weeks earlier she had found out the police were looking for her and she had gone to speak to Glennie. As she recalled:

> I said I did not know what they wanted me for; I did not know nothing about it. He said 'They can't touch you'. He told me that he went to Mrs Wright's house, and he said he struck her, and when he felt her a few minutes after she was cold. I told him I had seen the news. He said, 'Did you see the Frenchwoman running behind me?' I said yes, that was in the

picture. He said he was very sorry for what he had done, he
had no intention of doing it.

Dominey also suggested that Glennie might have got the idea
for the robbery from her friend Amy White, who had also
visited the house in Canonbury.

The police were now armed with two alleged confessions,
Glennie's carpetbag, an identification of Glennie as the man
running from the scene and an indirect link between him
and the Wrights' house. They had also recovered a black
coat which Phoebe Field claimed she pawned after Glennie
told her that it was the one he was wearing at the time of
the murder. It was enough to commit him for trial at the
Old Bailey.

The case began on 29 October 1888. One by one the
witnesses were called: Charles Cole Wright the husband, the
two French ladies living opposite, the members of the public
who saw the chase, the doctor, the investigating officers, and
the former colleagues at Eagle Range Co. Glennie's barrister,
Austin Metcalfe, reserved most of his fire for Mary Dominey
and Phoebe Field. It was suggested to Dominey that her baby's
father was in prison for highway robbery, that she had once
been charged with stealing boots, that she had been jailed for
three weeks for shoplifting, and that she was a prostitute. She
denied it all, but admitted that she was receiving a guinea a
week from the police while waiting to give evidence. Phoebe
Field was also receiving money from the police – in fact she
had been living with one of the sergeants for about a month.
Was she his servant, joked Mr Metcalfe. 'I have been taken
there because I am frightened for my life,' she told the court.

The defence also claimed she had changed her story. She
had allegedly told Sergeant Michael Walsh that Glennie's
accomplice was called Long Jack, not Long Bob, and that
Long Jack had been the one who hit Mrs Wright. Miss Field

was also forced to admit that she had worked on the street when she could not get a job at the laundry. That was one of the reasons she left her partner of three years to go with Glennie – 'I went to live with him on the understanding that he would keep me.'

Then Mr Metcalfe turned to Inspector Thomas Glass. 'Who had authorised the payments to Dominey? Was a guinea not an excessive amount?'

Glass replied, 'I advance it out of my own pocket, but I send my bill to the Treasury. I have got leave of the Treasury to give her that. I do not think a guinea a week is too much to give to a witness of that kind.' It was also suggested he had tried to trick Glennie into a false confession while holding him in custody, but he adamantly denied everything. 'I did not say to him "I have got your pal", I swear that. I did not say "he is going to split, I will give you half an hour", nothing of the kind.'

But the defence's real weapon was an alibi for the time of the murder. Glennie's sister Mary Ann Swallow testified that he came to see her in Neasden on 15 May and did not go out at all the following day. She was backed up by a dressmaker who was at the house on Wednesday 16 May. As for the black coat, Glennie's brother-in-law said that he was wearing it in May, and had only given it to Glennie a month later. Mr Metcalfe told the jury that there was no evidence to prove that Glennie went to the Wright house, and that the alleged confessions were unreliable. Mr Justice Cave summed up the case as one of 'grave suspicion', according to one news report, but added that he 'could not advise them to place much reliance upon the statements of the two principal witnesses [two loose girls named Phoebe Field and Polly Dominey] considering their conduct and the different allegations they had made at various times.' The jury took just five minutes to reach a verdict – not guilty.

It was yet another defeat for the detectives of Scotland Yard, and questions were raised about the case in Parliament on 12 November. In particular the Liberal MP Edward Pickersgill wanted to know why Glennie was repeatedly questioned by police, despite the practice being condemned by the courts. In 1888 there was no such thing as a recorded police interview and it was not until the 1950s that it became standard practice to interrogate a suspect. The Home Secretary assured the House of Commons that the questions were of the usual sort intended to allow a suspect to clear himself of involvement in a crime. With that, the case faded from public view.

For Charles Cole Wright, life went on. In December 1888, at the age of sixty-nine, he married a woman twenty-seven years his younger, Jane Collett, and moved to her boarding house in Highbury. His happiness was to be short-lived. Two years later he died at the address in Calabria Road, leaving an estate valued at £125.[94]

— Trouble and Strife —

Three days after the murder of Frances Wright, Islington was shaken by another 'outrage' reported by the newspapers. Robert Bright, a twenty-nine-year-old blacksmith, got out of bed as usual at 6.30 a.m., got dressed and arranged to meet his wife Maria later that day. Moments later, as he was leaving for work, he suddenly took up a hammer and battered her repeatedly over the head. Mrs Bright was fortunate to survive the attack and went on to give evidence against her husband, who was sentenced to nine months' hard labour. Yet while it was not a case of murder, it illustrates that all too often women were at risk from those living with them at home, rather than thieves or psychopaths. In earlier ages, domestic violence might have been shrugged off as an everyday occurrence, or at least a private matter between husband and wife. The Victorians however, purveyors of a different kind of sexism, believed that women should be protected and were more prepared to use the justice system to punish such behaviour. Domestic violence was now seen as a habit of the lower classes, along with overindulgence of alcohol. In many cases, both went together. Husbands returned home drunk at 10 p.m. to treat the neighbourhood to shouts, heavy blows and cries of murder until midnight when it was time to sleep. The social commentator Thomas Wright tried to intervene in one neighbourhood dispute, only to be battered over the head with a chair leg by the lady he had just rescued. 'He can hammer me if he likes without a meddling bugger like you a coming breaking people's doors open.' Wright returned home to the jeers of the crowd outside while the beating continued. Writing in the 1860s, he recalled:

Wife beating, so far from exciting the feeling of abhorrence with which it is regarded in decent society, is in our court looked upon, even by the beaten women, if not exactly as a proper and commendable practice, at least as a very commonplace one, and one which no person of a well-regulated mind would be guilty of interfering with.

Perhaps by the 1880s the situation had improved slightly. The charity worker and social campaigner Margaret Nevinson told how one husband in Whitechapel complained that he could never give his wife a beating in peace, 'All the neighbours come a-knocking and a-fussing at the door and a-carrying their tales to you ladies, so I'm now to a little house where we shan't be interfered with.' On the other hand, Nevinson also noted that, 'Saturday night is the time for fights and wife-beating of all kinds – any weapon handy – pokers, flat-irons, three-legged stools and one old soldier wounded in the Crimean War used to unstrap his wooden leg for the purpose.'[95]

Then, as now, domestic murders received much less attention in the press than the more sensational cases. And while the Year of the Ripper had more than its fair share of sensation, it also played host to the sadly familiar tales of women being beaten or stabbed to death by the men they loved and trusted.

In 1888 the novel *Vermont Hall* was published. It opened with a young girl reliving the nightmare of seeing her mother being murdered by her father. At the root of it, suggested the book, lay the vice of alcohol. The accused gives a speech in court warning of the dangers of drink: 'If there is here any young man who has begun to like the drink and who thinks he can keep that appetite and keep also home, and love, and friends, and honour and god, let him beware!' With that, he fell down dead in the dock.

That same year, two girls saw their mothers killed in separate incidents, both inflamed by drink. The first, thirteen-year-old Jane Newman, witnessed her father Charles Latham take a knife to the throat of fifty-year-old Mary Newman in the squalid single room they were renting at No. 53 Drummond Crescent in Somerstown, north London. Latham had a history of drunken violence and had only just got out of the workhouse. As Jane recalled:

> He was standing with his back against the fire. My mother was sitting in a chair. They were not talking at all, nothing was said by either of them. Then father got hold of a knife, and did that to mother. He put the knife across mother's throat while she was sitting on the chair. Mother halloaed out 'Don't do it'.

Jane ran upstairs to fetch the landlady. By the time help arrived Mary Newman had suffered nine wounds to the neck and face, one of which sliced open the jugular vein. She died ten minutes after being taken to hospital, on the evening of Saturday 19 May. Latham was charged and convicted of murder, but was spared the death penalty on the grounds that he was suffering from delirium tremens, a condition brought on by withdrawal from alcohol (*see* Chapter 15).[96]

Five months later, on Saturday 6 October, twelve year-old Emily Roberts saw her mother and father quarrelling in the street outside No.4 Essex Place in Hackney Road. They were both drunk. Her mother knocked her father to the ground with her hand, and then her father returned the favour by knocking her mother to the ground. Her mother – who was forty-three years old and also called Emily – then went indoors and lay down feeling ill. The next day Mrs Roberts went to her niece's home in the same street with two black eyes and told her, 'He knocked me down and knelt on my stomach and hit me in the face. The quarrel was all over the cat.' The husband, Joseph Roberts, a forty-one-year-old boot finisher, could not afford to pay for a doctor to visit immediately and so had to wait for the parish doctor to come round a week later. By that time Mrs Roberts's stomach was swollen and painful. She claimed that her husband had knelt on her stomach and punched her face and head. The doctor told Mrs Roberts that she was dying and asked if she had anything to add to her statement before she passed away. 'No, nothing, it is all true,' she replied. She died the next day, on Thursday 18 October, from inflammation of the bowels, which could have been caused by the kneeling on her stomach. Joseph Roberts was taken into custody after the jury at the inquest returned a verdict of manslaughter. His defence was that he had been drunk and had not meant to hurt her. A few days later, however, the case was dismissed by the magistrate and the prosecution offered no evidence at the Old Bailey.[97]

There was a similar conclusion to the case of Thomas Healey, a forty-six-year-old labourer charged with murdering his forty-two-year-old wife. This time the setting was in the working-class area of Rotherhithe, south London, described by Dickens as a place where the 'accumulated scum of humanity seemed to be washed from higher grounds, like so much moral sewage'. It was a community based around the docks and shipyards, warehouses and factories. On Paradise Street, a few hundred yards west from Brunel's Thames Tunnel, there were two schools, a police station, a fire station, a depot for Pickford's removal firm, and a series of alleyways crowded with dirty children and ramshackle housing. Thomas and Jane Healey lived at No.8 Donne Place, Paradise Street. On 25 October 1888, the neighbours were treated to a typical Saturday night of drunken 'wrangling' between the couple. Joseph Andrews decided to intervene after seeing Mrs Healey being beaten outside his door. He too received a blow for his trouble and retreated back into his home. Later, he heard Thomas Healey give his wife a shilling to fetch a pot of beer and on her return he began shouting once more, 'If you don't find the change, I'll have your life. I'll tear the skirt off you. It belongs to my daughter. You shan't live to wear it any longer.' Shortly afterwards there were more bangs and thumps and Mrs Healey flew past the Andrews' door and tumbled head over heels down the stairs. She trudged back up again for more punishment until it all went quiet. The next morning Jane Healey was found dead in bed with her skirt torn off, her face and body discoloured by bruises. 'It's a bad job,' Mr Healey told his neighbour, 'Do the best you can for me.'

The cause of death was given as internal bleeding on the brain, but the doctor was unable to say whether it was due to an assault or the fall. Although the coroner's jury returned an open verdict, unable to decide on the evidence, the police took up the case and hauled the husband before the magistrates charged with manslaughter. The neighbour's wife, Emily Andrews, told the court that the row next door had gone on until 1.30 a.m., at which point she heard Mr Healey say 'get up or I'll kick you up', followed by a thud. The next day Mr Healey had turned up at their door and said, 'I can't beat any sense into my wife, and I think she is in a fit or dead.' Rather implausibly, Thomas Healey denied that he had attacked his wife at all. The case was sent to the Old Bailey, but again the prosecution lacked confidence in getting a conviction and offered no evidence 'at the suggestion of the Court'.[98]

Both of these cases might have been expected to have at least gone before a trial jury. Even if the evidence was not strong enough for a charge of murder, it was still arguable that their actions had caused death. Neither husband sought to rely on the old 'right of chastisement' which was fading out by the end of the eighteenth century. The worst that could be said for Emily Roberts was that she had struck the first blow and appeared to be drunk, and perhaps this image of a 'bad wife' influenced the decision. It also seems odd that Thomas Healey should escape punishment for what was obvious domestic abuse, even if the defence were to suggest that she fell down the stairs of her own accord. Perhaps the old approach to domestic violence still lingered when circumstances were less clear cut. But generally husbands who killed their wives were more likely to be convicted than other murder defendants. This was particularly the case if they used a weapon – in November 1888, Levi Bartlett went to the gallows after murdering his wife by battering her with a hammer and stabbing her in the neck. He was the only person to be executed for a murder committed in 1888. Others were sentenced to death but were reprieved.[99]

'Warnings for "nagging wives" and brutal husbands!' was how one newspaper summed up the case of shoemaker James White. Yet that was hardly an explanation of how Mr White came to batter his sixty-seven-year-old wife Margaret to death with a poker. What had really driven him to commit such a terrible crime? It appeared they had been happily married for forty-one years. They had raised a son and a daughter, and were now grandparents. Even though he was sixty-five years old, James still earned a living as a shoemaker from their home in No. 1 Eden Place, off Pond Place in Chelsea. Essentially it was a single room, the front parlour on the ground floor of a house, furnished with a bed, chair, fireplace, chest of drawers and a workbench under the window. They lived in squalor in 'one of the poorest slums of the parish', but they got by with what they had. 'There could not be a more kind or affectionate husband on earth than the prisoner,' recalled neighbour Johannah Healey. 'There could not be a happier couple – she had a serious illness, bronchitis, some years ago – he nursed her always as well as he could, always got up in the morning and got her a cup of tea.' Another neighbour who had known Mr White for twelve years said he was a 'very quiet and peaceable man'.

There was also a darker side to James White, most noticeably when he had a drink. As his son David explained, 'When my father gets half a pint of beer his mind is not right. I have seen him take a knife and run it across his throat, as if to cut it.' The White family believed it was hereditary, as the men all tended to get shooting pains in the head, even the grandchildren aged eight and five.

'He sometimes broke out into violent fits of passion, with very little reason, if his tea was not ready,' said David's wife Catherine. 'He then said he would cut his throat and have done with it. His general demeanour was that of a kind, affectionate husband and father … he was unusually angry that afternoon – he was apt to get passionate after drink.' It was also clear that the couple were struggling for money. Business had been slow and Mrs White was careful with the little money that came in – it particularly upset her when James spent their precious pennies on alcohol.

On the morning of Saturday 3 March she travelled from Chelsea to Balham to drop off some mended boots with customers. Having collected 12s in payment, she returned home with her daughter-in-law Catherine, stopping off at the local pub for some bread and cheese for dinner and an eighth of gin. When they got back to Eden Place at about 12.30 p.m., James White was sitting at his workbench staring into space. After a minute or two he declared that he would like a pint of beer. It sounded from his voice like he'd had a few already. 'James, I think you have had enough, where did you get it?' asked his wife.

'I have taken a little job home, and I spent the money.' At this Mrs White began to cry, reluctantly handing over tuppence for his pint. When he returned a few minutes later with the beer, she gestured at the eighteen pairs of boots that needed his attention. 'Never mind those, I will see to those afterwards,' he said. Mr White then retired to bed, complaining that he felt ill.

This only increased his wife's tears – they had bills to pay and this was the first week in a long time that they had had any work. Catherine told her, 'Don't fret, Mother, let him sleep a little while, and when he wakes up he will go to work, don't disturb him.' Catherine then left, promising to come back once she had given her husband his tea at 5 p.m.

An hour later the couple's eight-year-old grandson Thomas Spinks arrived for his regular Saturday visit, and to give Margaret a bit of money from his mother to tide them over. The boy's grandfather soon had him at work making a cup of tea. Meanwhile, Mr White was demanding his wife give him the money from the boot mending. 'I have paid my way with it,' she replied.

James White was enraged: 'You had a right to come to me first.' Thomas then watched in horror as his grandfather suddenly turned violent.

'He threw grandmother off the chair. She fell on the floor against the table. I got frightened then and ran out.'

1 Postcard showing the RMS *Ormuz* leaving Sydney. (Reproduced by permission of Chris Tyrer)

2 Postcard showing Grosvenor Place, *c.* 1900; scene of the fatal accident involving Elizabeth Gibbs. (Author's collection)

3 Looking west down Piccadilly near the scene of the fatal accident involving James Langley. (Courtesy of *The Queen's London*, 1896)

4 Clare Market, 1891, scene of the alleged killing of George Best. (Courtesy of the *Illustrated London News*)

7 View of Trafalgar Square, scene of the 1887 riot. (Courtesy of *The Queen's London*, 1896)

8 View of New Scotland Yard, constructed on top of the basement where the torso of a woman was discovered. (Courtesy of *The Queen's London*, 1896)

9 Illustration of the Marylebone murder of Lucy Clark in the *Penny Illustrated Paper* of 4 February 1888. (Reproduced by permission of the British Library)

Left 10 *Punch* cartoon 'Blind Man's Buff' from 22 September 1888, poking fun at the police's inability to catch their man. (Author's collection)

Below 11 From the *Illustrated London News*, 1888: 'With the Vigilance Committee in the East End.' (Author's collection)

12 'The Nemesis of Neglect' from *Punch*, 29 September 1888, suggesting that the murders were the inevitable result of social deprivation. (Author's collection)

13 *Punch* cartoon 'Whitechapel, 1888' from 13 October 1888; another shot at the Metropolitan Police. The caption read: 'First member of criminal "Criminal Class" – "Fine body o' men, the Per-leece." Second ditto – "Uncommon fine! It's lucky for hus as there's sech a bloomin' few on 'em!!!"' (Author's collection)

14 *Punch* cartoon from 13 October 1888: 'Horrible London', suggesting some link between sensationalist publications and the Whitechapel murders. (Author's collection)

15 *Punch* cartoon from 20 October 1888: 'Is Detection a Failure?' It blames the 'sensationalist interviewer' for interfering with the detective's work. (Author's collection)

16 Collage of the Regent's Park murder and suspects, from the front page of the *Illustrated Police News*, 2 June 1888. (Reproduced by permission of the British Library)

17 At court in the Old Bailey. (Courtesy of *The Queen's London*, 1896)

18 View of Newgate Gaol before it was demolished and rebuilt in the early twentieth century. (Courtesy of *The Queen's London*, 1896)

19 Advert for Hudson's Soap in the *Graphic* in December 1888, which plays on the perception of crime in London. (Author's collection)

20 'New London' cartoon in *Punch's Almanac* for 1889. 'Mr Punch's Design for a Grand Historical Allegorical Almaniacal Picture for 1889 "The old order changeth, yielding place to new".' (Author's collection)

As the shouting and quarrelling continued, the boy went and fetched a police officer who was walking the beat in the Fulham Road.

'When I got in I saw the deceased lying on the floor in front of the fireplace on her right side,' recalled PC William Swinden. He continued:

> I considered her to be asleep. Mr White was lying on the bed. I asked him what the disturbance was about. He said there was no row. 'She is drunk and she will lie on the floor to sleep.' I did not wake her or disturb her. I told the prisoner not to make any disturbance, to keep himself quiet and I left the room.

Mrs White was still lying on the floor, with nothing on but a black dress bodice on her top half, when a customer called at 3.15 p.m. that afternoon. Rebecca Robson heard Mr White mutter from his bed, 'I suppose there will be no more work done today. They must come and fetch their things … I will see if I don't make you get up.' He then leapt from the bed, grabbed the poker from the fireplace and beat his wife three times with the round end, apparently unconcerned that Miss Robson was watching from the doorway.

'Oh, have mercy, and don't hit the poor creature with the poker,' Miss Robson cried.

'I don't care if I kill her,' he replied.

Miss Robson then left, but only after establishing that her boots were not yet ready for collection.

It was 4.30 p.m. when Mr White called on a near neighbour, Louisa Mayhew, for help. 'I want you to come over the way to help my old woman on the bed. I have very nigh settled her.' Mrs Mayhew found Mrs White lying on the floor on her left side, her bodice ripped open to expose her breasts. Her hip was swollen and bruised and there was blood on the left side of her head.

'Mr White, what have you been doing?'

'I don't care. She should have done what I wanted, and got me a cup of tea ready,' he said. 'She can get up if she likes. She is only shamming it.' Mr White then went and fetched a pint of beer in a can, sat on his work seat and smoked his pipe while Mrs Mayhew tried to get a response from his wife. They were joined first by Thomas Spinks and his mother Fanny, then Catherine White and finally at 7 p.m. the local doctor Daniel Lehane. By that time Mrs White was dead.

'A bloody good job too,' said Mr White. 'Fetch me my coat and I will go to the police station.' He then went out for another can of beer. When police constable William Davey arrived Mr White was happy to give a statement. 'My God, I settled her. She would not do as I wanted her, so I hit her three times on the head with the soft end of the poker.' On the way back to the station he added, 'We have lived happily together for forty-one years, but if she had done as I told her I should not have killed her. I suppose the Old Bailey will be my lot.'

James White was right, because on 2 May he stood trial at the Central Criminal Court. The blows he had dealt to his wife had fractured her left hip and her skull, but he claimed it was done 'in the height of passion'. His barrister claimed he was not responsible for his actions because of his history of a 'flow of blood to the head', but the jury rejected the insanity defence and convicted him of murder. Asked whether he would like to say anything before being sentenced to death, Mr White rambled – he never intended to kill her, and if she had let him have twenty minutes' sleep he would not have hurt her. His words were futile. The only thing in his favour was that the jury had recommended him to mercy because of his age and the lack of premeditation. As a result, the sentence was commuted to penal servitude for life. It mattered little in the end. James White died in prison two years later on 21 October 1890.[100]

One way of escaping trial after committing murder was to kill yourself before the arrival of the police. These 'murder-suicide cases' were and still are almost always committed by men – perhaps a reflection of the desire to be a 'dominant' figure even when the impulse is towards self-destruction. The perpetrators tend to be deeply depressed, whether because of financial or relationship problems. This was true of both Abraham Potzdamer in Whitechapel and Gordon Hare in Surbiton, and it was true of the third such tragedy in 1888.

Robert and Susannah Barrell had been happily married for twenty-two years. They ran the Bancroft Arms Tavern together in Moody Street, Mile End, and lived there with their four children. On Sunday 1 July, they went to bed in good spirits. The next morning at 8.45 a.m. their eldest daughter, Elizabeth, went to check why they had not yet risen. There was no answer when she knocked at their bedroom door and when she shook the doorknob the key dropped on to the floor on the inside. Elizabeth squeezed her hand underneath to retrieve the key and unlocked the door. When she got inside, she saw her mother lying on the bed with blood all over her face. There was a gaping wound to her right eye. Then Elizabeth saw her father on the floor with a gun lying next to his right hand. He too had been shot in the right eye. Both had been dead for several hours.

None of the children had heard anything, even though they were sleeping in a room next door. Neither had the police constable who passed the building every half an hour. A neighbour heard a gunshot sometime after midnight, but saw nothing suspicious in the street and went to bed. But whenever it happened, it was clear that Robert Barrell had killed his wife and then turned the gun on himself. He had been a chronic alcoholic for many years, and two or three months earlier his wife had confided in her mother about her husband's 'strange' behaviour and her fears that he was suicidal.

The public house had also been robbed twice in the previous eighteen months, and they had lost more than £68. Robert Barrell confessed to his mother-in-law, 'I am in great trouble, I've lost all Susie's money. I am entirely ruined.' In mid-June he had given up drinking and become teetotal, perhaps in an attempt to improve his health. The withdrawal may have contributed to the attack and the doctor believed he was suffering from delirium tremens, which may have brought on hallucinations, great anxiety and a terrifying sense of impending doom from which death was the only escape.[101]

～ The Neglected Wife ～

Not all domestic homicides are violent. Forty-five-year-old Mary Sandford was not the victim of a sudden or brutal attack. She had instead suffered a long, slow death from starvation and neglect. When the doctor was finally called to her bedside on the evening of 11 June 1888, her body was little more than skin and bone. Her clothes were filthy and her hair swarmed with lice. She had sores on her right hip and an ulcer on the left leg. Her internal organs had withered and it seemed as if her blood vessels were almost empty. All that remained in her stomach was a small amount of undigested lettuce. The police surgeon, Dr William Kempster, took the view that she had been lying on the bed for several weeks and had not eaten for three or four days at least. Gradually her body had shut down everything except breathing and blood circulation, until finally even they failed. If a doctor had been called earlier, they might have nursed her with a few ounces of brandy a day, barley water, arrowroot, milk, gruel or broth. 'Her condition indicated very slow death,' said Dr Kempster. 'I believe life would have been prolonged if she had had proper food and attendance or care.'

Mary had not lived alone in that room at No.9 Alfred Street in Battersea, south London. Her partner was William Jeffery, a fifty-one-year-old architect, described by the press as being 'well-connected'. The couple, who passed themselves off as husband and wife, had been together eight years and seemed to be loving and affectionate. But in 1886, Jeffery had been sent to a workhouse infirmary after being found wandering aimlessly in the street. After his release, Jeffery found it hard to get work, even as a lowly clerk. In early 1888 they moved from a house in Rollo Court to the room at Alfred Street, which had a cheaper rent of 2s a week and was furnished with two chairs, a bed and a table. Mary's health was also deteriorating and by May she had taken to bed complaining of her swollen ankles. Neighbours had urged Jeffery to apply for relief from the local authorities, but he never did.

On 11 June he asked his friend Mary Wyatt for a few half pennies and told her that his wife was very poorly.

'Why don't you get a doctor's order? Then she will have nourishment,' Mrs Wyatt said.

'I will,' he replied.

Two hours later he saw her again in the street and said, 'Will you come round with me? I think she is dead.'

Jeffery took her into the bedroom, picked up a lamp and held it near her head so Mrs Wyatt could see the lice in his wife's hair.

'Oh Mr Jeffery, you will get into trouble,' exclaimed Mary Wyatt.

'I think I shall,' he replied.[102]

Jeffery found out exactly how much trouble he was in at the inquest on 19 June when the jury returned a verdict of manslaughter. He was taken into custody and committed for trial at the Central Criminal Court by the Surrey coroner Athelston Braxton Hicks. The case, which began on Friday 3 August, rested almost entirely on the opinion of

Dr Kempster. He believed that Mary Sandford's death had been brought about and accelerated by the lack of care. 'The prisoner could have procured medicine and nourishment immediately by going to the relieving officer,' he told the court. However, he accepted that she would probably have died within three months anyway due to the long-standing condition of her lungs. Jeffery was not allowed to address the court in his own defence, but the jury heard evidence that he had told witnesses that his wife was an independent woman who refused his help or a visit from the doctor. In addition, he did not sleep in the same bed as her but on the floor. *The Times* rather harshly summed up the evidence as showing that 'the deceased woman was not only of an indolent and untidy disposition but had been at some stage of her life of unsound mind'.

The judge told the jury that it was their task to decide whether death had been caused or accelerated by 'gross and criminal neglect', but according to reports 'expressed the opinion that the charge against the prisoner could not be supported'. The jury accordingly found Jeffery not guilty. Mr Justice Hawkins ended the case by remarking that while Jeffery was under legal responsibility to provide proper nourishment and care to the woman he lived with, he was 'undoubtedly in a condition of great poverty, and he appeared to have done all that he could to provide for the woman, and to have treated her kindly, and he could in no way be said to have caused her death by wilful and criminal neglect'.[103]

~ The Triple Event ~

One night did more than any other to establish the legend of Jack the Ripper. In the space of three-quarters of an hour in the early hours of 30 September 1888, two women were found lying on the ground with their throats cut from ear to ear. The first, Elizabeth Stride, in Whitechapel, and the second, Catherine Eddowes, just under a mile away in Mitre Square in the City of London. Immediately the two murders were linked by the newspapers as being the work of the same man who was responsible for at least two other killings in the East End. An editorial in the usually reserved *Times* the next day asked:

> Have these been the freaks of a madman or the deliberate acts of a sane man who takes delight in murder on its own account, and who selects his victims by preference from the weaker sex, either as the safer and easier to deal with or as giving him the means of gratifying some horrid instinct of cruelty and perverted lust?

It was said that the killer had been interrupted during his attack on Ms Stride and had been driven to a second murder in which he indulged his bloodlust by cutting out Catherine Eddowes' left kidney and part of her womb. Together the crimes were known as the 'double event' and spread a ripple of fear across the capital. It was impossible to go anywhere without hearing about the Ripper, as he had apparently named himself in a letter to the Central News Agency a few days earlier. 'On my way back from Plumstead all the talk in the train was upon the two murders – the last exploits of the Whitechapel murderer,' wrote the playwright George Bernard Shaw in his diaries on 1 October.

Of course, there was other news to report in the papers that day – *The Times* contents listed a scientific report on the volcanic eruption at Krakatoa in 1883 and a 'fatal boiler explosion'. There was also a report on another murder that took place on the same night as the 'double event'. Like Stride and Eddowes the victim was a woman in her forties.

Like Stride and Eddowes, Sarah Brown was found lying dead in a pool of blood with her throat cut. But there the similarities ended. Sarah Brown was not killed on the streets of east London but in her own home in Westminster. Her killer was not a stranger or a serial killer; he was her husband, John Brown. The police did not have to work hard to solve her murder either, for the first they heard of the crime was when Mr Brown walked into the police station and told the officer on duty, 'I have stabbed my wife.' It was 11 p.m. on 29 September 1888, just two hours before Elizabeth Stride's body was discovered on the other side of the city.

John and Sarah Brown had been married for four years and lived together in a small three-roomed house in the working-class district around Regency Street. Their neighbours were hawkers, labourers, shopkeepers, beggars and prostitutes, although there were more modern buildings nearby which housed those with more respectable occupations like policemen, clerks and mechanics. John Brown had once worked as a porter on the London & South Western Railway between the capital and Plymouth, but he was sacked after repeatedly making false complaints against his colleagues. He then found a job as a labourer at St James' Park, but in June 1888 was admitted to Westminster Hospital with pneumonia. The doctor treating him noticed what he called 'peculiarities of his mind', depression or 'melancholia'. John brown returned home in July, but his mental state continued to deteriorate. His stepson Robert Young, aged twelve, recalled that:

> He seemed to have something the matter with him – he used to say to my mother that she let men into the house. She denied it, but he went on repeating it. He used to strike matches by day and night to look for the men. Before he came from the hospital they lived happily, but afterwards unhappily, by always making these accusations that led to disagreements between them.

By 14 August his behaviour had alarmed Sarah Brown so much that she tried to get help. In the late nineteenth century this meant applying to the local magistrate for a warrant to have her husband seen by the parish medical officer. During the examination she explained that following his return from hospital he constantly wanted to have sex with her, even though she was six months pregnant already. 'She said otherwise he was a kind and affectionate husband, always sober and very regular at his work,' reported Dr John Hunt. He continued:

> I spoke to him and remonstrated with him, and suggested his discontinuing living with his wife. Under those conditions I reported to the magistrate that I thought this would answer the necessities of the case – especially at the earnest request of his wife that I would not have him locked up.

Dr Hunt reported there was nothing wrong with him other than 'a little wildness about his eyes' and a morose manner.

John Brown argued against moving out for a time before finally agreeing, 'Well, I will go away, and that will settle it.'

The separation did not last long, most likely because Sarah could not afford to get by without his wages. By 15 September the couple were back together. Two days later Sarah attempted to get round the problem by applying for a summons against her husband for maintenance. It was dismissed because he had not actually deserted her and her two sons, and had only left on the order of the magistrate. She was caught in a catch-22 situation – it was impossible to live without him, but when he was at home she feared for her life. Sarah asked her daughter Mary Young, who was living elsewhere as a domestic servant, to come back home. 'He is always threatening me and I know he will kill me,' she confessed.

On Saturday 29 September, John Brown's delusions returned and he started pacing about, apparently searching the house for other men. After being threatened with a knife, Sarah went back to Dr Hunt to ask for protection, but he told her he could not do anything for her that night. She then went to a friend's house for help, begging her, 'What am I to do? Am I to go home and get murdered?' They decided to go to the police, but the local inspector said they could only act if her husband molested her. There was nothing she could do that night but hope for the best. She agreed to have an officer escort her part of the way home, but said she should return alone as she did not want her husband to know she had been to the police.

Minutes after her return at about 10.50 p.m. John Brown cut his wife's throat while her two sons slept upstairs. Neighbour Charles Redding recalled, 'I heard someone walk downstairs – immediately after I heard a scuffle in the front room and heard a woman call out "Oh, don't!". I went with my wife to the front door and heard a thud, as from somebody falling on the floor. Then all was quiet.' He knocked on the door, rousing twelve-year-old Robert Young from his bed. As the boy came downstairs he looked into the sitting room and saw his mother lying on the floor.

'I called to her and she did not answer,' Robert later told the Old Bailey. 'I saw a lot of blood round her head. She was dead.'

John Brown seemed unfazed by what he had done. As he sat in Rochester Row police station he told the officers, 'I hope she is dead; she has led me a pretty dance.' He then handed over a bloodstained knife. The next day, after being charged with murder, he was taken to Holloway Gaol for examination. The surgeon Philip Gilbert came to the conclusion that he was insane, reporting that:

He is under the delusion that he heard many voices speaking to him, neighbours and friends to his wife, saying that she ought to be ashamed of herself, that she ought to be killed, that men had been running in and out of his house all day, and that they had given her a good doing while he was away at the hospital, that seven or eight different men used to have connection with her of a night.

Brown also believed his wife drugged his beer to send him to sleep, so that she could let her men in and have them right next to him on the bed. But his paranoid fantasies were not just sexual – he believed that his wife put flammable liquid, 'naptha', in his boots which caused his feet to burn. The medical evidence was enough for the jury to find him guilty of murder while insane, which meant he would not face a death sentence.[104]

Although there was still a long way to go, protection for battered wives was improving. The police were still reluctant to become involved in domestic disputes and women were just as reluctant to take their husbands to court but these are issues that are still with us today, 125 years later. Change was taking place gradually, not just in public attitudes but also in the law. Sarah Brown had been able to apply for her husband to pay weekly maintenance as a result of the 1878 Matrimonial Clauses Act, but it applied only to husbands who had deserted their family. Magistrates could order that men convicted of assaulting their partners should seperate, although it was not until 1891 that a legal ruling finally 'settled the law' that it was illegal for a husband to beat or imprison his wife (R. v. Jackson). It was only in 1895 that the Married Women Act allowed women to separate from their husbands without an order from the magistrate. Neither drunkenness nor the infidelity of wives, real or imagined, was seen as much of a defence to a murder charge. Nevertheless, William Douglas

Morrison, the chaplain to Wandsworth Prison, suggested in 1891 that crime was brought about by increased pressure on the husband to maintain his wife in a respectable fashion. 'Household extravagance, extravagance in dress, the mad ambition of many English women to live in what they call a "better style" than their neighbours sends not a few men to penal servitude.' Poverty and financial pressures were a major factor – all the 1888 cases of domestic violence took place within poor or struggling households. This in turn may have exacerbated the tendency of the men, and sometimes the women, to drink heavily as a means of escape. Alcoholism and stress also contributed to deteriorating mental health. In a small number of cases the final result was the tragic death of one or both partners. Domestic violence would only decrease as living standards increased towards the end of the nineteenth century and into the twentieth. The consumption of alcohol would also decline from its height in the 1870s, with only a small rise during the First World War. The homicide rate would not increase to present levels until the period between the Second World War and the 1960s, a time of great social upheaval. This latter trend only really began to reverse in the early years of the twenty-first century.[105]

10

THE UNFORTUNATES

Most vulnerable of all were the women of the streets. Prostitutes, or, as the press and polite society preferred to call them, 'unfortunates' and 'fallen women', were not only at the mercy of their customers. They were also often viewed as being barely human. One of Europe's leading criminal anthropologists claimed in 1889 that: 'Professional prostitutes are incomplete beings ... they bear signs of physical and psychological degeneration that demonstrate their imperfect evolution.' The descriptions of the victims of Jack the Ripper only reinforced this stereotype. They were relatively old (mostly in their forties), in poor health, and lived in the worst type of housing in the worst area of London. Most had tragic back stories of lost innocence, violent spouses, poverty and a hopeless day-to-day existence relieved only by alcohol. Death might have been a merciful release had it not been for the cruel manner in which it was brought about.[106]

Social commentators had been fretting about 'The Great Social Evil' long before 1888. In 1869, the journalist James Greenwood listed it as one of the 'Seven Curses of London', adding that:

The monstrous evil in question has grown to its present dimensions chiefly because we have silently borne with it and let it grow up in all its lusty rankness under our noses; and rather than pluck it up by the roots, rather than acknowledge its existence even, have turned away our heads and inclined our eyes skywards and thanked God for the many mercies conferred on us.

Two years later William Logan, a former city missionary, called for the 'suppression of this widespread vice and the reclamation of its miserable victims'. He told of girls as young as eight giving themselves up to prostitution and stated that six years was the average lifetime of their career. Logan called for these women to be banned from walking the streets, having already remarked that, 'eight out of every ten are going about in a diseased condition ... reflect for a moment upon its fearful consequences on virtuous unsuspecting wives and innocent children'. The Contagious Diseases Acts of 1864 already allowed police to arrest prostitutes to check for venereal disease in an attempt to halt its spread through the armed forces, and there were calls for these checks to be extended outside the ports and garrison towns. There was also a vigorous campaign for them to be repealed, led by the feminist Josephine Butler, who saw the Acts as the unfair criminalisation of women rather than the men who paid for their services. The Acts were eventually repealed in 1886.[107]

That battle mirrored the debate over what should be done about these 'fallen women'. Should they be removed from the streets and locked away out of sight, as the antithesis of the Victorian domestic ideal? Or should they be given help, food and lodging and encouraged to abandon their lives of sin? Estimates of the number of prostitutes in London varied from the low thousands to 80,000. In 1888 the police gave a figure of 5,678 (with an estimated 1,200 in Whitechapel) and reported that over the year a total of 2,797 had been arrested; 1,475 were convicted of 'annoying male passengers for the purpose of prostitution', while fifty-two were acquitted of the same charge. Of course, not all prostitutes were in their forties and living in squalor in the East End. At least six 'types' were listed in Henry Mayhew's *London Labour and the London Poor*. There were 'kept mistresses and prima donnas' living in private houses, funded by their lovers; the 'board lodgers' paying brothel madams for their accommodation; those that lived in the disreputable 'low lodging houses' for 4*d* a night; those who serviced sailors and soldiers; the partners of thieves; and prostitutes who looked for business in the parks after dark. Mayhew also included 'cohabitant prostitutes', whose partners could not afford to marry and 'clandestine prostitutes', such as maidservants. There was even:

> The happy prostitute ... either the thoroughly hardened clever infidel who knows how to command men and use them for her own purposes ... and who in the end seldom fails to marry well; or the quiet woman who is kept by the man she loves and who she feels is fond of her; who has had a provision made for her to guard her against want and the caprice of her paramour.[108]

The 'higher class' prostitutes had traditionally gone about their business untroubled by the police at brothel-clubs like the Argyll Rooms in the West End before it was closed in 1878. 'The place was looked upon by many as an actual necessity,' wrote former Chief Inspector Cavanagh.

> It was far better for a particular class to be hidden away from the public gaze than that they should flaunt themselves in public thoroughfares ... but as time went on public opinion altered, and slowly but surely a change began to creep over

even those who were loudest in their protestations that the place was a necessary evil.

There was a determined move against brothels towards the end of the century, involving not just the forces of law and order, but also social campaigners like Frederick Charrington. He gave up his fortune as heir to a family of brewers to root out houses of vice throughout the East End. On 2 February 1888, he reported three brothels in Thames Street, Devonshire Street and Commercial Road, in Whitechapel, under the Criminal Law Amendment Act 1885. This piece of legislation had been passed partly as a result of a campaign by the *Pall Mall Gazette*, which had published an exposé of the alleged sale of London virgins to the sex trade. The 'story of an actual pilgrimage into a real hell' surpassed the antics even of the recently demised *News of the World*. The editor, W.T. Stead, set about finding a thirteen-year-old girl; he took her from her mother to a house off Oxford Street, doped her with chloroform, had her undress and then posed as a client. She was then handed over to the Salvation Army. Except the mother claimed she hadn't sold her daughter into sex slavery – she believed the girl was going to be a domestic servant. The set-up earned Stead a three-month prison sentence, but the Act was passed. One of its provisions raised the age of consent from thirteen to sixteen.[109]

The effect of this clampdown on brothels was to force prostitutes out on to the streets to ply their trade in alleyways, courts and darkened doorways. They were therefore exposed not only to violent sexual predators, but also to the police officers whose duty it was to arrest them for causing a public nuisance. In the early to mid-1880s, between 5,000 and 7,000 prostitutes were arrested every year, and the numbers charged with 'annoying male passengers for the purposes of prostitution' rose to 3,233 in 1886. However, by 1888 only

2,797 prostitutes were arrested and 1,475 were charged, a reduction of over half. Why? The main reason was that the Commissioner of the Metropolitan Police, Sir Charles Warren, had ordered that streetwalkers should not be arrested unless a third party came forward with a complaint. Police officers could no longer take action solely on the evidence of what they themselves had witnessed. This change in tactics came about as a result of a public scandal in 1887 after a police officer detained twenty-four-year-old Elizabeth Cass for soliciting in Regent's Street. Miss Cass turned out to be a respectable dress designer who had been taking a walk after leaving work in Southampton Row. The officer responsible, Bowen Endacott, who had been specifically tasked to bring in prostitutes, was put on trial for perjury at the Old Bailey. He was acquitted but the order remained in place and Warren was later criticised for encouraging prostitutes to once again throng the streets. At the height of the Whitechapel murders, Sir Robert Anderson, head of the CID, told the Home Secretary that he wanted to arrest every known 'street woman found on the prowl after midnight'. This was thought to be too drastic and instead he decided to 'warn them that the Police will not protect them'.[110]

After walking the streets, prostitutes would return to cheap rented rooms or, if they could not afford that, 'common lodging houses' which charged 4*d* a night in return for a filthy vermin-ridden bed. If they did not go out to work they would starve or end up in the dreaded workhouse. These common lodging houses had already received plenty of attention before 1888. They could be hugely profitable enterprises even though they catered for the poorest in society. Perversely, they thrived even as attempts continued to clear slums and rookeries to make space for wider thoroughfares and model dwellings for the working class. One result of slum clearance was that people were pushed into surrounding areas.

Overcrowding also increased as residents grouped together to pay the high rent bills. But the itinerant or casual worker who could not depend on a regular wage all year round was left with the lodging houses, which crammed as many beds as possible into their rooms to maximise revenue. Legislation was introduced to regulate them in 1851. It required them to be registered with the police and open to inspection but, in reality, there was little oversight and they became a byword for crime and depravity. That reputation did not dent their popularity and owners were able to use their profits to buy up even more properties to turn into common lodging houses. The celebrated 'Worst Street in London', Dorset Street in Whitechapel, was infested with them by the 1870s, but they were not just to be found in the East End. At the end of 1888, the Metropolitan Police Commissioner reported that there were 995 registered common lodging houses able to accommodate 32,172 lodgers, an increase of thirty-six houses on the previous year. Another 228 unregistered houses had been discovered and served with notices to register. Only twelve keepers of registered houses were convicted of infringements of the regulations. It was also noted that sixty-three residents had died of illness, mostly related to lack of warmth and food, or overindulgence in alcohol. There were twenty-four cases of infectious disease, including scarlet fever, typhoid and 'itch'.[111]

Howard Goldsmid visited common lodging houses across the East End as well as those in Borough and Covent Garden for his 1886 book *Dottings of a Dosser*. His investigation was intended to reveal living conditions worse than those found in the slums which had been the subject of previous journalistic exposés:

There is … a stratum of society even lower than that of the poor wretches who herd together in noisome courts and foetid filthy alleys. These are the unfortunate creatures whose only home is the doss'ouse, whose only friend the deppity; who have, perhaps, for years never known what it is to have the shelter of a room, save that of a common lodging house. There is no bitter cry from these, or at all events they have as yet found no spokesman to echo it in the public ear.

In the common lodging house he found boys of all ages, loafers, navvies, costermongers, thieves, unemployed artisans, ruined shopkeepers and even professional men whose careers as doctors and solicitors had ended in disaster. There were also prostitutes. Goldsmid claimed that lodging houses doubled as 'houses of ill-fame' despite the presence of corruptible children. He described a group of streetwalkers at one establishment called the 'Little Wonder' in Flower and Dean Street, another notorious slum in Spitalfields.

> All were smoking, sweating and shouting; and all, especially the women, were about as ill looking and undesirable specimens of humanity as one could meet in a lifetime. The unhappy women were by many degrees worse than the men. Their language was more obscene, their habits were more filthy, and they had abandoned even those primitive restraints of decency which hold sway over savages. Circes, they wallowed in moral filth, and seemed to revel in their degradation.

Yet for all his sensationalist prose, Goldsmid was highlighting common lodging houses and the lives of prostitutes because he believed something should be done to improve the situation. It was not enough just to appoint a committee or a royal commission, pass limited legislation and then move on to the next scandal. In a prescient warning about what might happen if the public sympathy for the most desperate in society went back to sleep, he wrote that:

'Its slumbers will probably last until the curtain which shrouds the only partially depicted scenes of London wretchedness be lifted with a ruder hand, and the "bitter cry" sound more bitter and perhaps more menacing.'

Two years later, between April and November 1888, eight prostitutes were murdered and others suffered life-threatening injuries. All were killed in the East End, although the last was out in Poplar on the other side of the River Lea. Only five are generally accepted to be victims of the Ripper.

In the early morning of 3 April 1888, Emma Smith staggered back to her home at the common lodging house at No.18 George Street, Spitalfields. Her face and head were battered and bleeding and her ear was torn. She was also clutching 'the lower part of the body'. Emma Smith told the deputy house keeper, Mary Russell, that she had been attacked and robbed. After being taken to the hospital, she told the doctor how she had been walking along Osborne Street in Whitechapel at 1.30 a.m. when she noticed three men walking towards her. One of them looked to be about nineteen years old. 'She crossed the road to avoid them, but they followed, assaulted her, took all the money she had, and then committed the outrage,' reported *The Times*. This outrage was the insertion of a blunt object into her vagina with enough force to rupture her peritoneum, the lining of the stomach cavity. She was unable to say what had been used, but the coroner later suggested that it was something like a walking stick. Emma Smith died of peritonitis the next morning, Wednesday 4 April. The lodging house deputy confirmed that the victim had stayed there for around eighteen months and had worked on the streets as a prostitute. She was known to act 'like a mad woman' when intoxicated and had often come home with black eyes. Once she claimed that she had been thrown out of a window. She was forty-five years old, 5ft 2in tall and had light brown hair. Her background remains unclear – she claimed to be a widowed mother of two who had left her husband in 1877, and that her son and daughter lived in Finsbury Park. Walter Dew claimed in his memoirs that 'there was a touch of culture in her speech unusual in her class'.

Witnesses stated that she had left home at around 7 p.m. on the Bank Holiday Monday and was seen talking to a man at the corner of Farrant Street and Burdett Road at around 12.15 a.m. He was dressed in a dark suit with a white silk handkerchief around his neck. She made no complaint to police and at the inquest on 7 April, the chief inspector of the Whitechapel Division admitted that he had no official information and only knew of the case through newspaper reports. The jury returned a verdict of 'wilful murder against some person or some persons unknown' but the police made little progress with their investigation. The case was listed as the first of eleven in the 'Whitechapel Murders' file and, like the others, it remained unsolved.[112]

While Dew believed Emma Smith was the first Ripper victim, Melville MacNaghten had 'no doubt that her death was caused by some young hooligans who escaped arrest'. One theory put forward by the press was that she was murdered by a 'High Rip' gang, which more than likely was a complete fabrication. Sir John William Nott-Bower, later Commissioner for the City of London police, said a gang with the same name was said to be responsible for a series of violent crimes in Liverpool. 'All this created considerable, and entirely unjustifiable alarm, though there was never the very faintest shadow of foundation for the suggestions made ... it was impossible, for such a gang could not have existed without the Police ever hearing of it.' Either way, said Dew, 'by most people the crime was merely regarded as a more than usually unpleasant incident in a district in which acts of violence were of daily occurrence.'[113]

Even before the murder of Emma Smith, at least two women had suffered serious assaults. On Saturday 25 February,

Annie Millwood was admitted to the Whitechapel Workhouse infirmary with stab wounds to the legs and lower body. She claimed to have been attacked by a stranger armed with a clasp knife. On 21 March she was discharged and went to another workhouse in the Mile End Road. Ten days later she collapsed and died from a rupture of the left pulmonary artery. Her death was certified as due to natural causes, unconnected to the attack. Then in the early hours of 28 March, Ada Wilson, said to be thirty-nine years old, was knifed twice in the throat on her doorstep in No.19 Maidman Street, Mile End. She survived and told the police that she had answered a knock at the door at 12.30 a.m. to find a stranger wearing a dark coat, light trousers and a wideawake hat; he looked to be aged around thirty and was 5ft 6in tall. He demanded money and stabbed her when she refused. Although she was described as a dressmaker or seamstress, a neighbour's account suggested she was a prostitute and had brought the male visitor back to her room. [114]

It was the murder of Martha Tabram in the early hours of Tuesday 6 August which the newspapers later seized upon as the first of the series. The attack took place less than 100 yards from that on Emma Smith, on the morning after a Bank Holiday Monday, and the victim was a prostitute. Her body was found on the first-floor landing of a block of model dwellings in Whitechapel, the George Yard Buildings. She had been stabbed thirty-nine times. It was reported at the inquest that her left lung had been penetrated five times, her right lung twice, her heart once, her liver five times, spleen twice and stomach six times. One of the wounds went through her sternum and the doctor concluded it must have been made with a strong blade such as a dagger or bayonet. Martha Tabram was thirty-nine years old, 5ft 3in tall and had dark hair. She was the youngest of five children of warehouseman Charles Samuel White and his wife Elizabeth. At the age of twenty she had married Henry Samuel Tabram, the foreman of a furniture-packing warehouse, and lived in Southwark not far from where she was born. They had two sons but the marriage ended because he was unable to stand Martha's heavy drinking. She took a warrant out against him after he refused to pay her sufficient maintenance and he was locked up. In 1879, he learned that she was living with another man, the carpenter Henry Turner. Her fondness for ale again plagued this relationship, and they separated three months before her murder. The couple had lived in a common lodging house off the Commercial Road in Whitechapel, but Martha was said to have frequently gone out at night on her own. She ended up at another lodging house at No. 19 George Street, Spitalfields.

On the night of 5 August she had visited a number of public houses in Whitechapel with a friend called 'Pearly Poll', Mary Ann Connelly. According to Connelly, they met two soldiers – one a private and one a corporal – and at 11.45 p.m. they paired off with the men and went their separate ways. Martha's body was first seen on the landing at 3.30 a.m. but the police were not alerted until around 4.50 a.m. when John Saunders Reeves discovered her lying in a pool of blood. Detectives focused on trying to identify the soldiers, and Connelly picked out two privates with the Coldstream Guards at Wellington Barracks. However, both men had alibis and the investigation stalled. Returning a verdict of wilful murder, the inquest jury recommended that a lamp be installed at the lodging house. The coroner George Collier called it 'one of the most dreadful murders anyone could imagine. The man must have been a perfect savage to inflict such a number of wounds on a defenceless woman in such a way'. But there was much worse to come.[115]

Three weeks passed. Then in the early hours of Friday 31 August 1888, while the East End sky was lit up by the huge fire devouring warehouses and workshops at the London docks, Mary Ann Nichols was found with her throat cut in Buck's Row, Whitechapel. Her lower clothing had been raised to her stomach to expose jagged wounds and slashes to her abdomen. Although her injuries were of a different type to those suffered by Tabram, the newspapers were soon linking the two cases because it made a better story.

Mary Ann Nichols, known as 'Polly', had turned forty-three five days earlier. She was 5ft 2in with greying brown hair; she had a scar on her forehead and was missing her front teeth. She was born near Fleet Street, the second of three children to blacksmith Edward Walker and his wife Caroline. At nineteen she had married a printer, William Nichols, and over the next fifteen years had five children. At first they lived off Fleet Street and then south of the river in Walworth and Southwark before breaking up in 1880. There had been a series of separations over Mary Ann's drinking habits, and eventually William Nichols had an affair with the girl who nursed his wife during her final pregnancy. As a result, she entered the Lambeth Workhouse, describing herself as a charwoman. Over the next seven years she went in and out of workhouses in Lambeth, St Giles, Edmonton and Holborn, and spent time on and off with her father. She was also said to be working as a prostitute. In February 1887 she was sleeping rough in Trafalgar Square and was sent back to Lambeth Workhouse. Then, in May 1888, she was given a chance of employment as a domestic servant with a married couple in Wandsworth. She wrote to her father, saying:

> It is a grand place inside, with trees and gardens back and front. All has been newly done up. They are teetotallers, and religious, so I ought to get on. They are very nice people, and I have not too much to do … So goodbye for the present. From yours truly, Polly.

Two months later, her father learned that she had run off with
£3 10s worth of clothing.

After this setback, Mary Ann gravitated towards the East
End. In the first three weeks of August she was staying in a
room with four other women at Wilmott's Lodging House at
No. 18 Thrawl Street, Spitalfields. This short and narrow road
was packed with similar establishments, and excited journalists
into florid condemnations of its 'destitution and depravity'.
Howard Goldsmid wrote:

> The dwelling houses are all poor and mean; the gutters in the
> daytime are full of squalling children; and refuse of all sorts
> is lying about in every direction. When closing time comes,
> and the dram shops and gin-palaces have sent their contingent
> to reinforce the representatives of sinning and suffering
> humanity that crowd the unwholesome street, Thrawl Street
> is a thing to shudder at, not to see. Women who have reached
> the lowest depth of degradation to which their sex can sink,
> are rolling unsteadily along the footpath, or quarrelling in
> front of the public houses from which they have just been
> expelled. Men are fighting, swearing and hiccoughing out
> snatches of objectionable songs. Babies, who have been taken
> in their mothers' arms to the drinking dens which rob them
> of their food and clothing, are wailing loudly; and the noise of
> quarrelling, intoxication and lamentation are to be heard on
> every side.

In the week before her death, Mary Ann was staying at a more
disreputable mixed doss-house at No. 56 Flower and Dean
Street, but on the night of 30/31 August, after visiting a pub
in Brick Lane, she returned to Wilmott's at 1 a.m. Her hopes
of staying there ended when the deputy lodging house keeper
threw her out because she did not have 4d for a bed. Mary Ann
is said to have pointed to her new black bonnet and replied,

'I'll soon get my doss money. See what a jolly bonnet I've got now.' Her friend Emily Holland, who had gone to see the fire at Ratcliffe dry dock, saw her at 2.30 a.m. staggering drunkenly down Osborne Street. She tried to convince Mary Ann to go back to Thrawl Street but was told, 'I have had my lodging money three times today, and I have spent it.' It seems she ended up in Buck's Row (now Durward Street), off Vallance Road, attempting to earn her doss money. It was a 'secluded place' with residential buildings on only one side. Neither of the police officers passing on their beat heard or saw anything suspicious. Emma Green, a widow living with her two sons and a daughter in the cottage next to the murder scene, heard nothing. The same applied to Walter Purkiss, his wife, children and servant, who lived in Essex Wharf across the road. Nothing of interest was noted by a night porter at the working lads' institute in Winthrop Street, which ran parallel to Buck's Row, or by the workers of a slaughterhouse 70 yards away. The alarm was only raised when Charles Andrew Cross saw Mary Ann's body on his way to work at 3.45 a.m. She was wearing a 'reddish Ulster, somewhat the worse for wear, a new brown linsey dress, two flannel petticoats with marks of Lambeth Workhouse on them, and a pair of stays, fastened'.

The Times of 3 September referred back to the two previous murders in Whitechapel and reported that the police 'had no clue' as to the perpetrator. It also claimed that detectives had abandoned the gang theory in favour of a lone male. Speculation was still rampant when the mutilated body of Annie Chapman was discovered in the backyard of No.29 Hanbury Street, Spitalfields.[116]

Like Mary Ann Nichols and Martha Tabram, Annie was not brought up in the East End. She was born Annie Eliza Smith in September 1841, six months before her parents George Smith, a soldier in the Life Guards, and Ruth Chapman, married in Paddington. The family then moved to Knightsbridge and

Annie appears to have stayed there when her parents moved to
Clewer in Berkshire in the 1850s. In 1869, aged seventeen, she
married a relative of her mother called John Chapman, who
worked as a coachman for wealthy gentlemen. Three children
followed. The first died of meningitis at the age of twelve and
the youngest was sent away to an institution for the disabled.
In 1881 they moved to Berkshire for John's work; but by this
time Annie was a heavy drinker and the relationship ended.
John Chapman, who was obviously fond of alcohol himself,
died of cirrhosis of the liver on Christmas Day 1886. With
no 10s weekly maintenance to fall back on, Annie returned
to London and began living at common lodging houses in
Whitechapel and Spitalfields. It is said she tried to make a
living by selling flowers and matches on the street, but she
was known to bring men back with her at night. Annie also
formed brief relationships with two men, one of them being
a forty-seven-year-old bricklayer's labourer nicknamed 'The
Pensioner'. She continued to battle her addiction to alcohol,
particularly rum, and was at times successful. By September
1888 she was living at Crossingham's Lodging House at
No.35 Dorset Street and attempting to restrict herself to only
drinking on Saturday nights.

In the week before her death she was seen with bruises
to her head and chest, possibly as a result of a fight with
another woman, and complained of feeling unwell. On Friday
7 September, she claimed to have got some money from her
sister in Vauxhall which she used to buy some beer and a hot
potato but, by 1.35 a.m., she did not have enough to pay the
8d needed for her bed that night. She promised she would
be back with it soon and left in the direction of Spitalfields
Market. She was forty-seven years old, with dark brown
wavy hair, blue eyes and a thick, flat nose, and was wearing a
long black coat, black skirt, brown bodice, two petticoats, red
and white striped woollen stockings and boots. She was last

seen at 5.30 a.m. with a man outside No.29 Hanbury Street, a three-storey house occupied by seventeen people, including an elderly woman selling meat for cats, two cabmen and their families, and a widow running a packing-case business with her son. None of them heard or saw anything. The man was heard asking Annie, 'Will you?' to which she replied, 'Yes'. The pair would have had no difficulty completing their transaction in the backyard of No.29, as the front and back doors were left open all day, possibly because there were so many lodgers.

At the inquest, the coroner Wynne Baxter, aware of the frenzied interest in the case, and perhaps keen to play to the gallery, laid out his interpretation of what happened next:

> After the two had passed through the passage and opened the swing door at the end, they descended the three steps into the yard. On their left-hand side there was a recess between those steps and the palings. Here, a few feet from the house, and a less distance from the palings, they must have stood. The wretch must have then seized the deceased, perhaps with Judas-like approaches. He seized her by the chin. He pressed her throat, and while thus preventing the slightest cry, he at the same time produced insensibility and suffocation. There was no evidence of any struggle. The clothes were not torn. Even in those preliminaries, the wretch seems to have known how to carry out efficiently his nefarious work. The deceased was then lowered to the ground and laid on her back; and although in doing so she may have fallen slightly against the fence, the movement was probably effected with care. Her throat was then cut in two places with savage determination, and the injuries to the abdomen commenced. All was done with cool impudence and reckless daring; but perhaps nothing was more noticeable than the emptying of her pockets and the arrangements of their contents with business-like precision in order near her feet ... There were two things

missing. Her rings had been wrenched from her fingers and had not since been found, and the uterus had been taken from the abdomen.[117]

The graphic nature of the injuries to Annie Chapman needed no spin or exaggeration, but the similarities between the latest murder and that of Polly Nichols gave the press the freedom to indulge in their taste for sensation. Allusions had already been made to Robert Louis Stevenson's 1886 novella *Strange Case of Dr Jekyll and Mr Hyde*,[118] and now the editorials overflowed with speculation about the nature of the killer. He was 'labouring under some terrible form of insanity', was filled with 'hideous malice, deadly cunning, insatiable thirst for blood', and responsible for crimes 'so distinctly outside the ordinary range of human experience that it has created a kind of stupor extending far beyond the district where the murders were committed'. Newspapers competed to describe the panic and terror that was undoubtedly spreading through the city at that time. Molly Hughes, in her 1936 memoir *A London Girl of the Eighties*, wrote that:

> No one can now believe how terrified and unbalanced we all were … it seemed to be round the corner, although it all happened in the East End and we were in the West; but even so, I was afraid to go out after dark, if only to post a letter. Just as dusk came on we used to hear down our quiet and ultra-respectable Edith Road the cries of newspaper-boys, in tones made as alarming as they could: Another 'orrible murder! … Whitechapel! … Murder! … Disgustin' details. … Murder!

For her, what was alarming was the way the killer seemed to strike quickly and then disappear as if by some kind of supernatural force. Likewise, the writer Compton Mackenzie, then aged five, remembered the autumn of 1888 as 'the most difficult time of my childhood because it was then that the nightly fears and fantasies became acute'. He wrote in his memoirs that:

> It was Jack the Ripper who first made the prospect of going to bed almost unendurable … Whitechapel became a word of dread, and I can recall the horror of reading 'Whitechapel' at the bottom of the list of fares at the far end inside an omnibus.

There were also reports of crowds of men and boys gathering in the streets chanting:'Down with the Jews.'[119]

Sir Charles Warren viewed the hysteria with dismay. 'A moment's serious thought would have been sufficient to show that the only people to whom the fiend was a menace were the poor women of the streets,' he wrote in his memoirs. 'But I am afraid that the respectable women of Whitechapel derived small comfort at the time from any such reflection, and everywhere extreme precautions were taken against the Ripper's coming.'There may also be a hint of moral judgement that the victims were 'only prostitutes', who were putting their own lives at risk by maintaining an immoral lifestyle. 'The victims, without exception, belonged to the lowest dregs of female humanity, who avoid the police and exercised every ingenuity in order to remain in the darkest corners of the most deserted alleys,' was the verdict of the future Assistant Commissioner, Melville MacNaghten. Prostitutes were treated as outcasts by pretty much every section of society, even the poorest. At the height of the Ripper murders, the socialist John Burns noted in his diary for 1888 how customers of a coffee house were avoiding the only vacant seat because it was next to a 'dirty, bedraggled and diseased' prostitute. 'Repulsive though she was I thought it necessary to remind the workmen that I was not influenced by her poverty and degraded condition and sat down beside her. This unexpected consideration visibly affected her and increased her sympathy and secured her gratitude.' He noted that the only distinction between her and the workmen was that 'they prostitute another part of their body – their hands'.[120]

Elizabeth Stride was well known to the police for prostitution and drunken behaviour. Stride was actually Swedish, born Elisabeth Gustafsdotter on 27 November 1843, on a farm in Torslanda, north of Gothenburg. At the age of seventeen she was working as a domestic maid, but three years later her life was beginning its unhappy trajectory. She left her job, her mother died, she contracted a venereal disease and she gave birth to a stillborn child. In March 1865, at the age of twenty-one, she was registered by Swedish police as a prostitute.

The following year, attempting to turn her life around, she travelled to England using her inheritance. In 1869 she married a carpenter from Regent's Park, John Thomas Stride, and opened a coffee shop with him in Poplar. She was later to claim that her husband and two of her nine children died on the paddle steamer *Princess Alice*, which sank in the River Thames in 1878, although this seems to be a total fabrication as he died of heart disease in 1884. By then the couple had separated, most likely because of Elizabeth's heavy drinking, and in January 1882 she was living in Flower and Dean Street in Spitalfields. In 1884 she was sentenced to seven days' hard labour for soliciting for the purposes of prostitution, and throughout 1887 and 1888 she was repeatedly hauled before the magistrates for drunk and disorderly behaviour and using obscene language. During this time she was living on and off with a waterside labourer, Michael Kidney, who later said: 'It was drink that made her go away … She always returned without me going after her. I think she liked me better than any other man.' He claimed he last saw her on 25 September 1888. She was nearly forty-five but looked younger, was 5ft 5in in height and had curly brown hair.

The following day she was seen at No.32 Flower and Dean Street by the philanthropist and 'do-gooder' Thomas Barnardo. Writing of his visit to the lodging house, among others, in the November issue of his magazine *Night and Day*, he described talking to girls and women in the kitchen about the Whitechapel murders.

> The female inmates of the kitchen seemed thoroughly frightened at the dangers to which they were presumably exposed ... One poor creature, who had evidently been drinking, exclaimed somewhat bitterly to the following effect. 'We're all up to no good, and no one cares what becomes of us. Perhaps some of us will be killed next!' And then she added, 'If anybody had helped the likes of us long ago we would never have come to this!' I have since visited the mortuary in which were lying the remains of the poor woman Stride, and I at once recognised her as one of those who stood around me in the kitchen of the common lodging house on the occasion of my visit ... surely the awful revelations consequent upon the recent tragedies should stir the whole community up to action and to the resolve to deliver the children of today, who will be the men and women of tomorrow, from so evil an environment.

On the afternoon of Saturday 29 September, Elizabeth Stride was paid 6*d* for cleaning rooms at the lodging house. At 11 p.m. she was seen with a man leaving a pub in Settles Street, Whitechapel, and there were further sightings of her with a man in Berner Street at 11.45 p.m. and 12.35 a.m. Ten minutes later Israel Schwartz, who lived off Backchurch Lane, saw Elizabeth Stride being pushed to the ground in the gateway leading to Dutfield's Yard and the International Workingmen's Educational Association at No.40 Berner Street. She screamed three times. Schwartz then ran off and did not see what happened next. At the time, there were between twenty and thirty people singing in the club following a discussion about the 'necessity for socialism among Jews'. Their merriment stopped abruptly at around 1 a.m. when they were told that a woman had been found outside with her throat cut. Elizabeth Stride had not suffered any other injuries and this was immediately taken to indicate that the killer had been interrupted before he could begin his mutilation. It might also suggest that it had nothing to do with the murders of Mary Ann Nichols and Annie Chapman. But when another prostitute was found dead forty-five minutes later, it seemed too much of a coincidence.[121]

Catherine Eddowes was a year older than Elizabeth Stride but, like Mary Ann Nichols and Annie Chapman, she appears to have turned to prostitution much later in life following the breakdown of her marriage. She was born in Wolverhampton in 1842 but the following year she moved with her parents to London when her father found a job as a tinplate worker in the City of London. Her mother died at the age of forty-two in 1855, having given birth to twelve children, and her father followed two years later. Catherine left the family home in Bermondsey and returned to Wolverhampton. After working as a tinplate stamper and a tray polisher, she began a relationship with a former soldier, Thomas Conway, and had his initials tattooed on her arm. Their first child, a daughter, arrived in 1863 and they moved back to Westminster in London. Two sons followed, but the family was being torn apart by Catherine's alcoholism and she is said to have regularly disappeared for months at a time. Conway is also said to have beaten her during their rows. In 1880 she left their home in Chelsea and ended up in the East End, possibly because her sister was living in Spitalfields. She fell in with a man named John Kelly and lived with him at Cooney's common lodging house at No. 55 Flower and Dean Street. Cooney's was almost a brand – they had several other branches in Thrawl Street, all offering single beds for 4*d* and doubles for 8*d*. One of the Thrawl Street outlets was described by Howard Goldsmid as being 'stuffy, close, ill-ventilated, and stenchful beyond expression'. He also complained that it was populated by half a dozen cats chasing rats, a malnourished eight-year-old girl carrying out domestic chores on the orders of her drunken mother, and a man enthusiastically pontificating on religion, the economy, the law, medical science and the higher education of women.

Although they were living in a notorious slum, witnesses claimed Catherine was not habitually walking the streets and it is likely that she only resorted to it when money was tight. She is also said to have worked as a domestic servant for Jewish families in the area, while John Kelly tried to earn a wage on the markets, and every year they joined the crowds heading out to the country for the hop-picking season. In 1888 they went to Hunton near Maidstone in Kent but 'didn't get on any too well' and they returned to London almost penniless on Friday 28 September. Kelly had to pawn his boots for 2*s* but this didn't last long and the following day, at 2 p.m., Catherine went out alone. Kelly claimed that she was going to try to get money from her sister in Bermondsey, but by 8.30 p.m. she was slumped drunkenly on the pavement of Aldgate High Street. Her condition attracted the attention of a police officer and she was taken off to Bishopsgate station, where she gave her name as 'Nothing'. It was one of the safest places for a prostitute to be at night, but tragically for Catherine Eddowes she was found fit to be released at just before 1 a.m. She gave her name as Mary Ann Kelly and her address as No.6 Fashion Street, adding, 'I shall get a fine hiding when I get home.' Her last words to the constable as he ushered her out were, 'Good night old cock.'

Instead of heading towards Flower and Dean Street and home, she went the opposite way towards Houndsgate and

Aldgate High Street. She was 5ft tall with dark hair and wearing a black straw bonnet, a black cloth jacket with imitation fur collar, a piece of apron round her neck, a dark green skirt printed with Michaelmas daisies and golden lilies, brown stockings and a pair of men's laced boots. At 1.35 a.m. she, or another woman with a black bonnet, was seen standing with a man at the entrance to the passage between Duke Street and Mitre Square. There were at least two patrolling uniformed officers and three plain-clothes officers in the area at the time, but none saw anything suspicious. 'Never in the history of the East End of London had such elaborate precautions been taken to prevent the very thing which had not only been done, but repeated,' claimed Walter Dew. 'Hundreds of police, in uniform, in plainclothes and in all manner of disguises – some even dressed as women – patrolled every yard of every street in the "danger zone" every few minutes.' But it was not enough. At 1.45 a.m. PC Edward Watkins entered Mitre Square and found Catherine Eddowes' mutilated body slumped in a darkened corner, 'ripped up like a pig in a market'.

The killer had used what few minutes he had to inflict even more gruesome injuries than those suffered by Annie Chapman. Not only was the uterus missing, but also the left kidney too. A piece of intestine had been cut out and left between the body and left arm. There were knife wounds to the lower eyelids, cheeks and right ear, and the tip of her nose had been cut off. Further mysterious clues added to the Ripper legend – a piece of Catherine Eddowes' apron was found in the entrance to a building on Goulston Street. Above it were three lines of writing in white chalk: 'The Juwes are not the men who will be blamed for nothing.'[122]

It was at this point that the legend of Jack the Ripper was born. A letter, supposedly received by the Central News Agency on 27 September, was printed in the 1 October editions of the newspapers. Not only did it give the killer a memorable name, it also contained a reference to clipping ears off that was similar enough to actual events for people to believe it was genuine. A postcard postmarked 1 October, signed the same way, appeared to predict the 'double event'. Then on 16 October, the chairman of the Whitechapel Vigilance Committee, a group set up by local businesses to patrol the streets, received a box containing part of a human kidney that was believed to have been taken from Catherine Eddowes.[123]

Here was a killer who delighted in taunting the authorities and who was equipped with surgical skill, speed, stealth and an inhuman lust for the blood of middle-aged women walking the streets after midnight.

Mary Jane Kelly was different. She was much younger, at around twenty-five years of age, and stood 5ft 7in tall. She was also said to have possessed 'rather attractive features'. What is known of her early life comes from the account she told to her partner and friends, and may or may not be reliable. Even her true hair colour is in doubt, as indicated by her various nicknames: 'Ginger', 'Fair Emma', and 'Black Mary'. Kelly claimed to have been born in Ireland and moved to Wales as a child. She married a collier at the age of sixteen, but he was killed in a mine explosion. After that she turned to prostitution in Cardiff before travelling to London to work in a high-class West End brothel. She claimed to have gone to Paris with a gentleman, only to return after two weeks because she did not like it. One way or another she ended up in the East End, in the parish of St George's in the East, in and around Ratcliffe Highway (then known as St George's Street). By 1886 she was living at a common lodging house in Thrawl Street, Spitalfields, and the following year she began a relationship with Joseph Barnett, a porter at Billingsgate Market. The couple settled in a small room costing 4s 6d a week at No.13 Miller's Court, accessed via a passage from Dorset Street. There was a fireplace, two windows looking out on to the court (one of which was broken), a bed with a tin bath underneath, a bedside table, and a chair. The set-up worked for a while, but then Joseph lost his job in the summer of 1888 and Mary Kelly returned to prostitution to pay the rent. It was perhaps during this period that Walter Dew saw her 'often … parading along Commercial Street, between Flower and Dean Street and Aldgate or along Whitechapel Road. She was usually in the company of two or three of her kind, fairly neatly dressed and invariably wearing a clean white apron but no hat'. Her decision to go back on the streets and to invite other prostitutes back to her room appears to have been the reason behind Joseph Barnett's decision to go and live elsewhere on 30 October. He last saw her on the evening of Thursday 8 November, a few hours before her murder.

According to her friend Lizzie Albrook, Mary Kelly was in a melancholy mood that night:

> About the last thing she said was, 'Whatever you do don't you do wrong and turn out as I have.' She had often spoken to me in this way and warned me against going on the streets as she had done … I don't believe she would have gone out as she did if she had not been obliged to do so to keep herself from starvation.

She did go out that night, and was seen taking a man back to her room at around 11.45 p.m. Two neighbours claimed to have heard her drunkenly singing the song 'A Violet I Plucked from Mother's Grave':

> Scenes of my childhood arise before my gaze,
> Bringing recollections of bygone happy days.
> When down in the meadow in childhood I would roam,

No one's left to cheer me now within that good old home,
Father and Mother, they have pass'd away;
Sister and brother, now lay beneath the clay,
But while life does remain to cheer me, I'll retain
This small violet I pluck'd from mother's grave.

At 2 a.m. she was back outside asking an acquaintance, George Hutchinson, for sixpence. He did not have any money and watched her walk off down Flower and Dean Street towards Thrawl Street. According to Hutchinson, she was approached by a well-dressed Jewish-looking man who put his arm round her shoulders and walked with her back to Miller's Court. Two other witnesses heard a cry of 'Murder!' between 3.30 a.m. and 4 a.m. that night, but the alarm was not raised until Thomas Bowyer went to collect the rent at around 10.45 a.m. The scene inside No. 13 Miller's Court traumatised those who saw it in 1888, and it is still shocking people today, thanks to the photographs taken by the police. Mary Kelly was lying in bed, with her throat cut, and her nose, lips, cheeks, and eyebrows sliced. Joseph Barnett could only recognise her by her ears and eyes. She had also been disembowelled and the internal organs were placed around her body. Her heart was cut out, but it is unclear whether it was taken away by the killer or not.

The authorities appear to have made a deliberate attempt to clamp down on the Ripper frenzy following this murder. Three days after the discovery of the body, the inquest was concluded quickly without fully describing the injuries or revealing new details for the next day's papers. Whereas previously reporters had been able to see the body in the mortuary or examine the scene, on this occasion they were left to try and pick up information by speaking to local residents. At the same time, the focus of much press criticism, Sir Charles Warren, was allowed to resign. The reporting of the

Kelly murder did not scale the heights of the 'double event' and in terms of column inches returned to the level seen in relation to Annie Chapman.

By now the killings had attracted the keen interest of Queen Victoria. After spending the previous four months fuming about the behaviour of her grandson, the German Emperor Wilhelm II, she sent a cipher telegram to the Prime Minister Lord Salisbury on 10 November:

This new most ghastly murder shows the absolute necessity for some very decided action. All these courts must be lit and our detectives improved. They are not what they should be. You promised, when the first murder took place, to consult with your colleagues about it.

Salisbury replied that the cabinet had agreed to issue a proclamation offering 'a free pardon to anyone who should give evidence as to the recent murder except the actual perpetrator of the crime'. Three days later, after being told that Warren's resignation had been accepted, the Queen drafted a letter to Matthews stating that: 'the Queen fears this resignation will have a bad effect in encouraging the lawbreakers to defy the police!' Victoria even offered her own views on how the investigation might be improved:

At the same time the Queen fears that the detective department is not so efficient as it might be. No doubt the recent murders in Whitechapel were committed in circumstances which make detection very difficult; still, the Queen thinks that, in the small area where these horrible crimes have been perpetrated, a great number of detectives might be employed and that every possible suggestion might be carefully examined and if practicable, followed.

She suggested that the police examine the cattle and passenger boats, look into the number of single men living alone and ensure that there was sufficient surveillance at night. 'These are some of the questions that occur to the Queen on reading the accounts of this horrible crime.' There were even discussions with Lord Salisbury about replacing Matthews with Charles Ritchie, the Tower Hamlets MP who had recently and successfully brought the 1888 Local Government Act through Parliament.[124]

The murders also spurred on churchmen and charity workers like Dr Barnardo, the Revd Samuel Barnett and William Booth of the Salvation Army to put forward their own suggestions as to how to solve the problems of the East End. Barnardo, who often complained about the state of his organisation's finances, wrote to *The Times* after the double event, noting that 'stimulated by the recently revealed Whitechapel horrors, many voices are daily heard suggesting as many different schemes to remedy degraded social conditions'. He then put forward his own plan to take over a common lodging house in Flower and Dean Street and to turn it into a home for:

> Those unfortunate children ... who from the very earliest age have been condemned to the vilest associations, who must as a matter of fact and of necessity be degraded by constant contact with fallen women, with thieves, with criminals of every type, and with persons who are veritably the pariahs of society. It is from amongst just such scenes ... that I am daily snatching as from the very fire children who without such aid must become in a short time by the sure process of natural and moral laws assimilated to the degradation of their surroundings.

To do this he required generous donations from readers.

Booth, who claimed to rescue 1,000 prostitutes a year, also exploited the Ripper murders to raise money to carry out his mission. In one issue of the Salvation Army newspaper,

War Cry, he printed an appeal from one of his staff, James J. Cooke:

> Of course we are taking advantage of this terror, and are doing our utmost to bring the people to repentance. A few are getting saved. It was so sad to hear of the last murdered woman – Kelly – that she was quite recently on a Sunday morning in a lodging house where Capt Walker and her lieutenant were holding a meeting and sang from the same hymn book as the captain. Alas! She did not get saved. Who will help us to get the thousands of worse than heathens still living in Whitechapel and other slums saved? Send us your money or come yourself.

In December 1888, Booth presented a memorial to the government asking for £15,000 to open ten rescue homes and ten shelter depots. The request was rejected by the Home Secretary and clearly upset some members of the Church who felt that Booth's 'well-meaning but uninstructed philanthropy' hindered the work already being carried out. The rector of Christ Church in Lisson Grove complained that 'food and shelter thus supplied would in all probability have the effect of increasing destitution rather than diminishing it'. Booth was not deterred, and in 1891 he came up with an even more ambitious plan to raise £1 million and set up a series of 'colonies', including a 'Whitechapel-by-the-sea', to do for the poor what Brighton did for the middle classes.[125]

Smaller organisations also saw their chance to appeal for donations from concerned members of the middle and upper classes. The chairman of the Metropolitan Association for Befriending Young Servants wrote to *The Times* on 17 October:

> Particular attention is now being drawn to a class of unfortunates, the flotsam and jetsam of that huge ocean of misery collected in this metropolis. While much may be done,

and is done, by rescue work, clearly the preventive agencies are those into which our strength should be thrown … We have, I think, proved statistically that our work of befriending young servants of the helpless class does influence the girls for good … We are at the present moment grievously in want of money (our balance at the bank is nearly £200 to the bad, and our monthly cheques to the branches are withheld till more funds are available) …

Others were less disposed to helping. One reader, who sent a letter to *The Times* after the double murder on 30 September, opposed attempts to disperse the 'vicious inhabitants' of Dorset Street and Flower and Dean Street. 'There are no lower streets in London, and, if they are driven out of these, to what streets are they to go?' The writer suggested that the 'unknown surgical genius … has made his contribution towards solving the problem of clearing the East End'. This kind of viewpoint had already been parodied by George Bernard Shaw in an anonymous letter sent to the *Star* on 24 September. He noted that public interest in the poor and helpless of the East End had only been brought about because 'some independent genius has taken the matter in hand, and by simply murdering and disembowelling four women, converted the proprietary press to an inept sort of communism. The moral is a pretty one'. Even the victims' pasts were used for political point scoring – on 6 October the *Graphic Illustrated Newspaper* rejected what it called the 'socialist theories' that the victims were oppressed by 'capitalist tyranny', and asserted that 'they were all originally well brought up, fairly well-to-do persons, the wives of respectable men; and their terrible downward course into vice and wretchedness seems chiefly chargeable to their own misdoing'.[126]

The debate about 'what is to be done' was still raging when an eighth prostitute was found dead in east London. Police sergeant Robert Golding was patrolling along Poplar High

Street with a colleague in the early hours of 20 December when he noticed a woman lying on her left side in Clarke's Yard between Nos 184 and 186. Unlike the previous cases, there was no obvious sign of any injury to the body. It was only when the woman was taken back to the mortuary that Dr Matthew Brownfield found evidence that she may have been murdered. 'There were slight marks of blood having escaped from the nostrils, and the right side of the nose showed a slight abrasion, while on the left cheek was an old scar,' *The Times* reported. The report continued:

> On the neck there was the mark apparently of a cord extending from the right side of the spine round the throat to the lobe of the left ear. He had, by experiment, found that a piece of four-fold cord would cause such a mark. On the neck he also found marks as of the thumbs and middle and index fingers ... The marks ran perpendicularly to the line round the neck before described. There were no injuries to the arms or legs as if any violent struggle had taken place.

The doctor believed that the killer would have wound the cord round his hands and then pulled it tight round her neck from behind.

Although this was a completely different method to that used on previous victims, the newspapers were only too willing to pose the question that must have been on many lips: 'HAS THE WHITECHAPEL MURDERER ADOPTED A NEW METHOD?' The *Star* newspaper suggested that 'preliminary strangulation' may have been used to stop the victims crying out, and that any marks on the neck would have been obliterated by the cutting of the throat. There were also concerns raised by a juror at the inquest that 'the inhabitants of Poplar are left far more unprotected than the people of Whitechapel and it is a great wonder that more murders of this kind have not been done in the neighbourhood'. On the other hand, it was reported that the neighbourhood and the police seemed uninterested in the case, and that life in Whitechapel continued as normal. 'There has been nothing like the panic which followed the previous murders,' read one account in the *Birmingham Daily Post* on 27 December. It continued:

> The district from which the Whitechapel fiend has drawn his victims was yesterday the scene of terrible debauchery, which unfortunately characterises that portion of London during this season of the year. The gin palaces were thronged with women reclining under the influence of drink and the police officers who have been stationed many years at the east end of the Metropolis declare that the terrible series of crimes which have been perpetrated during the present year has had no effect in deterring or softening the women of the unfortunate class who infest certain thoroughfares in Whitechapel. On the contrary they appear to pursue their calling with greater callousness and brutality than ever.

It took several days for the victim to be identified. The head nurse at Bromley-by-Bow sick asylum recognised her as a patient by the name of Rose Mylett, who was admitted for treatment on 20 January and then discharged on 14 March 1888. In Poplar she was known as 'Fair Alice' Downey, but she was also known to frequent the areas of Whitechapel, Spitalfields and Bow, and had the nickname 'Drunken Lizzie' Davis. She was described as being 5ft 2in tall, 'very poorly dressed, but … fairly good looking'. According to Walter Dew, she had been 'driven out of Whitechapel by her dread of Jack the Ripper' and police discovered that she had been staying at a common lodging house at No.18 George Street, Spitalfields – the same address as Emma Smith, and next door to an address used by Martha Tabram. The deputy described Mylett as 'a very respectable person'. Eventually officers also tracked down Mylett's mother, Margaret, at Pelham Street off Baker's Row in Spitalfields. Mrs Mylett, described as an Irish-born widow, said her daughter's real name was Catherine. Recent research suggests that she was born in Whitechapel in 1859 and had two brothers and an older sister. According to her mother, Rose went on to marry an upholsterer by the name of Davis and in September 1880 the couple had a daughter, Florence. A year later, mother and child were living together in Mile End, Old Town. Rose also appears to have had a son named Henry in 1883, before separating from her husband. By 1888 her daughter was at a school in Sutton, Surrey, and twenty-nine-year-old Rose was earning a living through prostitution. One of her friends in that line of work was Alice Graves, a fellow resident of No.18 George Street, and likely to be the same Alice Graves who had come to the attention of police a year earlier when she was charged with the murder of her fourteen-month old son. Graves was said to have admitted throwing the boy into the Thames from London Bridge on Christmas morning 1887, but police were unable to find any evidence that she ever had a child and the case was thrown out.

Rose appears to have left her lodgings at George Street between 6 and 7 p.m. on Wednesday 19 December, after borrowing 2*d* from her landlady Mary Smith for the tram fare to Poplar. She was dressed in brown and black, with a tweed jacket, red petticoat and red and blue striped stockings. It didn't take her long to get there, because by 7.55 p.m. she was talking to two sailors not far from the scene of her death on Poplar High Street. According to Charles Ptomoley, a 'lunatic attendant' at the Poplar Poor Law Union, she was telling one of them, 'No, no, no!' At around midnight she was spotted in the same street by Jane Hill, who ran a boarding house at No.152, and who gave her 2*d* when she complained she had no money. Then at around 2.30 a.m., according to Alice Graves, she was with two men outside the George in Commercial Road, Stepney. Rose appeared drunk. If this is true, less than two hours later she was back in Poplar High Street. Clarke's Yard, so named because it belonged to a builder named Clarke, was described in the *Daily News* as:

> A long narrow lane leading from the main thoroughfare down to some workshops and stables. It is about eight to ten feet wide, it is not lit up; one of the two gates which formerly kept out intruders at night time has disappeared and lately the yard has become a nuisance from a sanitary point of view, while it is much frequented by women of the unfortunate class.

Nobody witnessed the attack, which must have taken place not long before the discovery of the still-warm body at 4.15 a.m. Rose was still carrying 1*s* 2*d*, so robbery seemed an unlikely motive. There was also the account of a woman named Neos Green, who claimed that shortly before the body was discovered two sailors had rushed up to her in the High Street and asked for directions to West India Docks. As they left she heard one say: 'Make haste, Bill, and we shall be in time to catch the ship.'

Like all the previous 'unfortunate' victims, the murder of Rose Mylett would remain unsolved. But it is also easier to see why the police were unable to catch the person responsible. It was not because he was the legendary Jack the Ripper, but because they were not convinced it was a murder at all. Sir Robert Anderson, the Assistant Commissioner of Police, was convinced that she had died of 'natural causes' and 'but for the "Jack the Ripper" scare, no one would have thought of suggesting that it was a homicide'. Three more doctors examined the body, all of them agreeing with the first report of strangulation. Anderson asked a fifth doctor for his opinion. This was Dr Thomas Bond, who had told Anderson the previous month that Nichols, Chapman, Stride, Eddowes and Kelly were killed by the same person.

At first, Bond agreed that Mylett had been strangled. However, after consulting with Anderson and making a further examination, he reported that while the fingermarks on the neck remained, the mark of the cord had disappeared. Bond suggested that the mark on her neck might have been caused by her collar when she slumped to the floor drunk and unconscious. He told the inquest that in his opinion was that it was ' ... not murder – that the amount of violence required to strangle an able-bodied woman would leave a mark which would not disappear in five days'. Dr Bond also stated that he found a teaspoon of alcohol in a tablespoon of her stomach contents, whereas the doctor who carried out the first examination found none. In common with the previous murders there were plenty of loose ends. As the coroner summed up: 'The usual signs of strangulation, such as protrusion of the tongue and clenching of the hands, were absent, there being nothing at all suggestive of death from violence.' Therefore, if she had been strangled then it had probably happened quickly and while she was in a weakened condition. In the end, the inquest jury rejected Bond's opinion and returned a verdict of wilful murder.[127]

The police failed to solve any of the eight murders of prostitutes in 1888. This partly reflects the status of 'unfortunates'. They were outcasts, shunned by respectable society and forced outdoors to walk the most dangerous streets of the city at night. They were untrustworthy and could easily be discredited in court. Even in the twenty-first century, sex workers are still one of, if not the most, vulnerable and overlooked sections of society. In 2006, Steven Wright murdered five women who worked as prostitutes in the Ipswich area over six weeks, and more recently Stephen Griffiths was convicted of killing three prostitutes in Bradford. It is almost as if the authorities only take notice when the bodies start piling up. The reality is that prostitutes have fewer community ties and are less likely to be reported missing. They can be chosen at will and tempted into deserted yards and alleyways away from prying eyes. Their friends on the street are less willing to help police, and evidence of their final movements is harder to obtain. Their lifestyle also means that they are a natural target for the killer driven by hatred of women and women's sexuality. And because it is easier to 'get away with it', their killers are able to strike again and again.

11

UNDER THE KNIFE

One early theory surrounding the Jack the Ripper case was that the gruesome mutilations could only have been carried out by a surgeon or someone with anatomical knowledge. This suggestion was later dismissed by other doctors, who were perhaps keen to disassociate their profession from the crimes. Whatever the truth, there were other murders in 1888 that police suspected had been carried out by doctors. These three female victims all died following suspected 'unlawful operations', a term generally used by newspapers to refer to abortions. Before 1803 terminations were allowed if they took place before the baby began to move in the womb (known as the 'quickening'), but by 1861 the punishment was life imprisonment. Doctors were prepared to carry out the procedure if the mother's life was in danger, but otherwise the choice was either visiting a 'back-street' abortionist or taking the pills and miracle cures advertised in the newspapers. The ultimate risk of both options was death.[128]

On 14 February 1888, a twenty-seven-year-old chimneysweep's widow called Elizabeth Gorman died at her home at No.4 Callow Street, Fulham Road, Chelsea.

The post-mortem revealed that she had suffered internal injuries from an unlawful operation which could not have been self-inflicted. According to witnesses, Mrs Gorman had called a series of medical men to see her in the days before her death, but later claimed she was only suffering from a cold. Emma Young, a neighbour, said she recommended that Mrs Gorman cure her 'violent chill' by putting her feet in mustard and hot water and bought her some pills from a dispensary. The newspapers reported no details of what exactly her internal injuries were, but did note that she had been living with a man named Miller since her husband's death a few months earlier. The jury were satisfied with the evidence enough to return a verdict of wilful murder against person or persons unknown. The inference is that one of the medical men had performed a botched abortion, but it appears that nobody was ever arrested or charged.[129]

A botched abortion was also responsible for the death of a twenty-one-year-old woman in Somerstown, north London. Emma Wakefield was 'a good looking, well-conducted girl' with a steady job as a shell-box maker at a factory in Charrington Street. She was engaged to her boyfriend of five years, Thomas Price, and was due to be married the following May. He too had good prospects, earning £1 a week at a local printing works. On 23 September 1888, she was staying with Mr Price at the home of his married sister at No.60 Aldenham Street. Shortly after going out for an hour and a half with finacé, she suddenly fell ill. The following day she went to see a doctor, but he diagnosed her as having a chest infection and recommended that she rest in bed. Emma's condition gradually deteriorated and she died on Saturday 29 September. The post-mortem revealed the cause of death was blood poisoning following an abortion. 'There were two internal abrasions which could not have been caused naturally,' reported the *Reynolds's Weekly Newspaper*. 'An instrument had been used.'

Who had carried out the operation? Thomas Price, his married sister and his mother denied all knowledge of any pregnancy. Emma Wakefield had not told the doctor of her condition and her mother had been away in the country at the time. But Mr Price did reveal a strange conversation that he had with his fiancée shortly before her death. 'She said an angel was waiting to receive her, that she was leaving the world a prudent upright girl, that she was quitting this life without a fault upon her tongue and that she was cut down in the midst of her bloom,' he told the inquest. At other times she sang hymns 'oh so sweetly' or launched into random outbursts, pointing at Mr Price's mother and shouting: 'Look at that woman in the corner, you liar, you liar! You deceived me. Go out of this room.' She was clearly delirious as a result of her illness. Thomas' mother claimed that Emma mentioned a 'Mr Johnson', the fifty-year-old married foreman of the factory where she worked. Mr Johnson had called to see her while she was ill and after he left she had rambled: 'Stand up, Mr Johnson! Father, look at him! Mrs Price, get out of the way … Ah! I have got you!'

Police searched No.60 Aldenham Street but found nothing to indicate what had happened. It seemed likely that at least one of the witnesses was covering something up, but nothing else emerged to clear up the mystery and Emma's father insisted that Mr Price 'would not hurt a hair of her head'. The jury returned a verdict that Emma Wakefield had 'died from the effects of blood poisoning following abortion, caused by the illegal use of instruments', and they were of opinion that some person or persons at present unknown were guilty of causing her death. The coroner William Wynn Westcott added: 'Your verdict is tantamount to one of wilful murder. I think perjury has been committed.'[130]

As in the Gorman case, no further action was taken. In the third case, however, there was a trial at the Old Bailey.

Eliza Schummacher was convinced that she was pregnant. She was a thirty-nine-year-old married dressmaker and already had two children. By 1888 she had lived apart from her husband, a gentleman's servant, for several years, but nobody knew whether he was the father or if it was somebody else. Either way, she did not want to have the child and decided to seek help from a doctor. Eliza chose James Gloster, a thirty-four-year-old Irishman practising in Upper Phillimore Place, a row of grand late-Georgian terraced houses in Kensington. 'She told me that she believed she was in the family way and asked if I could help her to get rid of it,' Dr Gloster said, recalling the meeting in early June 1888. 'I told her most certainly I could not, that no doctor could hear of such a thing.' She went to another doctor in Soho instead, the Italian-speaking Louis Tarrico, from South America.

Three weeks later, Eliza was bedbound and in excruciating pain. Her local doctor Charles Crane visited her home at No.21 Moreton Place, Pimlico, and asked her what had happened. What she told him shocked him so much that he decided to write it down. Her statement, dictated on the afternoon of 27 June, a few hours before her death, appeared to implicate Dr Gloster:

> I thought I was pregnant and I went to see Dr Gloster ... he said as I had mentioned the subject for which I had gone to him he could not have anything to do with me. He said go to Dr Tarrico. I wanted him to write the address and he said no, no one can mistake a name like this. He told me to ask Dr Tarrico if he would examine me for something for the womb and if Dr Tarrico did so examine me then he Dr Gloster would take on the case. Then I went to Dr Tarrico and he passed an instrument – that was on the same day in the evening as I went to Dr Gloster that was last Tuesday four weeks. Dr Tarrico did not hurt me, he was gentle. I went to

Dr Gloster next day and he passed an instrument into my body which hurt me very much. He came to see me here on the 11th June and he again passed an instrument which hurt me very much. I have been in pain ever since and unable to get up. He said if I was very bad I was to send for him. I did send for him, I was in great agony. I cursed him. He did not pass an instrument that day. He brought some medicine. He applied some cotton wool. I thought he had left the cotton wool inside me. I did not see him again. I have never been very well since and I do not think I am going to be so. I make this statement with the fear of death before my eyes.

Eliza Schummacher had never been pregnant – it was all in her mind. At the post-mortem, Dr Thomas Bond found that she did indeed still have a piece of cotton wool inside her – but in the pelvic cavity rather than the womb. The cavity was also full of pus. At first he could not explain how the cotton wool had got there, but on closer examination he found a slight scar which he was able to pass a probe through. Somehow it had been forced through the lining of the uterus by a pointed instrument, possibly a doctor's speculum. 'I have no doubt death was caused by peritonitis,' reported Dr Bond. 'I should think the wound was caused at least a week before death … it would have caused great pain.'

Both Gloster and Tarrico were arrested and charged with causing Eliza's death. Gloster denied involvement, claiming he had sent the woman to another doctor, and reacted angrily to her allegations. 'I don't know what made her say that when she was dying. It must be in spite. You don't know her. She is a drunken woman.' He even denied that he mentioned the name of Dr Tarrico to Mrs Schummacher, whereas Tarrico told police that Dr Gloster had asked him to see 'a friend and patient' with congestion or ulceration of the womb. 'He brought a lady upstairs to my front room. I examined her and said I do not know what it is, perhaps it might be congestion.' Tarrico prescribed rhubarb pills and never saw her again.

On 3 July, the inquest jury returned a verdict of wilful murder against Dr Gloster alone and two weeks later Dr Tarrico was discharged by the magistrate. The problem for the prosecution was that there was no direct evidence that Dr Gloster had caused the fatal injury except for the statement of Eliza Schummacher, who of course could not testify in court. At Westminster Magistrates' Court, Gloster's barrister Charles Gill argued that the dying declaration was contradicted by other evidence, particularly on dates. 'It was not likely that a man of the skill and even special ability of Dr Gloster would perform an operation for which there could be no necessity,' said Mr Gill. 'The fatal injury was either occasioned by the woman herself or by some unskilled person.' Dr Gloster insisted that he had ordered Mrs Schummacher to leave when she told him what she wanted. The magistrate also heard the bizarre evidence of an American surgeon who claimed that a certain 'Dr Robertson' had confessed to taking part in the operation. But when cross-examined, the American admitted that he just wanted 'to get the poor beggar off'. Gloster was committed for trial for murder at the Central Criminal Court.

On 25 September, James Gloster surrendered to bail at the Old Bailey and entered the dock. He struck reporters as 'a fine gentlemanly-looking man' as he entered a plea of 'not guilty' to the charge. The prosecution case was that Dr Gloster, unaware that Eliza was not pregnant, had performed an operation intending to cause a miscarriage but instead caused the fatal injury. There was evidence that Mrs Schummacher had been perfectly healthy after seeing Dr Tarrico on 8 June. Three days later, she had returned to Dr Gloster and was given a note reading 'please change cheque for me'. As the prosecutor Harry Bodkin Poland observed, 'It was strange that instead of the patient giving the doctor money, the doctor was giving the patient money.' The operation was said to have taken place on 18 June, and the following day Mrs Schummacher fell ill. She sent a telegram to Dr Gloster asking him to come immediately, but he told her that she was just suffering from inflammation and that she should call her local doctor instead. A few days later, Mrs Schummacher's sister asked Dr Gloster to visit Eliza again because she was complaining that her 'inside feels like a burning hell'. Unmoved by her plight, he replied, 'No I won't come again. She has deceived me. She sent a telegram, open, with my name on in full. I would not go if you were to lay me down £500 this minute. I would not be seen again in the neighbourhood. My name is my name.' Was this because he knew he had done wrong, and wanted to avoid being connected to the victim?

The prosecution lawyer Harry Bodkin Poland admitted that it was difficult to understand how a properly qualified doctor could make such a mistake. He came up with another theory: 'Could it be that the person did not intend to procure a miscarriage, but in consequence of the deceased's persisting that she was pregnant he examined her with an instrument and so injured her in this way?' If so, then Dr Gloster was guilty not of murder but of manslaughter due to gross negligence. Or was it, as the defence contended, a case of a delusional woman making a false charge against the doctor?

The key evidence was the dying declaration, but the defence argued that it should be declared inadmissible. Dr Crane had admitted that the final part of the statement in which she had the 'fear of death before my eyes' was his own wording. He may even have encouraged her to believe she might survive. Did she really have 'a settled and hopeless expectation of impending death'? All she said was that she did not think she would recover. The judge, Mr Justice Charles, after considering the case law, said that it was not enough that the person thought they would die the following day and concluded that Mrs Schummacher did not 'ever entirely give herself up for good.' The judge told the jury that they would not be hearing the statement of the deceased, and as a result the prosecution were dropping the case. The doctor was found not guilty.

James Gloster continued in practice in Upper Phillimore Place and went on to have a son and daughter with his wife Aphra. His name would be printed in the newspapers again in 1895, but not because of any alleged criminality. Instead he had ventured into business as a director of a company hoping to strike gold in Africa. In January 1895 shares were offered for subscription to back up their attempt to buy 140 claims 'located on the best gold reefs in Matabeleland'. It was not entirely successful, as the £1 shares were selling for only 7s four years later. Still, when he died in September 1916, he left an estate worth £1,900.[131]

The dangers of illegal abortions highlighted just how desperate some women were to avoid having a child. Eliza Schummacher had told Dr Gloster that if she was unable to have a termination she would be 'ruined'. This fear led some mothers to resort to drastic measures to rid themselves of their newborn babies. Infanticide was so prevalent in late nineteenth-century London that nearly half of the recorded homicide victims were children younger than three months old.[132]

12

DEAD BABIES

The Irish Exhibition at Olympia opened its doors to the pleasure-seekers of London in the summer of 1888. For the price of a shilling, visitors gained entrance to an underground cave of limestone and sandstone with glistening stalactites and stalagmites. On the other side, blinking in the sunlight, they gazed in wonder at a mock village complete with peasants and pigs, a genuine dairy – churning butter from the milk of sixty cows transported from Kerry – and a replica castle hosting mock sieges and military displays. Their stomachs churned at the sight of the roller coaster and a 450ft toboggan slide. For the less adventurous there were displays of textiles, shipbuilding, engineering, mining, brewing, printing, furniture and 'women's industries'. And at the centre of the attraction, for those of higher cultural leanings, was the gallery of ancient and modern Irish art, including the Book of Kells – the illuminated Latin manuscript containing the four Gospels of the New Testament. The effect, it was hoped, would be to educate the English about the country lying off their western coast, and the money raised would go towards improving the situation in Ireland.

On Monday 13 August, a married woman by the name of Elizabeth Doyle was making her way home from the exhibition. She decided to take the underground Metropolitan District Railway from Kensington towards the East End and her home just north of Bethnal Green. It was just after 9 p.m. when she took her seat in a third-class carriage. The first thing she noticed was the terrible smell. None of the other passengers seemed to be doing anything about it, so she looked around the compartment. Under the seat she spotted a brown paper parcel. The source of the stench was inside, wrapped in copies of the *Morning Advertiser* and the *Sporting Life* newspapers. What she had found was the decomposing body of a newly born baby girl.

The dead child was quickly passed on to a guard at Mansion House station and then to Inspector Simon Hoskins of the City police. He instructed one of his plain-clothes officers to investigate and the following morning William Saunders visited the mortuary in Golden Lane to view the body. What he was looking for was a clue as to who had placed the child on the train. And there, on the brown paper wrapping, he found printed out the details of a Miss Max, of the Falcon Hotel near Fleet Street.

Emmeline Max was a barmaid at the Falcon on Gough Square – an address most famous for its connection to Dr Samuel Johnson, who lived at No.17 while he compiled his dictionary in the mid-eighteenth century. Miss Max told the officer she had received the parcel containing a dress at the end of July, but denied having a child. Saunders then questioned the other staff to see if they knew of anyone there who might have been pregnant. The next day he and Inspector Hoskins returned to the hotel to question Ruth Newman, a twenty-one-year-old housemaid, who had been off work sick for at least a week. Asked about the child found on the train, she replied, 'I know nothing about it whatever.'

'Have you been ill?' queried Inspector Hoskins.

'Yes, I have been in bed all the past week and have been seen by Dr Ryan of Dean Street, Fetter Lane,' said Miss Newman.

'What did the doctor treat you for? What was the matter?' he pressed.

Miss Newman hesitated for a few moments before replying, 'I have been suffering from irregularity of the system. The doctor only came once and only sent me one bottle of medicine.'

Inspector Hoskins then revealed his hand. 'Certain circumstances have come to my knowledge that you are the mother of this child, is that so?' When she failed to reply, with a nervous, frightened look on her face, he repeated his question. Her resistance broke.

'Yes, I'll tell you the truth,' she sobbed. She then told the inspectors the whole ghastly tale:

> What I have previously told you is false. I was delivered last Sunday week in the kitchen and I was alone. My fellow servant the cook had gone out. I hardly knew what I was doing but as soon as I was able I went on the landing, got some paper and wrapped the body of the child in it. It was quite dead. It never moved or breathed, and I placed it in my box where it remained until last Monday when I took it out and went to Kensington and left the body in the carriage. No one knew anything of it but myself.

Inspector Hoskins then told her that she would be charged with concealing the birth and she was taken off to see a doctor. On Thursday 16 August, Ruth Newman was brought before the magistrate and taken into custody until the inquest. At that hearing, the doctor who had carried out the autopsy referred to the blisters all over the body caused by boiling water and the marks on the throat suggesting a ligature had been used.

The child's eyes appeared to be bulging, and the tongue was protruding, suggesting strangulation. In the opinion of the doctor, the appearance of the lungs indicated that the baby had breathed after being born. This satisfied the legal test of a 'separate existence' from the mother and Miss Newman now found herself accused of murder.

The young maid was committed for trial by both the coroner Samuel Langham and the magistrate Sir Andrew Lusk. However, Lusk thought it was more a case of concealment of birth, a much less serious charge punishable by a maximum of two years imprisonment. In the end, the Grand Jury at the Old Bailey agreed and ignored the murder bill. Miss Newman was found not guilty of murder, but pleaded guilty to concealing the death of her child after its birth on 6 August 1888. In mitigation, it was said that there was a 'very pathetic story' behind the crime. Her father had died fifteen years earlier and she and her sister had left their mother's home in the country to enter domestic service. Miss Newman had been seduced by a man who abandoned her as soon as he learned of the pregnancy. She fell ill and made no preparation for giving birth, and the child was stillborn. The chaplain of Holloway Prison and the secretary of the St Giles' Christian Mission asked the court to allow them to place her in the care of her mother and spare her a prison sentence. The judge, Mr Justice Charles, agreed and released her on condition she forfeit £50 if the terms of the order were broken.[133]

The Newman case was 'solved' thanks to good detective work, but there were countless others in 1888 involving babies that were never identified. In May it was reported that a male child had been found in a brown paper parcel lying in a doorway in Wheatsheaf Alley, Thames Street in the City. He had suffered fractures to the head and right arm, as well as a severe brain haemorrhage. The inquest jury returned a verdict of wilful murder, but nobody was ever charged. Later that month another dead baby boy was recovered from the Thames near Tunnel Pier, Wapping. He had a piece of string tied tightly round his neck. The child had also suffered a large cut to the side through which the intestines had protruded.

On 2 July a newborn girl was found in Spring Gardens in Westminster, only yards from the offices of the Metropolitan Board of Works (the London County Council from 1889).

On 23 July, a male child was found wrapped in a brown paper parcel in an alley running off Burdett Road, Limehouse. Finger-sized marks on the neck indicated that it had been suffocated, and the police issued a description of the young woman believed to have left the body – nineteen or twenty years old, 4ft 10in, dressed in a blue serge dress, black hat trimmed with blue ribbon, high-heeled boots and a leather belt. In all three cases the jury returned a verdict of wilful murder 'against some person or persons unknown'.[134]

It is estimated that there were 300 suspicious infant deaths in London every year during this period. Some were ruled as accidental suffocations, caused by the parent or sibling rolling over them in bed. Others may genuinely have died during, rather than after, birth, or died suddenly from unexplained reasons. If the mother was identified, they were often given the benefit of the doubt by magistrates and juries at coroners' and criminal courts. In November the *Pall Mall Gazette* reported, under the headline 'Mutilation of a child at Woolwich', that a twenty-two-year-old domestic servant called Lily Smith had cut off her baby's head, arms and legs and burnt them, leaving only the torso at her room in Ogilby Street. Her partner, a soldier, had left for India after the birth. She said the child had been born a month previously but had died and that she was 'very sorry, and that if she had not been half-starved it would not have occurred'. Her tears and moans of distress in the dock may have influenced the magistrate's decision to commit her for trial only for concealment of birth, rather than murder.

The same applied to Eugenie Blanchard, a twenty-two-year-old French nurse who hacked up the body of her illegitimate newborn and stuffed it down the servants' lavatory at the home of a wealthy couple in Sumner Place, South Kensington. A week later, a local bricklayer was called in to sort out the blocked drains. In front of the lady and gentleman of the house, he dug up the ground and opened the junction pipe to find the remains of an infant, cut in half lengthwise. The doctor was unable to say whether the child had been alive at birth and Eugenie was cleared of concealment by a jury at the Old Bailey. In May 1888, three baby girls were found dead in the room of Elizabeth Robson, said to be a highly respectable servant at a hotel in the Strand. One of them had been tied up in a bundle with a cord twisted around her neck, while the other two were loosely wrapped in a towel. The jury concluded that the first died of suffocation, but stated had there was not enough evidence as to how it was caused. The other two had died through want of attention at birth. Robson was charged with concealment of birth rather than murder, but the case was dismissed by the magistrate at Bow Street. It may have helped that her employer at Osmond's Hotel testified that Robson had an impeccable eight-year record and was 'a most invaluable servant and highly respectable'.[135]

Domestic servants were frequently involved in cases of suspected infanticide because they had so much to lose if they kept their baby. They would have to leave their jobs and their status as 'respectable' women would be ruined. In desperation they could resort to a practice known as 'baby dropping'. Catherine Morgan, a nineteen-year-old Welsh girl employed as a servant at a house in Lordship Road, Stoke Newington, left the dead body of her newborn boy in a cask in the cellar. Her mistress, noticing her condition, asked whether she had given birth but Morgan denied it and walked out. The child was only found later that evening on 1 July 1888. Although there was no indication as to the cause of death, Catherine Morgan was at first charged with manslaughter. By the time the case reached the Old Bailey it had been reduced to an allegation of concealment of birth. She was acquitted by the jury. This might not have attracted much attention in the newspapers had it not been for a stinging attack on the police by the judge Mr Justice Hawkins, popularly known as 'Angin' 'Awkins because of his tough sentences. It emerged during the trial that officers had arrested Miss Morgan at her uncle's home in the middle of the night without a warrant, and had taken her back to the station to be examined by a surgeon. 'I consider that there has been harshness and severity in the treatment this poor girl has received which amounts to positive cruelty, and I trust that this is the last time I shall ever hear of such conduct,' he said. The judge's comments were raised in the House of Commons, but the Home Secretary, Henry Matthews, replied that the police might have acted differently if she had admitted the truth straight away. In the House of Lords, the Lord Chancellor went further and claimed that Catherine Morgan should have been found guilty of concealment. 'The police might occasionally be guilty of error of judgement, as everyone else might be, but he believed it would be difficult to find a finer or more respectable body of men.' This statement was greeted by cheers.[136]

The case against Annie Burbridge was much more serious. 'Horrible Child Murder At Battersea' read the headline in *Reynolds's Weekly Newspaper*. On the night of 1 July 1888, the twenty-year-old servant girl was found lying ill in bed at her master's home in Park Road, Battersea. A doctor attended and immediately realised that she was in labour. 'That can't be the case because I never had connection with a man,' Annie replied. She was given a painkiller but refused to be examined. A few hours later it became clear she had given birth. Her mattress was stained with blood but there was no sign of the baby.

'I asked her where she had placed the body of the child,' said Dr John Oliver.

> She gave me no direct answer at first and hardly seemed to know what she was about but after a while she told me it was in her box. I went to the box but it was locked. She told me she had hid the key under the mattress. I opened the box and I found the body of a child hidden underneath all her clothing. It was wrapped up in a white petticoat and a pair of drawers and three diapers round the child's neck and all were saturated with blood.

There was a gash just below the baby's jaw.

'Where's the knife you killed your child with?' asked Dr Oliver.

'It's not a knife, it's a pair of scissors. I have hidden them in some boxes in the drawer.'

Annie seemed to admit that the child had been alive when it was born, but was in such distress that the doctor believed she was suicidal. At the inquest, the jury concluded that she was not responsible for her actions at the time of the death of the child. Nevertheless she was charged with murder and committed for trial at the Old Bailey. Again the charge was dropped and Annie was instead prosecuted for concealment. The jury found her guilty and she was sentenced to one month in prison. She was taken from the dock of the court sobbing.[137]

It was not just young single servants trying to cover up illegitimate children. Julia Magson, a cook, was married and already had a two-year-old daughter. Her colleagues at the home of Mrs Leon at No.104F Mount Street, Mayfair,[138] had noticed the bulge in her stomach but she denied that she was pregnant. 'I am going under an operation,' she said. 'I have a tumour in my inside.' The following month, at 4.30 a.m. on

3 June 1888, a maid living in the next room heard an infant crying. She knocked on Magson's door and asked what was the matter. 'There is nothing the matter, it is all right,' replied Magson. The maid went to fetch the caretaker and when they returned Magson was washing towels. There was a bath upside down in the room with blood on the floor, on the bed and on her clothes. Magson admitted, 'I had a baby but it is dead.' The caretaker, Emma Batty, asked her what she had done with the baby. Magson held out her hand and said, 'It was only that size … I have put it in the fire.' Sure enough, the kitchen stove was blazing even though it was the middle of the night. Once it had died down, the caretaker raked out the fire and found the charred thigh bone of an infant child. Julia Magson was charged with murder, but the problem for the prosecution was proving that the baby had been alive when it was born. The other servants had heard what they believed to be a baby's cry but the medical evidence did not contradict Magson's claim that it was born six months premature. The case was dropped before being put before a jury at the Old Bailey.[139]

The large number of discarded babies each year was also a sign of the public perception of the value of infant life. Attitudes were changing, but in November 1884 Revd John Mirehouse still felt able to post a stillborn baby girl in a box to the then Home Secretary Sir William Harcourt in protest at a decision concerning burial grounds in his parish in Lincolnshire. The coroner called it a 'gross outrage on public decency' but the reverend escaped punishment. In May 1888, a cook was charged with murder after she posted the dead body of her newborn illegitimate daughter to its absent father in Northampton. Mary Sarah Lambert, who was in service at a house in Queen's Gate Terrace, Kensington, told the magistrate, 'I swooned as soon as it was born and when I came to it was dead. I put it in a box and sent it to the father.' She stood trial only for concealment of birth and was acquitted.[140]

The same year there was a case of a grandmother accused of murdering her daughter's two illegitimate children. On 31 January, after a difficult labour, thirty-year-old Dora Hart gave birth to twins – a boy and a girl – at the family home at No.206 Upper Fore Street, Edmonton. The doctor and nurse who attended the delivery called again the next day only to be told that the babies had been sent to Southgate. The day after that, Dora's mother Jane, aged fifty-four, admitted that they were dead and that under the Jewish religion all children who died within twenty-eight days of their birth were considered as stillborn. 'I have not laid a finger on the little dears,' she told police. The girl was later found wrapped up in a parcel in the schoolyard of a Wesleyan chapel in Tottenham and Dora's brother Harry admitted to police that the boy had been buried in the back garden in a brown paper parcel.

The first doctor to examine the bodies believed that the boy's death was not natural, while the girl had died from starvation. Both mother and grandmother were arrested and charged with causing their deaths, but only Jane Hart went on to stand trial for murdering the male child at the Old Bailey. The medical evidence was conflicting – a professor believed that the boy had died of asphyxia, which might have arisen from natural causes, while another doctor believed that the boy had died of natural causes due to 'imperfect expansion of the lungs'. In his summing up, the judge declared there was no evidence to support the charge and she was acquitted by the jury.[141]

The murders of newborn children were generally of far less interest to the newspapers than other cases, and tended to be reported in brief. There was no mystery, no salacious detail, only tragic circumstance. Occasionally the press picked up on unusual details. When Florence Lovett, a twenty-five-year-old single woman, was charged with killing her illegitimate newborn daughter, the *East End Observer* headlined its report: 'The shocking child murder at Mile End – The career of Mad

Florrie.' Miss Lovett was known in the neighbourhood for her strange behaviour. One witness told the inquest: 'We used to call her Mad Florrie. She used to tell such stories. She would say she had been to Wales, when she had not. She would say she was engaged to people when she was not.' She lived with her father Edward, a builder, her stepmother and her two-year-old child at the family home at No.175 Skidmore Street. On Friday 6 January, 1888, her sister Minnie became suspicious after Florence claimed that she was ill with neuralgia. Minnie looked under the bed but the chamber pot was missing.

'I looked in a cupboard in the bedroom and there I found the chamber with some blood in it,' said Minnie. A dead infant girl had been wrapped in a bundle of clothing inside a box, and a piece of tape was tied tightly round her neck. A doctor gave the cause of death as strangulation, and Florence was committed for trial for murder by the coroner, despite her father's claims that she was not responsible for her actions and that there was mental illness running in the family. The jury at Old Bailey appears to have taken pity on her condition and cleared her of both murder and concealment of birth. The outcome was noted in *The Times* of 29 February with the statement that 'the case did not present any features of public interest'.[142]

Another case took place in Spitalfields at the height of the Ripper murders. On the morning of 10 October 1888, a dead newborn baby was found at the home of a twenty-two-year-old tailoress, Dinah Israel, at No.16 Church Street. One of her roommates had heard her moving around and groaning the previous night, but Dinah claimed that she had diarrhoea. The truth only emerged when they saw the state of her bedding. A post-mortem revealed that the infant girl had been born alive but died 'from want of proper attention at birth'. It was Dinah's second illegitimate child. The inquest jury returned a verdict of manslaughter, but the Grand Jury at the Old Bailey ignored the bill and she was found not guilty.[143]

13

CHILDREN

The 1880s saw impressive developments in child welfare. Education was now compulsory between the ages of five and ten, and the London Society for the Prevention of Cruelty to Children was campaigning for a new law to protect victims of neglect and abuse. In 1889, the 'Children's Charter' was passed, giving the state power to intervene when a child was thought to be in danger. The same year the newly formed NSPCC and its network of inspectors dealt with 3,947 cases across the country.[144]

Murders of children by their parents, on the other hand, were often sudden and unpredictable. None of the 1888 cases appear to have involved systematic, long-term abuse and most of the accused were said to be loving and affectionate. Their terrible acts were often rooted in mental illness or stress of circumstance, rather than deliberate cruelty.

➤ The Runaway Soldier ➤

On 11 October 1889, a young private in the 29th Steel Battery of the Royal Artillery at Newbridge Barracks in Ireland made a sudden confession.

'I wish to give myself up,' Edwin Shuttleworth told his sergeant-major.

'What for?' came the reply. Shuttleworth was already in trouble for leaving his post early and going off to get drunk, but it was hardly a major offence.

'For child murder,' he said. Shuttleworth explained that there was a warrant out against him over the death of his three-month-old son. 'I did not do it,' he hastily added, before revealing that his real name was Clarence Henry Longman. He was only nineteen years old.

Exactly two years earlier, Longman had married a young woman called Elizabeth Carmichael, the respectable daughter of a clerk in the bankruptcy court. She was then seven months pregnant and their son, Clarence Junior, was born on 18 December 1887. From the beginning, the relationship was troubled thanks to Longman's short temper and failure to find work. He was clearly not cut out for family life at the age of seventeen and did not appear to have any affection for his son. He referred to the baby as a 'little sod' and repeatedly suggested that it should be given to somebody else to look after. On several occasions he told his wife, 'If you want to live you will have to go on the streets and work for me as I shall not work for you.' They lived only on the money they got from Longman's father, an advertising agent based in Ludgate Hill.

The situation only got worse when they moved into a single room, costing 2s 6d a week, at No.12 Clayton Road, Peckham, south London, on Tuesday 20 March 1888. The following night, Longman and his wife were in bed with the baby when he again brought up his suggestion that she work the streets. 'If you don't do that you will have to go home to your mother and ask her advice about you going to service.' He said he would keep the baby while she was away, adding, 'Are you afraid of me hitting him? You must think I'm a coward, go on, make haste and go.' She left on the understanding that he would bring the baby round to her mother's house in Brixton the following day. When he finally turned up, he no longer had the child.

Longman first claimed that his sister had it, but Elizabeth was adamant that he take her to see her son. At first, he refused, and then said the boy was at Arlington Street, Westminster. There was no Arlington Street in Westminster. Next he claimed that he had given the baby to three young women he knew. Finally, after Elizabeth's mother, Catherine, confronted him at his father's house in Peckham, he agreed to take his wife to see the child. This time he pointed out a door at No.26 Monk Gardens, Westminster Bridge Road, but when Catherine Carmichael went round to check, the occupants knew nothing about any baby.

Longman continued to be evasive despite his wife's increasingly despairing pleas to tell her where he had taken her child. On 31 March, as they took a tram from New Cross to Camberwell, she was so upset that a fellow passenger alerted a police officer and the couple were taken down to the station at Camberwell Green. 'I want my baby, my baby,' she sobbed. Longman told the sergeant in charge that it was 'out at nurse', but claimed he did not know the address. After waiting some time while officers tried to locate his father, Longman announced that he would take his wife to the child.

Once they were back on the tram, he turned to his wife and said, 'Well look here, I'll tell you the truth of it, the baby is not out at nurse, it's dead … I gave it some peppermint and laid it on its face thinking it would break the wind. I have not killed him. I suppose I have given it too much peppermint …

I ought to have called a doctor in at once, I was so excited and I knew how it would upset you that I was afraid to tell you.'

'What have you done with the baby?' Elizabeth again demanded.

Longman said, 'I've wrapped it up nice and warm and put it in a little box and buried it at some place beginning with B.' He then asked her not to say anything and made her write a letter.

'My dear mother,' it read. 'I have seen the baby, Harry and I went together this afternoon. I shall be home tomorrow morning. I remain your affectionate daughter.'

He then had the cheek to go and see Elizabeth's father, Charles Carmichael, to ask for some money to keep him and his wife going while he looked for a job. Mr Carmichael recalled:

> I said if he would bring my grandson back then I would talk to him. I think I said I should be the happiest man in the world if he would only bring the child back. He said it was somewhere not very far off – Whitechapel, I think he said, and he should want some little time to write for it.

Longman promised to bring the baby back the following day. Again he failed to keep his word.

The truth finally emerged when the Carmichael family learnt that the body of a child had been recovered in Battersea. A waterman had spotted a bundle of sacking on the south foreshore of the Thames underneath the Albert Bridge and opened it to reveal a parcel tied with string. He undid the package and saw a child dressed in a white shirt and white flannel petticoat.

When the Carmichaels got to the police station, Elizabeth was too distressed to identify the body, but her mother was instantly able to recognise the clothing and confirmed the boy was her grandson Clarence Junior. He had died of suffocation rather than drowning. Although the find had been made on 28 March, and the information circulated to all police stations, the link was not made until 5 April. By then Clarence Longman had vanished.

He failed to attend a single hearing of the inquest and his parents said they had no idea where he had gone. The coroner issued a warrant for his arrest and a description:

Seventeen, 5ft 2in; complexion, swarthy; hair, dark brown (worn on forehead, and when oiled appears to be black); high forehead, eyes, full, very dark hazel; very thick black eyebrows; nose well formed; two large scars back of head, one extending to left; small feet; swinging gait; carried hands in pockets. Dress: short blue serge jacket, green or black cloth vest; grey mixture trousers; black hard felt hat, worn on one side of head; spotted silk tie; patent high-heeled boots.

The police also circulated a woodcut portrait of the murder suspect.

Longman had travelled to Dover and enlisted in the Royal Artillery under a false name on 1 May 1888. He kept his secret for fifteen months before finally coming clean on his second wedding anniversary while stationed at Newbridge. He was handed over to the Royal Irish Constabulary and returned to London to stand trial at the Old Bailey for murder. During the hearing, Elizabeth's mother recalled a conversation she had had with Longman while her daughter was in hospital a few days before giving birth. She had said to him: 'It is a pity the baby is coming so soon. It would be well if the poor little thing would die, as it would then give you a chance to get on.'

Longman replied, 'Yes, I wish it would die.'

Faced with all the evidence, the defence case was that the child had been accidently smothered while in bed. Longman had panicked and tried to cover up the death, and had no motive for killing his son. The argument was only partially successful. Longman was cleared of murder but convicted of manslaughter and sentenced to twenty years' penal servitude.[145]

∼ One Night in Judd Street ∼

In 1888, the twenty-one-year-old Herbert George Wells was still finding his way in life. He had finished his studies in biology at the Norman School of Science in London, spent four months teaching at a school in Wrexham and had given up on his first attempt to write the novel which would become his breakthrough 1895 work *The Time Machine*. It was June and he was back in London, 'lean and unkempt' with £5 in his pocket to live on until he found some work. 'I arrived, with that old small portmanteau of mine, at St Pancras and found a lodging that night in Judd Street, which I considered to be just within my means; a rather disconcerting lodging,' he wrote in his autobiography. He continued:

> The room had three beds and one of my fellow occupants, the lodging house keeper told me, was 'a most respectable young man who worked at a butcher's'. The next morning I breakfasted in a coffee house – one could get a big cup of coffee, a thick slice of bread and butter and a boiled or fried egg for fourpence or fivepence – and then set out to find a room of my own.

The room in Judd Street may have been chosen because his geology professor had the surname Judd, but it was hardly suitable lodgings. He quickly moved into a more respectable place in Theobald's Road and spent the next six months gradually using up his savings, visiting the British Museum reading room, loitering in the streets and watching the crowds. Eventually the loneliness of his wanderings got to him and he went to stay with his aunt, Mary, and cousin, Isabel, whom he would marry in 1891.[146]

A few months after Wells' brief stay in Judd Street, the neighbourhood was shocked by the murder of a five-month-old boy at No.125. Mary Ann Reynolds and her husband, William, had moved into the house with their four children in April 1888. The youngest, Frank, had been born about a month earlier, but they had been forced to move from their last place because of difficulties with their landlord. They were also suffering financially because William had lost his job. The pressure was starting to tell on Mary Ann, and something didn't seem to be quite right. Every so often she would knock on the top of her head and announce, 'It is here', without further explanation. She told her sister that she had a burning pain at the top of her head, but did not seem to want to get medical help. Despite all her problems, she remained an affectionate mother and doted on her youngest. Then in the early hours of 9 August, the landlord Robert Hough heard a loud knocking upstairs and ran up to investigate. Mrs Reynolds told him that her baby was dead.

The doctor arrived to see Mary Ann sitting on the bed with her hands clasped, swaying backwards and forwards with her eyes shut. 'I clutched the baby round the neck and found it dead,' she suddenly answered, before continuing with her strange rocking movements. She had scratches and a wound to her throat and two large bruises to the back of the head. A hammer and a pair of scissors lay next to her. Beside the bed, the baby boy was lying on the floor with obvious bruising to the throat. He had been suffocated.

Mary Ann was taken to the Royal Free Hospital and two days later tried to cut her throat in the middle of the night using a knife left in another patient's locker. When a police officer came on duty to watch over her during the day she told him, 'I killed my baby, I put a handkerchief round its neck and squeezed it, I was loving it, I don't know what I did it for. My husband was asleep and I took the hammer, striking my head with it, and that woke him up.' She then exclaimed, 'Oh, look, the ceiling is falling' and asked if the officer would catch one of the butterflies fluttering about the ward. She saw dogs on her bed and claimed to hear children crying. The same day she was moved to Holloway Prison to be put under constant observation. It was no surprise when in September 1888 an Old Bailey jury found her 'guilty but insane' and she was taken to Broadmoor Lunatic Asylum.[147]

― At the Workhouse ―

On 5 November 1888, PC Herbert Lee was on duty in Marylebone Lane when he saw a woman lying on a doorstep. In her arms was a baby. Approaching them, PC Lee noticed that the child was dressed only in a nightshirt. He told the woman that she should wrap her baby up warm because the cold winter air would do it no good at all. 'Mind your own business,' replied the woman, slurring drunkenly. The officer decided it was best for everyone if he arrested her and took her down to the station.

Ellen Mulchay was a thirty-year-old widow and variously described as a charwoman or an ironer, who had been deserted by her partner. She had already been charged twice before with drunkenness. But it wasn't her condition that concerned the police. The child, a seven-month-old girl named Jane, was in dire need of food and a wash. Her weight, 5lb 14oz, was lower than that of a newborn. The officer put the girl in a blanket and took her to the nearest doctor, the medical officer at Marylebone Workhouse.

In 1888, the workhouse could hold 1,600 people, having added a new block for 240 women to its site between Marylebone Road and Paddington Street. It took in vagrants, the poor, 'idiots', the insane and the elderly, whether men, women or children, and gave them food, a bed and a wash. But it was not a place you would choose to live, even if conditions had improved since the early Victorian era popularised by Charles Dickens' famous workhouse child Oliver Twist. Dickens had served as a juror on an inquest held at the site in 1840, and considered the case of a young maid suspected of killing her newborn son. He seems to have almost single-handedly ensured that the woman stood trial at the Old Bailey only for concealing the birth rather than murder. Ten years later, he revisited the workhouse for an article for *Household Words* magazine. One scene he described involved a nurse in the 'Itch Ward' wringing her hands and sobbing in great distress. 'Oh, the child that was found in the street, and she had brought up ever since, had died an hour ago, and see where the little creature lay, beneath this cloth! The dear, the pretty dear!'

Dickens saw the 'dropped child' she was referring to, and noted how it 'seemed too small and poor a thing for Death to be in earnest with, but Death had taken it; and already its diminutive form was neatly washed, composed, and stretched as if in sleep upon a box'.

Sadly little Jane Mulchay would share the same fate. The staff had tried to feed her without much success, for most of it came back up as vomit. They even gave her the traditional sip of brandy in an attempt to revive her spirits. Her mother made several visits, but always seemed to be drunk and in no fit state to have her child returned. As the days went by, the girl's condition seemed only to worsen, and on 17 November she died.

Three days later the inquest was held, at the Ossington Coffee Tavern rather than Marylebone Workhouse.

The doctor told the hearing that the girl had died of exhaustion 'following mal-assimilation of food' and the coroner remarked that he had 'no doubt this was a case where the mother had neglected the child, owing to her drunken habits'. The jury returned a verdict of manslaughter against Ellen Mulchay and she was taken into custody. The following week, however, the magistrate, considering the charge, refused to commit her for trial at the Old Bailey because the doctor was unable to say why the child had starved at the workhouse. 'That the prisoner had behaved in a disgraceful manner was quite clear and if it had been proved that the death was the result of that disgraceful conduct, he should have committed her for trial. But it had not and she must be discharged.' The Grand Jury at the Old Bailey appeared to agree and dismissed the case.[148]

~ A Telegram for Mr Spickernell ~

Just as the late twentieth century was revolutionised by the emergence of the internet, the Victorian era also saw the benefits of long-distance communication using telegraphy. At the forefront of this technology was the Submarine Telegraph Co., who in 1850 had laid the first copper cable across the English Channel. Over the next three decades, they laid more cables to France, Belgium, Germany and Denmark. It was a period during which British companies operated two-thirds of the world's telegraph cables, another demonstration of the power of the Empire.

On 29 December 1888, the Submarine Telegraph Co.'s army of 'telegraphists' tapping out Morse code messages across the world included a certain Frederick Spickernell. That morning, he had gone through his usual routine before kissing his wife and four children goodbye and setting off for work. Later that day, he was at his desk when he received a telegram asking him to return home. Immediately he feared that something had happened to his thirty-seven-year-old wife Julia. She had been ill for some time and often complained of headaches. That Christmas Eve he had urged her to rest instead of washing one of the children's nightclothes and she had thrown herself at him screaming, 'Oh Fred, I will murder you. I will murder you and then I shall be a murderess.' He put it down to overexcitement, because she was stressed about her mother's visit for Christmas. When he got home to No.93 Milton Road in Stoke Newington he learned the horrible truth. She had killed their nine-month-old daughter Mabel.

Earlier that morning at around 11 a.m. Julia Spickernell had knocked on the lodger's door in the basement. 'Mrs Goldring!' she pleaded.

'Tea, dear,' replied Mary Ann Goldring, expecting to be asked for a drink.

'I wish to speak to you a minute,' Julia said. 'Come now.'

Mrs Goldring opened the door and immediately sensed something odd about Mrs Spickernell's behaviour.

'I have something to show you,' Julia said, insisting that she come right that minute and bring her servant Ada too. She then led them to the kitchen door before announcing, 'I have done it.'

'Done what?' asked Mrs Goldring.

Julia appeared excited. 'Give me Mr Goldring's razors,' she said, and then started screaming.

Mrs Goldring ran out of the house and fetched the next-door neighbour Lucy Cavalier before calling for a doctor. Then the two women returned to No.93 and went up to Julia's bedroom. They knocked, and after a few moments Julia opened the door.

'I have done it,' she repeated. 'The devil made me do it. He has been following me about up and down stairs the last five weeks.'

Eventually Mrs Goldring managed to calm her down and went into the bedroom. There she found the baby drowned in a bucket of water.

When Dr Edward Spencer arrived at the house, Julia Spickernell was in such an excited state that he had to throw her to the ground and pin her down until she blacked out. When she came round a few minutes later she asked him to give her a rope. 'Let me hang myself, let me hang myself,' she cried. It seemed clear to both the doctor and the police surgeon that she was suffering from some kind of homicidal mania and it was arranged for her to be taken to Holloway Prison for further assessment.

It took two months for her to recover enough to be put on trial at the Old Bailey for the murder of her child. The key evidence came from Dr Philip Gilbert, the medical officer at the prison. 'I formed the opinion that she was insane when I first saw her,' he told the court.

> She was intensely dejected. She took no notice of her surroundings, she was moaning and rocking herself to and fro, it was with difficulty I could make her speak. When she did she sobbed and said she had been an extremely wicked woman, that she had gone through hell, that she had been a wicked wretch all her life and was unfit to live. Besides this she was under the delusion that she heard a voice that came from the devil, continually accusing her of doing nothing but taking care of herself. It kept her awake at night.

In his opinion, the madness had been brought on by 'excessive lactation' – that her health had been damaged by breastfeeding her child too much. Dr Gilbert told the court that it was a temporary form of insanity and that she had now recovered. The jury found her 'guilty but insane' and she was sent to Broadmoor Lunatic Asylum.[149]

～ Want and Murder ～

Emma Aston could hardly be said to look like a double murderer. Yet somehow this frail, sobbing thirty-nine-year-old mother and factory worker had killed her two young sons. She had suffocated them both, first twelve-month-old Frank and then two-year-old Bertie. It took a long time for the eldest to die, for he was old enough to put up a struggle. Now she was under arrest. 'Why did you do it?' she was asked. 'Want,' she sobbed, and began to tell her tragic story.

At the bottom of it was a man. John M. Morris was the foreman of the clothing factory where she had worked for more than a decade, in Old Change near St Paul's Cathedral in the City of London. He was also married, but that did not stop him embarking on a relationship with Emma Aston and fathering both of her children. She had given up her job as forewoman to look after them in 1886, and at first Morris was attentive in sending her letters and money once a week to pay for her food and lodging at No. 36 Whitfield Road, Upton Park, east London. Emma – who was using the false name Mrs Styles – told her landlady that the letters came from her husband who was often away from home because of his work as a commercial traveller. But shortly before Christmas, the money started arriving through the letterbox less and less regularly. The bills were starting to mount up and she hadn't received any reply to the three messages she had sent. When a letter finally came on Saturday 18 February 1888, she had received no money for three weeks and the £1 postal order inside wasn't enough to cover what she owed to her landlady, the baker and the doctor who had come round to check on her two boys. She read the letter over and over again, trying to find a glimmer of hope for her situation. 'Just a line to hope you are all well. I am so sorry I could not send it before, I have not had it in my possession ten minutes. Will write on

Monday. Hoping you are getting on pretty well, ever your loving Jack.'

Her landlady's daughter, Alice Jones, was sympathetic to her plight and suggested that she go and see her husband on Monday. As Miss Jones recalled:

> She was very much disappointed and distressed at the letter. She had been complaining for some days of acute neuralgia in the head, and of a weight on the top of her head. Her face had been very much swollen and she had to wrap something round it. She also complained of a sore mouth and of a constant pain in the back. I know she had been up with the children for a fortnight, and that her rest had been disturbed. From what I could judge of her she was very ill – she had nursed the children day and night, giving them the most tender care, and never leaving the house all that time. She was completely worn out. She was a most devoted mother to the children.

On the Sunday, seeing Emma was still ill, Miss Jones kindly gave her and the children their dinner at midday. For the rest of the day they remained in their room.

The next morning, 20 February, Miss Jones got up at around 7 a.m. to light the kitchen fire and was startled to see Emma Aston sitting fully dressed on the sofa with a shawl over her head. She seemed to be reading the letter again.

'Oh, Mrs Styles, how you did frighten me!' Miss Jones exclaimed.

'Oh, Miss Jones, I have killed my two dear little children,' Emma said, and sobbed uncontrollably. 'Oh my pretty little dears, my pretty little dears.'

They both went upstairs to the bedroom and Emma Aston pulled back the sheet on the bed to reveal both boys lying on the bed, dead. The youngest had some blood around his mouth. Then Emma broke down in tears and made a full confession:

> I am not married, and I knew if I went to that man this morning he would not give me any money ... I was mad, I was mad. I felt such a weight on the top of my head, something impelled me to do it ... I tried to cut Frank's throat with a knife, the knife was blunt, and seeing the blood I put my hand over his mouth and kept it there till he died. He was not long in dying. I used the bedclothes to Bertie, he took a long time to kill, he struggled so.

She would have killed herself too but, perversely, she felt that would be wrong. 'She did not seem to think she had done anything criminal in killing the children,' recalled Miss Jones.

The following month, Emma Aston was found 'guilty but insane' at the Old Bailey and was sent to Broadmoor Lunatic Asylum. The witnesses at the trial did not include the man who shared some responsibility for events, John Morris. The police had tried to track him down, but it appeared that he had left his £300-a-year job the day after the murder. Perhaps he had eloped with yet another woman, for there was a rumour that he was also cheating on his wife with a second lover who he was keeping at a hotel somewhere in London. As the *Lloyd's Weekly Newspaper* reported: 'There was no doubt that the prisoner had been treated scandalously.'[150]

～ Ten Shillings ～

It was Saturday, 26 May 1888, and William Pierrepoint had not paid his rent for six weeks. His landlady Sophia Moon had been sympathetic at first – he had lost his job as a wheelwright and had a wife and two children to look after – but he now owed a total of 19s 6d. Mrs Moon had given him two weeks' notice, but when the deadline came his pockets were still empty. After three years at No.158 Neate Street in Camberwell it was time for them to leave their single room and find somewhere else to live.

At 10 p.m. Pierrepoint and one of his friends were still loading a barrow with their bed and other belongings when Mrs Moon asked him if he had the 10s he had promised. They had agreed that if he could not find the money he would leave the bedstead behind.

'No, I have not,' he replied gruffly. He told his friend, 'Take the bloody things back.'

'We don't want them Mr Pierrepoint,' Mrs Moon replied, trying to avoid trouble.

'You can have the bloody bed. You can have the bloody lot. I won't touch a bloody thing.' He seemed to have been drinking. He picked up his twenty-two-month-old son Sidney in his arms and went downstairs to his wife. By now a few neighbours had come out into the street to see what all the fuss was about. Pierrepoint was crying into a handkerchief and seemed inconsolable. Suddenly he kissed little Sidney on the head and sobbed, 'They said I starved you.' He put the handkerchief back in his pocket and added, 'You shall be the victim.' Pierrepoint then took up the boy and swung him down on to the pavement, smashing his skull on the asphalt.

'He was holding it on his arm, he lifted it up with both hands and threw it on to the ground,' recalled Eliza Howell, a mother of ten who lived at No.172. 'I believe its head fell on the ground first. I screamed "Murder".'

Another witness, Kate McCormack, saw it slightly differently: 'I saw a man with the child by its two legs and dash it on the ground. He had it by its heels. I saw the child strike the ground and as it struck the ground I ran away.'

The screams quickly brought a crowd out on to the street to surround Pierrepoint who was standing in a daze, perhaps unable to comprehend what he had just done. For a moment it looked like he might be given a thorough beating, but after a few punches were thrown, a neighbour, Sarah Store, shielded him behind her and shouted, 'Don't knock the man about, let him alone he will have enough to suffer.'

When PC George Lunn arrived a few minutes later, Pierrepoint was nursing a black eye and drowning his sorrows in the nearby Little Wonder beerhouse. The officer walked into the pub to arrest him and was told that he had run out the back and over the wall. PC Lunn took up the chase but the suspect didn't make it far before being stopped by some men in the street.

'I shall take you to the station for assaulting your child,' Lunn told him.

'All right mister,' replied Pierrepoint. As they walked back he added, 'We had notice on Tuesday to leave. I have been out of work and have had a lot of trouble. We had our bed stopped by the landlord for the rent. I had no intention of doing such a thing.' But by the time they got back to the station in Rodney Street his story had changed slightly. 'I dropped him off my arm,' he said. 'No one saw it.'

Half an hour later they learned that Sidney had died at Guy's Hospital from a severe skull fracture and brain damage. William Pierrepoint was remanded in custody until his trial for murder at the Old Bailey.

The jury really only had one issue to consider. Did the child fall or was he thrown? The defence did its best to persuade the witnesses that it might have been accidental. Perhaps the boy had slipped and Pierrepoint had grabbed him by the ankles to try and stop him hitting the ground? Sarah Store did not accept the suggestion, but Eliza Howell wavered. 'He threw it down … it might have fallen as you say … I have described what I saw.'

Miss McCormack, however, was adamant. 'I am quite sure that the child did not slip out of his arms. He held it by its two legs, close down to the ankles.'

On 5 July 1888, Pierrepoint, aged thirty-one, was found guilty and sentenced to death. He would escape the noose, partly thanks to the jury's strong recommendation of mercy.[151]

14

TEENAGE GANGS IN LONDON

It was Whitsuntide and the population of London was celebrating the beginning of the summer season. That bank holiday had seen hundreds of thousands of sightseers, holidaymakers and pleasure-seekers take to the roads and railways for trips across the country, to Brighton and the South Coast, to Windsor Palace, Southport and Skegness. Others took the opportunity to visit the attractions of the capital – 4,500 to see the pygmy skeleton at the Natural History Museum, 7,000 to the National Gallery, 26,000 to Regent's Park Zoo and 70,000 to Hampstead Heath. At the Alexandra Palace crowds were entertained by a troupe of Russian gymnasts, ventriloquists, puppeteers, a roller coaster, panoramic railway, shooting galleries and a pyrotechnic reproduction of *The Last Days of Pompeii*. The weather was fine and the whole city was enjoying itself.

The holiday mood was still in the air a few days later on Thursday 24 May 1888, when two young couples set off for a walk to Regent's Park. There was Joseph Rumbold, a twenty-one-year-old printer, and his date Elizabeth Lee, her cousin Emily Lee and a colleague of Joseph's called Alonzo Burns.

They entered the park by York Gate, just down the road from the new Madame Tussauds' building on Marylebone Road, and turned left on to Outer Circle along the fence up towards Clarence Gate. It was about 9 p.m. and there was an organ playing to a small crowd enjoying the last light of the day. Just past a bend in the road, not far from Cornwall Terrace, Elizabeth noticed five young men were 'larking around' playing some version of tag. The group then walked past them a few yards before turning round and blocking their path. One of them said to Joseph, 'Are you Macey?'

'So help me God, I don't know what you mean,' Joseph replied. Then three more young men – they were all about sixteen or seventeen – came across and joined the group.

'Yes, that's him, that's him,' they shouted. The first man grabbed hold of Joseph by the neck and repeated his question, 'Are you Macey?'

At this, Joseph decided to run. Twisting his neck away from his attacker, he dropped his hat and fled back towards York Gate followed by the gang. Elizabeth picked up the hat and ran after them. By the time she caught up to him he was leaning on the railings next to the park-keeper's house with blood on his mouth. 'Call me a cab, I am stabbed,' he gasped.

Elizabeth left her cousin to get help and chased after the gang as they ran out of York Gate, yelling, 'Stop thief' in an attempt to attract aid. She did not get very far before two of the group punched and kicked her to the ground. The next she saw of Joseph was at the Middlesex Hospital. He had been brought in just before 10 p.m. with two stab wounds to the neck and back, but nothing could be done. The second injury was the fatal one, penetrating just below the shoulder blade into the right lung and severing a branch of the pulmonary artery. Joseph had bled to death within minutes.[152]

Alonzo Burns and Emily Lee had been 20 yards behind Joseph and Elizabeth when the scuffle started. A group of young men had run up to them and recognised Burns as being local to Lisson Grove in Marylebone. 'Hallo Lonnie,' one said. Another added, 'Oh, he is all right, I know him.' They ran off round the bend in the path. Moments later the couple saw Joseph being attacked.

'I saw a scuffle and I saw him dart out from the midst of him,' recalled Alonzo. 'He ran right past me. I saw blood coming out of his mouth. I said "Joe!" – he could not answer me, he squirted out some blood.'

The first clue as to why Joseph had been attacked came when they approached a member of the group who had stayed behind rather than join the chase. 'What have you done to Joe?' Burns asked. The young man said they were getting revenge for a rival gang 'banging our fellows and giving a girl a black eye'.

The 'banging' had occurred the previous evening at around 9 p.m. A member of the 'Fitzroy Place lads' gang, eighteen-year-old Francis Cole, had strayed into the territory of their rivals from Lisson Grove in Marylebone with his girlfriend Louisa 'Cissy' Chapman. They were in the Marylebone Road near Madame Tussauds when two men approached them and asked where Cole was from. Cole replied that he was from the Hampstead Road.

'Do you know any of the Fitzroy Place lads?' one of them asked.

'Yes, and glad to know them too,' said Cole, either out of bravado or because he was unaware of the danger.

With that, one of the two young men whistled and about twenty others came running down the road. One of them punched Cole in the face and knocked him down, and some of the others began kicking him while he lay on the ground.

'How many more of you?' shouted Cissy, taking up the challenge.

'Take that you cow,' one of the youths replied, punching her in the face. The gang ran off with Cole's hat.

This was just the latest incident in a long-running feud between the two gangs and news of the attack quickly spread round the other Fitzroy Place lads, who were all based in and around the Tottenham Court Road. Frank Cole and his friends David Cleary and George Galletly immediately began rounding up recruits for a revenge attack on Marylebone. The following evening Galletly approached Adolph Fontaine at a pub called the Blue Posts and asked, 'Have you heard about Frank being bathed? Frank has got a bash in the eye and Ciss has got a black eye.' Fontaine agreed to go with him to meet Cole at the 'Fair', half an acre of disused land between Tottenham Court Road and Whitfield Street, but sensibly backed out of the plan to go to Marylebone by claiming he had to meet his 'young lady'. Others were more keen to join and Cole soon had a small expeditionary force of up to sixteen young men aged between fifteen and nineteen.

They found their first Marylebone lad in nearby Howland Street, but he was able to run off after being punched and kicked. This didn't satisfy them, and after failing to find more prey in the Green Man pub on Union Street, they headed for Regent's Park.

What followed appears to have been a tragic case of mistaken identity. But for the newspapers it was the inevitable result of 'roughs' being allowed to terrorise areas of London with impunity. There was even a suggested link to prostitution. On 26 May, *The Times* printed a report that: 'The gang is supposed to be a number of men who are in connection with a number of disorderly women who gain their living by visiting the Outer and Inner Circle [of Regent's Park] for immoral purposes.' Another piece stated that: 'For some months past a gang of roughs has infested this district nightly, some of them being in the habit of levying blackmail on respectable couples walking around the park. They are also the companions of a number of disorderly women that frequent this and other portions of Regent's Park.'

The reports sparked a series of letters to *The Times*, beginning with one from someone calling themselves 'Regent's Park', who claimed that the area had been neglected by the overworked police because of 'the public taste for monster processions and demonstrations'.

The letter continued: 'Whatever happens the moral of this sad occurrence is plain. Places in the heart of a great city like London, which are exceptionally quiet by day, want very careful attention at night, and if this be withheld society will some day be awakened by a very rude shock.'

This prompted a local resident, George Romanes of Cornwall Terrace, to complain that the Regent's Park district 'is becoming more and more generally recognised as the happy hunting-fields of the worst rowdyism of London … For several years past my neighbours and myself have found it prudent as much as possible to avoid the precincts of the park when returning home after night-fall'. Concerns over the policing of the park were raised in Parliament the following month and it was announced that the Commissioner of Police, Charles Warren, had made changes to ensure 'a better control of disorderly persons'.[153]

Although the case was covered in detail by the newspapers, and featured on the front page of the *Illustrated Police News*, it did not cause anywhere near the prolonged excitement of the Ripper murders. This was partly due to the success of the police in rounding up all the suspects by the end of the week. Two of the suspects had decided to turn 'Queen's' and gave evidence against their fellow gang members after reading about the offer of a full pardon in the *Daily Echo* on 26 May.

David Cleary, an eighteen-year-old out-of-work baker with a previous conviction for stealing bacon, and Thomas Brown, a sixteen-year-old polisher, both pinned the blame on George Galletly, known as 'Garry'. According to their statements, the group that had gone to Regent's Park also included:

Francis Cole; William Elvis, a sixteen-year-old porter from Euston Road; William Graefe, a nineteen-year-old cutter from Tottenham Court Road; William Henshaw, a sixteen-year-old French polisher from Hampstead Road; Charles Govier, a sixteen-year-old farrier's boy from Drummond Street; Michael Doolan, a fifteen-year-old porter from Sexton Street; and Peter Lee, a nineteen-year-old sailor. As they left 'the Fair' Lee couldn't resist boasting about a knife he kept in a sheath on his belt. He took it out and twirled it round.

'Show me that knife,' Galletly told him, taking the knife from Lee's hand. 'This will do for one of them.' Later, when they reached Portland Place, Galletly asked Lee to lend him the knife and put the belt with the sheath round his waist.

According to Cleary, it was also Galletly who suggested they go to Regent's Park. The group then split up, with some going round to Clarence Gate via Marylebone Road, while Clearly and the rest entered through York Gate and headed left round the Outer Circle. The second group soon came up behind Alonzo Burns and Emily Lee, but Cleary recognised him and told Galletly, 'He is all right, I know him.' The group then ran past towards Joseph Rumbold.

Neither Cleary nor Brown admitted seeing the stabbing, perhaps in an attempt to conceal their true involvement. Their story was that they had run ahead to meet Elvis and Doolan before turning back. As they rounded the bend near Cornwall Terrace they came up to Galletly, red-faced and out of breath.

'I have stabbed him,' Galletly said.

'Who?' asked Brown.

'One of them,' Galletly replied. Asked where he stabbed the victim, Galletly indicated the back of his neck. As they walked back to Tottenham Court Road he boasted that he had 'laid one out' and showed off the bloodstained blade. He had exacted his revenge for the attack on his friend Cissy Chapman.

After taking Cleary and Brown's statements, the police began to round up the suspects. Inspector George Robson arrested Galletly the same night, 26 May at 10.30 p.m. outside the Duke of York pub in Charlotte Street off Tottenham Court Road. 'I know nothing about the murder,' said Galletly. An attempt to rescue him was made by one of his friends as he was being led away to the station, but Robson held tight to his suspect.

'That bleeding Dave and Brown have turned coppers to try and hang me,' muttered Galletly.

Four hours later, at 2.30 a.m. on the 27th, Inspector Thomas Bannister, accompanied by Cleary and Brown and several police officers, went down to No.23 Whitfield Place to arrest Peter Lee.

'I hope you don't think that I stabbed the man,' said Lee. In his defence he said:

> I know I was with the mob, and the man that did it had my knife, but I don't know his name. I never spoke to him till that night, and I have not had my knife since. Them other two chaps that was with you were there as well, and they know the man that stabbed him.

By 4 a.m. Bannister also had Graefe in custody. Henshaw was arrested near his home in Frederick Street that afternoon. The rest handed themselves in after hearing that Brown and Cleary had turned Queen's. Govier came to the police station with his mother at 6.30 p.m. and an hour later Elvis and Doolan turned up. They all admitted they were with the mob, but denied being there when Joseph Rumbold was stabbed. The last of the group, Francis Cole, was brought to the station at 11.30 p.m. by his father. Rounding off what was turning into a highly efficient investigation, the murder weapon was discovered in its sheath in a sewer in Upper Rathbone Place three days later.

All eight young men were charged with murder and committed for trial at the Old Bailey. The case was due to start in the session beginning in early July, but was postponed until September because two of them had yet to find a barrister to represent them in court. While they waited, safely behind bars, the feud between the Fitzroy and Marylebone lads continued. 'They walked about with sticks concealed up their sleeves, and complaints were daily received at the Tottenham Court Road police station about the pavement being impassable owing to their conduct,' reported *The Times*. 'They went about in gangs, used foul language, and respectable persons were afraid to go near them.' On 30 July, two gangmembers were convicted of disorderly behaviour following a disturbance in Fitzroy Square and were ordered to put up 40s on promise of good behaviour in future.[154]

The trial, which began on 1 August 1888, centred on the evidence of Cleary and Brown, and both were heavily cross-examined by counsel representing the eight defendants. Neither was entirely convincing, particularly when it came to their involvement in the attack. Both denied being a Fitzroy Place lad or a 'Decker lad' from the Seven Dials, although Brown eventually admitted that he had been present at an earlier 'combat' between Fitzroy Place and Marylebone. Further questioning revealed that Brown had pawned his trousers shortly after the murder. Also suspicious was the way that Cleary and Brown had decided to go to the police together on the night of the 26th. According to Brown it was Cleary's idea. Brown told the court:

He said, 'Will you come up to the station with me and give information about the murder?' It took us about five minutes to go to the station. We were not talking about the case on our way… we were talking about other things, but not a word about this case.

At the close of the prosecution evidence, it was clear that there was little tangible proof to show that anyone but Galletly and Lee knew of the knife. Following a submission by the defence, the judge Mr Justice Hawkins directed that Graefe, Henshaw, Govier, Doolan, Elvis and Cole should be found not guilty. Only Galletly and Lee remained. It was now up to the jury to decide whether or not Galletly had intended to kill or seriously injure Joseph Rumbold at the time of the attack. To find Lee guilty of murder, they would have to find that Lee had contemplated that his knife might be used to stab somebody and then encouraged its use.

It was almost 5 p.m. when the jury returned to convict Galletly of murder. They also tried to find Lee 'guilty of being an accessory before the fact, and aiding and abetting', but after being told by the judge that this amounted to murder, they changed their verdict to not guilty.

The clerk of the court then stood up to ask, 'George Galletly, have you anything to say why sentence of death should not be passed on you?'

'All I have got to say is that I only used the knife once,' replied Galletly.

Unusually, Mr Justice Hawkins did not put on the black cap to pass the death sentence:

> It is a painful thing to contemplate a lad of your age standing to receive sentence for a crime as cruel and brutal as it is possible to conceive. You and the gang who accompanied you found this unfortunate young man walking with a girl in Regent's Park. He had done you no harm, had not wronged one of your party, but simply because you thought he lived in the district where some men resided who had insulted and outraged two of your comrades on the previous evening, you cruelly stabbed him twice, defenceless as he was.

'Only once,' interrupted Galletly.

> You stabbed him once in the neck and once in the back and
> he died from the act of brutal and cruel violence on your part.
> For you, even a long life would be too short to pray for pardon
> for the great sin which you have committed and if it should
> be that He in the exercise of His duty – stern imperative duty
> – should see no reason to interfere with the due course of the
> law, then it would behove you to spend the time that remains
> to you in earnestly imploring forgiveness from the Almighty.[155]

Galletly's execution was fixed for 24 August but on the 15th it
was reported that the death sentence had been replaced with
one of penal servitude for life.[156]

It only remained to sentence the remaining seven prisoners
on their guilty pleas to the lesser charges of assault and
unlawfully conspiring to assemble and commit a breach of the
peace. Lee, the owner of the knife, and Govier, who was said
to be the one who first grabbed Joseph Rumbold, received
fifteen months' hard labour; Henshaw nine months; Cole
eight months; Graefe seven months; and Elvis and Doolan
six months. 'Your imprisonment will operate as a warning to
others in the future not to be parties to such grievous outrages
as those for which you have been convicted upon your own
confession,' said the judge.

On the same night that the verdicts were returned, there
was another fight between the Marylebone and Fitzroy lads.
Arthur Charlton, a sawyer from Somerstown, was confronted
by a mob in Stanhope Street off Euston Road, knocked to the
ground and repeatedly punched and kicked. Police arrested
two of the attackers, Patrick Gorman, a twenty-two-year-old
plasterer, and Henry Lee, the nineteen-year-old brother of the
trial witness Emily Lee. When the case came to Marylebone

Police Court, Lee explained that he had gone with his sister to collect their witness money from Albany Street police station. As they passed through Fitzroy Place they were approached by Charlton and asked how the trial had gone. When they told him the result he replied, 'It served them right.' But a few minutes later he reappeared with a gang of lads who began to attack them with belts. Emily Lee suffered a serious injury to her eye.

The magistrate had no sympathy for Lee's story and sentenced both him and Gorman to two months' hard labour, remarking that he hoped the punishment would 'put a stop to this sort of ruffianism'.[157]

The Times welcomed the verdicts by dwelling on 'the painful interest on the revelation which the trial gives of the thick stratum of barbarism underlying our civilisation'. London was 'the theatre of systematic local feuds' between rival gangs, each with its own 'codes of fellowship' that demanded retribution for an assault on one region by the other. The paper expounded that:

> Ruffianism of this organised kind must be put down, even though the motive of it may be to punish attacks upon women, and attacks by the many upon the few. The only condition upon which life is possible in a great city is that feuds of the sort which have come to light in this trial should not be allowed to settle themselves by violence.[158]

By contrast, the liberal *Pall Mall Gazette* saw the Regent's Park murder as proof that the police and particularly the Commissioner Sir Charles Warren were at fault. 'The hoodlum and the larrikin of civilization is the standing difficulty of our sentimental age,' it declared, in a report on 'The Bandit Gangs of London'. Its list of gangs included those in Marylebone and Fitzroy Place, the Black Gang of Borough and the aptly named 'Gang of Roughs' from Norwood, as well as more unlikely sounding groups like 'The Monkey Parade Gang' of Whitechapel, and 'The Jovial Thirty-Two' of Upper Holloway. The report also portrayed Lisson Grove as an uncharted land of savages, much like Whitechapel. Groups of up to a dozen youths roamed about blocking pathways, yelling obscene and blasphemous abuse into the ears of women and children, and hung about with prostitutes. According to a local shopkeeper, they were thieves and blackguards, associates of 'immoral women' or members of the part-time militia (in fact most of the defendants in the trial were working men). They had no fear of the police and frequently got the better of them in street riots, it was claimed.

The *Gazette* had not forgiven Sir Charles Warren for Bloody Sunday, and took the chance to blame him for 'this recrudescence of violence and ruffianism' on the basis that he had stopped his officers from cracking down on brothels. It asserted that gang members were almost always pimps who worked with prostitutes to steal from the public. 'Every one of these really disorderly houses is a centre and breeding ground of crime and indolence and dishonesty and violence,' it concluded. 'Need we wonder that disorder riots in our streets, when its nesting places are specially preserved by the order of the Chief Commissioner?'

The Regent's Park murder also demonstrates that modern fears of teenage gangs, 'postcode wars' and knife crime are nothing new. Neither is the belief that society is at risk from spoilt children with no respect for authority. 'A generation is growing up around us which has never been disciplined, either at home or at school,' said the *Gazette* in 1888. 'So they grow up like wild asses' colts, and are the despair of law and order.'[159]

15

MADNESS

Queen Victoria survived eight assassination attempts during her reign. Between 1840 and 1882 she was shot at as she travelled around London in her carriage, menaced by a teenager with an unloaded pistol, and beaten over the head with a walking stick. None of the attacks caused any serious injury and, in fact, they only seemed to increase the popular sympathy for the monarch – Victoria reportedly said it was 'worth being shot at to see how much one is loved'. But the final attempt also brought about a change in the law which affected several 1888 murder cases.

On 2 March 1882, a deranged poet called Roderick McLean fired at the Queen as she was being driven out to Windsor station in a carriage. He was charged with High Treason and after a short trial was found not guilty on the basis that he was insane and could not be held criminally liable for his actions. This didn't mean he would be walking free from court – McLean spent the rest of his life at Broadmoor Asylum – but the Queen was disturbed by the use of the phrase 'not guilty' and insisted that 'if this is the law, the law must be altered'. She wrote in a letter:

Punishment deters not only sane men but also eccentric men ... a knowledge that they would be protected by an acquittal on the grounds of insanity will encourage these men to commit desperate acts, while on the other hand certainty that they will not escape punishment will terrify them into a peaceful attitude towards others.[160]

The Trial of Lunatics Bill was passed quickly through both Houses of Parliament to change the special verdict of 'not guilty by reason of insanity' to 'guilty but insane'. In reality it was a change only in name, as the end result remained the same – detention in an asylum 'during Her Majesty's pleasure'. It is, however, a fact that there were no further attacks on the Queen for the rest of her reign.

How did the jury decide whether a prisoner was insane or not? Legally they had to follow what were known as the M'Naghten rules, named after the man who tried to assassinate the Prime Minister Robert Peel in 1843.

To establish a defence on the grounds of insanity, it must clearly be proved that at the time of the committing of the act, the accused was labouring under such a defect of reason, from disease of the mind, as not to know the nature and quality of the act he was doing, or if he did know it, that he did not know what he was doing was wrong.[161]

This insanity could be demonstrated in a number of ways and by a variety of medical conditions. In the case of Charles Latham, the thirty-year-old alcoholic who cut the throat of his long-term partner Mary Newman in Somerstown on 19 May 1888, the evidence was that he was suffering from delusions and hallucinations. Three weeks before the murder, he had been taken away to the insane ward of the St Pancras Workhouse and diagnosed with delirium tremens.

Latham remained there for a week before returning to live with Mrs Newman. A neighbour who had witnessed the killing told the court that Latham 'did not appear to recognise me ... he did not appear to notice anything ... he did not appear the least to understand what he was doing'. He looked 'strange' and 'wild about the eyes' when he was arrested and appeared to think his partner had been cheating on him with two police officers and a fellow lodger. On being charged with murder, he replied:

> I had cause. I could not go outside my place without the man who lived in the next room was in my room with my missis. I could not go to bed without this man getting in at the window. I have heard that they have chloroformed me and taken liberties with me, but I know nothing about it. [Inspector] Dod and [Sergeant] Cobb, I have heard that they have taken a liberty with me and have had my missis all over the place.

Both officers and the twenty-eight-year-old lodger, Edward Salmon, insisted that they had had nothing to do with Mrs Newman. Latham's only other explanation for his actions was given to the police surgeon, 'I could not help giving it to her, for she was always nagging at me.'

According to the expert evidence given at the trial, Latham's delusions were brought on by long-term heavy drinking. Henry Bastian, a physician at University College Hospital, said, 'The excessive drinking had undoubtedly damaged his brain. A sane man may hold a suspicion not amounting to delusion, but a delusion is suspecting something that no sane man could suspect ... the prisoner cannot even now be said to be actually of sound mind.' It was for the jury to decide whether it was more likely than not ('on the balance of probabilities') that Latham was not responsible for his actions. After hearing the arguments of both prosecution and defence, and the directions of the judge, the jury returned their verdict that: 'Latham committed the act but was of unsound mind so as not to be responsible for his actions.' Mr Justice Hawkins, slipping into old habits, announced, 'That is a verdict of not guilty on the grounds of insanity', when it was in fact 'guilty but insane'.[162]

Delusions were also the basis of the same verdict in the cases of John Brown, who killed his partner, and Mary Ann Reynolds, who suffocated her child. For Sarah Procter it was epilepsy. In the case of Emma Aston, it was one doctor's opinion that 'want of rest and want of food' could have contributed to a temporary attack of insanity. It may be that the murder of both her children was simply too shocking to be explained in any other way. The police surgeon Charles Bass told the court, 'I am of opinion that at the time this was done the prisoner was certainly suffering under an uncontrollable impulse to kill, and therefore was not conscious of the nature and quality of the act which she was committing, or conscious that what she was doing was wrong.' Julia Spickernell, on the other hand, was said to have been suffering puerperal mania when she drowned her baby daughter. Her doctor, Edward Spencer, explained to the jury:

> There are three kinds of puerperal mania: one which comes on in the puerperal state before the child is born, another which comes on during the state of labour or soon after, and another kind which is recognised as the insanity of lactation; she was still suckling her child at this time. It is common to get this condition in women of delicate constitution, who have borne children rapidly, and have a profuse supply of milk, especially after loss of rest or anything likely to exhaust the nervous system ... I believe that at the time she did this she was unconscious of the act, that she was incapable of appreciating the nature and quality of the act.[163]

Murderers might also be so insane that they could not stand trial. This happened in the case of Louisa Ostler, the twenty-three-year-old wife of a chemist's assistant who killed her two-year-old son Percy at their home in Greenwich. Louisa, who was heavily pregnant, had been suffering from religious delusions and melancholia since December 1887. A local doctor, Charles Hartt, had decided not to place her in an asylum and advised that she be watched over by her sister Henrietta Brown at the family's basement flat at No. 55 Trafalgar Road. Dr Hartt also made daily visits to the house to check on her condition. 'I advised the husband that if she was carefully looked after and had someone with her she would be perfectly safe and I believed that after her pregnancy was over she would probably recover. She was always a quiet and inoffensive person.'

At around 10.45 a.m. on 11 January 1888, Miss Brown decided to go out briefly to get something for dinner and left Louisa with the child in the kitchen. A few minutes later, Louisa's husband, James, who was working at the chemist's shop on the ground floor, decided to go and check on them while his sister-in-law was away. He entered the kitchen to find his wife standing over the body of his son, lying in a pool of blood on the floor. He had been decapitated.

'What have you done?' Mr Ostler asked his wife.

'My Jim, I had only one life to take,' she replied.

From the pools of blood it appeared that the boy's head had been cut off with a table knife while he was sat on a chair at the end of the table. The bloodstained piece of bread he had been eating was on the tablecloth next to a child's cane and a ha'penny.

Mr Ostler had just taken his wife to the bedroom and got her to lie down on the bed when Miss Brown arrived back at the house to discover the grisly scene in the kitchen.

Asked why she had done it, Louisa Ostler explained, 'I've had a command from God to offer a sacrifice for the whole world. We shall all be redeemed and caught up and God will make known to us the mystery.' Later she added:

> I have a Beast's nature and the child had two natures; go down and cut its other heart and feel if he is cold. The judgement will come. I am cloven and have no feeling. God has taken away my intellect and wisdom, knowledge and power and I am Satan himself.

Although Mrs Ostler had been ill for at least six weeks, both her husband and the doctor claimed that she had never shown any sign she was homicidal. Mr Ostler told the inquest, 'My wife has never threatened to do herself or anyone else any injury … she has religious delusions and has never been left alone for any length of time of late – I have guarded against this.' Miss Brown said that Mrs Ostler had always been very affectionate towards the child, and earlier that morning she had washed and dressed him, kissed him and given him an orange.

Dr Hartt gave evidence that not only was she unaware of the nature of her act, but she did not appreciate the nature of the proceedings against her and was unable to give instructions. The medical officer treating her at Greenwich Union Infirmary also agreed that she was 'of unsound mind'. The result was that when she appeared before the Old Bailey on 1 February it was accepted by the prosecution that she was 'hopelessly insane'. Legal formalities meant that a jury was sworn in to hear brief evidence before returning a verdict that she was unfit to plead. Louisa Ostler was detained during 'Her Majesty's pleasure' at Broadmoor Lunatic Asylum.[164]

The asylum (now known as Broadmoor Hospital) was located outside London, about a mile from the village of Crowthorne in Berkshire. It had opened twenty-five years earlier on 27 May 1863, with space for around 500 inmates in seven blocks for men and two for women. During 1888,

Henry Cullum; Emma Elizabeth Aston; John Brown; Mary Ann Reynolds; Sarah Ellen Procter; Charles Latham; and Louisa Ostler were all admitted and given a number and a uniform. Julia Spickernell followed in early 1889. All eight were still there at the time of the 1891 census, which reveals a total of 477 male inmates and 152 females, as well as more than fifty members of staff, including the assistant medical officer, male and female attendants, laundry women, a baker and a gatekeeper. Later censuses recorded inmates only by their initial, but it is likely that they remained there for the rest of their lives. They may have learned trades like carpentry and upholstery in the workshops, or laboured in the kitchen, the garden or the farm. They may also have heard gossip and speculation about the patient who managed to escape from the asylum on 23 January 1888.

James Kelly had been convicted of murder in August 1883 after stabbing his twenty-two-year-old wife, Sarah, in the neck with a carving knife at their home not far from Angel Islington. He was sentenced to death, but just three days before his scheduled execution date he was certified insane and taken to Broadmoor. In 1885, he took up the violin and was allowed to play in the asylum band. Two years later, he came up with a plan to fashion a key from a piece of metal he found buried in the kitchen garden. After spending weeks filing it down so that it could open the door, the key was concealed in a secret compartment in his violin case. On the chosen night, he put on the suit he was allowed to wear for band practice, went downstairs, unlocked the door to the courtyard and walked out. He had only to clamber a 6ft-high wall (later increased to 16ft) and he was free.

For the next eight years he remained on the run. Kelly, who was twenty-seven at the time of his escape, later claimed he went first to see friends at a lodging house near the docks in the East End of London. His travels then took him to Liverpool,

Dieppe, New York, Pennsylvania, Los Angeles, Arizona, New Mexico and Dallas. Then, in 1896, he walked into the British Consulate in New Orleans and announced that he was handing himself in with the hope of being granted a pardon. He was put on board a steamer for Liverpool and preparations were made by police to have him taken into custody upon his arrival. However, when the two warders turned up at the dock on the evening of 26 February, they discovered that the ship had arrived a day earlier than expected. Kelly had disappeared.

Thirty-one years later, at the age of sixty-six, grey-haired and half deaf, Kelly walked up to the main entrance at Broadmoor Asylum and begged to be allowed back in. This stunning twist was reported in the *News of the World* under the headline: 'Fiction and the Films outdone – returned to Broadmoor after thirty-nine years.' Kelly was said to have told the authorities that he now wanted to 'set his conscience at rest and pass peacefully out of existence'. He added:

> I have no friends and I am alone in the world. I have wandered all these years feeling that I am a fugitive who might be pounced on by any policeman I passed. I am getting feeble now from the constant fear and I dreaded the idea of dying alone.

Kelly died two years later from pneumonia on 17 September 1929.[165]

16

DEATH

Finally it was time for him to die. Levi Richard Bartlett had been waiting for this moment for three weeks, readying himself, preparing for the end while at the same time hoping that somehow he might be saved. Every effort had failed. He had made his farewells to his family and now the date of execution had arrived: 13 November 1888.

At 6 a.m., Bartlett woke up and saw the familiar walls of his cell at Newgate Gaol, the most famous prison in the country. He was offered breakfast but felt no inclination to eat. He had only two hours left on earth. Two hours interrupted only by the arrival of the chaplain and, a few minutes before 8 a.m., the executioner. James Berry was a solid-looking sandy-haired man with an unsettling deep scar down his cheek and a reddish complexion that suggested a fondness for drink. Overall, he had a surprisingly gentle face, considering his occupation. Berry introduced himself in a broad Yorkshire accent before getting to work, slipping a broad leather belt around Bartlett's waist. The prisoner's arms were pinioned using two straps around the elbow and another strap around the wrists, and fastened to the body belt at the front. Bartlett was then taken from the condemned cell to join the ceremonial procession towards the gallows. Ahead of him were the chief warder and the chaplain, reading aloud from the burial service. Berry, the executioner, was directly behind him, followed by the warders, the governor Colonel Milman, two under-sheriffs, the prison surgeon and an attendant. As they set off, a white cap was placed upon Bartlett's head.

All too soon, they were at the foot of the scaffold. Bartlett managed to keep his composure as he was helped by the warders to the trapdoor beneath the beam. Once in place, his legs were tied together with a leather strap below the knees. He was asked if he had anything to say. 'I wish only to give my love to all my family and to thank the governor and sheriffs and all the officials for the kindness they have shown me,' he replied. Berry placed the noose over his head and checked the knot was in the correct position to ensure a clean execution. He also had to make sure that he had correctly measured the rope's length. This was something Berry was very particular about. If the 'drop' was too short Bartlett would not suffer instantaneous death by dislocation of the neck, and would instead suffer a slow, undignified strangulation. If it was too long then the head might be torn clean off the body. Berry calculated that 4ft would be enough. Bartlett was a large man, but more importantly he had a large wound to his neck which had only recently healed. There was a risk that it could reopen when the noose tightened and spray blood everywhere. They wanted as little mess as possible.

Finally the preparations were complete. Berry pulled down the white cap to cover Bartlett's eyes and gave the signal for the trapdoor to be released. There was silence as the spectators held their breath.[166]

Levi Richard Bartlett was sixty-six years old. He had led a colourful life, for in his time he had been a soldier in the Crimea, a 'ganger' on the Millwall docks and a milk dealer.

He sometimes went by the name of Richard Freeman, using the surname of his first wife, while others knew him by the nickname 'Mad Dick the Jockey'. In 1872, he had spent seven weeks in hospital after an unloading accident at the docks and since that time he hadn't been quite right. He was well known in his neighbourhood on the Isle of Dogs for his strange and eccentric behaviour. William Leslie, a local surgeon, remembered how 'several times when driving I have seen him come up with an unmeaning grin on his face, put his arms round the horse's mouth and kiss it, and sometimes he would take the foam from the horse's mouth and put it into his own'. Despite his bizarre behaviour, Bartlett formed a relationship with a divorcee ten years his junior and in 1884 they were married. Elizabeth Bartlett was described as a hard-working and industrious woman, who sought to control her husband's errant ways. This was fine when he was sober, but a drink or two almost inevitably meant a blazing row, the throwing of sticks and bottles, and drunken threats to cut off her head and throw it in the street.

Levi made attempts to turn teetotal, but by August 1888 he had been drinking pretty much solidly for the whole month. The only way his wife could stop him was by withholding money, but this just meant another argument. On Saturday 18 August, the rows started at 9 a.m. after Levi returned from finishing the milk round. Levi wanted $2\frac{1}{2}d$ to buy some more gin, but Elizabeth was determined not to give him anything.

'You won't have it out of me this day if I know it,' she told him.

'You cow, I will mark you for this tonight,' he replied.

Levi moved towards a display of cakes, intending to go out into the street and sell them, but was intercepted by his wife. Levi kicked her between the legs and grabbed an iron bar while she ran round into the shop and grabbed a knife from behind the counter. Levi then ran out the house, ripped the bell from the gate and threw it at his wife. When that missed he took the gate off its hinges and hurled that at her as well, telling her, 'You cow, pick that up.' Eventually he got the money and spent the rest of the day sitting in a drunken haze in the armchair in the parlour. At 11 p.m., after yet another row, the couple shut up shop and retired to bed.

It was around 4 a.m. when the lodgers Thomas Jones and Benjamin French were woken by a knock on their door. It was Levi Bartlett asking if they had any alcohol. When they told him they hadn't, he shook both their hands in turn and told them, 'Goodbye, you won't see me no more alive … I have done for my missis and I am going to do for myself.' He left the room but returned a few minutes later with a razor in his hand and blood pouring from his throat. They followed him back to the couple's bedroom to find Mrs Bartlett lying in bed. Her head had been smashed in with a hammer. There was blood spattered over the pillow, up the wall and across the ceiling.

Mrs Bartlett was still breathing when the doctor arrived at the house, followed shortly by her sister Emma Mears, who lived just down the road, a police inspector, a sergeant and three constables. The officers managed to disarm Levi after a struggle, and held him on the bed while Dr Charles Smythe examined his wife, but there was little he could do to save her life. She had been stabbed three times in the neck and had suffered a severe fracture to the left temple. 'The bones were quite broken in, and the brain substance knocked out … that blow alone was quite sufficient to cause death,' he later recalled. She was pronounced dead an hour later. Dr Smythe sewed up the wound to Levi Bartlett's neck before he was taken off to Poplar Hospital.[167]

It was another month until Bartlett had recovered sufficiently to be charged with murder and attempted suicide, and to be brought before Thames Police Court. 'Owing to the weak state the prisoner was in he could not be put in the dock but sat on a seat close to the solicitors' table,' reported *The Times*. He listened as his wife's sister, Emma Mears, described him as a 'treacherous vagabond' who used to rob money from the shop to spend on drink. His milk carrier, Thomas Jones, was also called to speak about the violent confrontation the day of the attack. It was more or less a formality. Bartlett was remanded in custody at Holloway Prison to await trial at the Old Bailey on 24 October.

His only hope of avoiding a death sentence would be to prove that he was insane at the time of the attack. The prosecution relied on the surgeon at Holloway, Philip Gilbert, who told the court that there was nothing wrong with him apart from gout. Bartlett's defence barrister was the Irishman Gerald Geoghegan, who went on to represent the serial-killer Thomas Neill Cream, and was described as 'the outstanding figure at the Old Bailey' until his powers were diminished by drink. Geoghegan played upon Bartlett's nickname of 'Mad Dick' and called evidence to suggest he should be locked up in an asylum. Bartlett's sister, Sarah Ann Fitch, who lived in Westminster, told the court that one sister had tried to drown herself and another had twice attempted to poison herself. Charles Serel, the warden at Christ Church and a resident of Manchester Road, described him as 'very strange and eccentric'. Finally, William Leslie, a surgeon who treated Bartlett for a dislocated arm, told the jury, 'Even when sober I could not honestly say he was quite sane, when drunk he is a dangerous lunatic … he was the most furiously mad man I ever saw.'

The jury took nearly three hours – an unusually long time in those days – to reach a verdict. It was guilty, with no recommendation to mercy. The judge, Mr Justice Cave, passed the death sentence and Bartlett was taken to his cell at Newgate Gaol.

His solicitors quickly gathered together a petition calling for a reprieve but the reply from Whitehall was disappointing:

Sir, I am directed by the Secretary of State to inform you … that he has had this case under his careful consideration but he regrets that he has not been able to find any sufficient ground to justify him in advising Her Majesty to interfere with the due course of the law.

The execution would go ahead.[168]

Twenty years earlier it would have taken place in public, outside the prison walls. Now, there were only a handful of press and officials to witness the death of Levi Bartlett. At 8 a.m. precisely, the massive oak doors swung open beneath his feet. He felt gravity take hold, his stomach lurching as he plunged downwards. All too soon the rope snapped taut around his throat, dislocating his neck.

'Death was instantaneous,' noted the reporters, watching the body swing slowly below the scaffold. Outside the prison a small crowd cheered as the black flag was raised.[169]

Epilogue

31 DECEMBER, 1888

As 1888 drew inexorably to a close, London was enveloped by a dense fog rolling up the Thames. Darkness descended well before the sun slumped beneath the horizon and by 6 p.m. the temperature had plummeted below zero. The muddy roads began to freeze into icy death traps, and the major thoroughfares of the metropolis seized up as cabs, buses and carts slowed to a crawl. Pedestrians, unable to see more than a few feet in front of them, struggled to keep their heads as they threaded their way through the traffic. To the shouts and cries of drivers and the shrieks of horses were added the bleats and moans of sheep and cattle being driven home from the markets. Everywhere was chaos and confusion as London shivered and bolted its doors until morning.[170]

It was perhaps a fitting end for the Year of the Ripper. At times during those twelve months it had seemed as if the normal order of things had broken down and the city was on the verge of sliding into the depths of Hell. That once proud capital of civilisation had been tarnished by 'a series of unique atrocities revolting to humanity' which outdid any work of fiction. The legend of Jack the Ripper played upon a host of

Victorian fears about the future, and exploited a variety of stereotypes – the mad doctor, the depraved aristocrat, the Jewish immigrant and the fallen woman. The fact that the killer, or killers, evaded capture despite leaving a series of tantalising clues and loose ends only heightened the terror and deepened the mystery. It is no wonder the case still fascinates the public more than a century later.[171]

Yet when the hysteria subsided, and people had time to reflect, it seemed that 1888 was not such a momentous year in the scheme of things. The world had been pretty quiet. 'Those colossal calamities of which no year is altogether deficient have been far below the average in number and magnitude,' remarked the *Liverpool Mercury*, '… there has been no great war and only a few small ones.'[172] Parliament had busied itself with domestic issues like housing, immigration and the conditions of 'sweated labour', but little was actually done. The task of sorting out London's problems would fall instead to the London County Council, set up under the Local Government Act of 1888. It was the passing of the Act that the *Graphic Illustrated Newspaper* concluded was the most memorable event of the year.

Jack the Ripper did, however, play an important part in focusing national and international attention on the problems that a capitalist society faced. The modern era was fast approaching, and in many ways 1888 marks a symbolic dividing line between the old and the new.[173] This changing of the guard was depicted in a *Punch* cartoon at the end of the year called 'New London'. It showed the forces of light, backed by science, art, literature, and the standard of municipal reform driving away the forces of darkness represented by slums, money lenders, sweaters and crime.

At the same time, the 'Great Powers' of Europe were also sliding towards war. The 1880s saw the beginning of the 'Scramble for Africa' and the arms race as they competed for dominance over land and sea. The year 1888 marked the deaths of two German emperors in the space of three months, and the arrival to the throne of the confrontational Kaiser Wilhelm II, who bears as much blame as anybody for the First World War twenty-six years later. In Britain, the Prime Minister, Lord Salisbury promised Queen Victoria that the navy would adopt the 'two power standard' by maintaining a fleet big enough to face both France and Russia.[174]

This was also an age of important developments in science and technology. Electricity was emerging as an alternative to gas and coal, and the inventors Thomas Edison and Nikola Tesla were squaring up to each other for the 'War of Currents' between AC and DC.[175] In 1888, George Eastman invented the first Kodak hand-held camera and marketed it with the slogan: 'You press the button, we do the rest.' Edison, having pioneered the lightbulb and the phonograph, began researching a prototype moving film camera known as a kinetoscope. Meanwhile, Karl Benz continued to work on the internal combustion engine and began selling the first commercially available automobile. It would only be another fifteen years until the Wright brothers successfully made their first flight. Authors like H.G. Wells were inspired by the rapid speed of progress, and began writing science fiction novels featuring time machines, alien invasions and invisible men. One of the bestsellers of 1888 was Edward Bellamy's *Looking Backward 2000–1887*, about an American who fell asleep and woke up in a socialist utopia in the year 2000.

Socialism was now starting to attract the support of workers as well as intellectuals like George Bernard Shaw, thanks to the 'Great Depression' and the focus on social problems in the East End. The 1880s saw the formation of the Social Democratic Federation in 1881, and the Fabian Society in 1884, the extension of the vote to higher-paid workers, the Bloody Sunday demonstration of 1887, the Bryant & May 'matchgirls' strike and the 1889 dockers' strike. The last two events revitalised the Trade Union movement and spurred on its growth throughout the industrialised areas of England, Wales and Scotland. This 'New Unionism' would lead to the formation of the Labour Party at the beginning of the twentieth century.

The decade saw increasing agitation for women's rights by feminists such as Emmeline Pankhurst, and the emergence of the so-called 'New Woman'. In 1888, the *Woman's World*, edited by Oscar Wilde, featured an article on 'the fallacy of the superiority of man' by Laura McLaren. 'No age was ever so favourable for the development of female talent as the present and every day the conditions of male and female become more equal,' she wrote.

> It has taken many centuries to develop the intellect of man. If, by the year 1987, the position of women in the artistic, musical, scientific and literary worlds is not equal to that of the other sex in their day, men will then be able to write a plausible essay on the inherent inferiority of women.

Likewise the 'New Journalism' was revolutionising the newspaper industry with its ever more inventive attempts to attract readers. Matthew Arnold, who coined the phrase in 1887, praised its 'ability, novelty, variety, sensation, sympathy, generous instincts' but mourned its feather-brained tendency to 'throw out assertions at a venture because it wishes them true; does not correct either them or itself, if they are false; and to get at things as they really are it seems to feel no concern whatever'. The *Star* newspaper, born on 17 January 1888, was one of the new breed that made their names and circulations on the back of the Ripper murders. Its first editorial promised to look at every issue 'from the standpoint of the workers of the nation, and of the poorest and most helpless among them'.

Fifty years later the newspaper looked back on the changes wrought on society:

> In 1888 we had not heard of the submerged tenth ... but we had the real thing, plain to all our senses. The poor in 1888 were poorer by far than they are today, they had fewer alleviations of their poverty. Perhaps too they had less reticence concerning it. The streets were full of beggars. In the poorer districts barefooted children were a common sight. And at night the noble river embankment was a mile and a half of sheer misery, with homeless people sleeping out in all weathers. The Salvation Army was doing its best. Private but badly organised charity did something. But the city's conscience had not yet been aroused to a realisation that this misery was a public concern. In this respect it is safe to claim that there has been a marked advance since 1888. There is still plenty of poverty ... but by legislation, or by municipal energy, or by private benevolence, or by all combines, the submerged tenth has been reduced to a smaller fraction, and that fraction brought nearer to a surface where life is endurable.[176]

Even Whitechapel was able to cast off some of its hellish reputation. In 1938, the police officer George W. Cornish wrote that it was:

> ... as law abiding as any district in London, and perhaps more so than some. It is still cosmopolitan, and in parts rather picturesque. The two great roads to the eastern suburbs and the docks run through it, but they are very different from the cobbled, badly lit streets of thirty-five years ago. There are still mean streets and dark alleys but the coming of buses and the Underground, restaurants, big shops and cinemas altered it completely.[177]

31 December, 1888

Revisiting London in 1888 has revealed some eerie similarities to the present day. Again capitalism is in crisis. The city is labouring through an economic depression and has been visited by riots, strikes and occupations of public spaces. Our head of state is an elderly Queen who has just celebrated a jubilee. The government is again led by an Old Etonian Conservative. The police force is under pressure, morale is low and a commissioner has been forced to resign.

Since the Year of the Ripper we have seen a massive increase in state intervention and the establishment of public services like the NHS to protect the most vulnerable in society. It now seems that the state can no longer afford such generosity and we may have to rely once again on charity and philanthropy.

Just as in 1888, when some feared the spectre of revolution, it is difficult to predict what might happen next. Hopefully we will not have to face our own Jack the Ripper.

APPENDIX

Metropolitan Police statistics on murder and manslaughter 1881–1891

Year	Population	Murder	Manslaughter
1881	4,788,657	11	84
1882	4,990,952	10	85
1883	5,042,556	16	83
1884	5,147,727	16	74
1885	5,225,069	9	97
1886	5,364,627	8	98
1887	5,476,447	13	96
1888	5,590,576	28	94
1889	5,707,061	17	34
1890	5,825,951	16	41
1891	5,713,859	12	32

★The figures are taken from the Report of the Commissioner of Police of the Metropolis for the year 1891. The population count between the census years of 1881 and 1891 were estimates on behalf of the Registrar General.

Homicide by gender in England and in London, 1883–1893

Year	England M	England F	London M	London F
1883	188	134	39	38
1884	178	148	29	32
1885	172	138	25	30
1886	181	130	34	26
1887	181	171	30	45
1888	155	146	30	39
1889	159	131	42	37
1890	160	126	38	35
1891	158	157	31	39
1892	153	147	31	38
1893	185	152	28	32

*Figures taken from annual reports of the Registrar General.

Homicide cases featured in this book

Unsolved murders (chapter number in brackets)
Total number of victims: 14

Annie Chapman (10)

Lucy Clark (9)

Catherine Eddowes (10)

Annie Mary French (8)

Elizabeth Gorman (11)

Mary Jane Kelly (10)

Rose Mylett (10)

Mary Ann Nichols (10)

Elizabeth Stride (10)

Elizabeth 'Annie' Smith (8)

Emma Smith (10)

Martha Tabram (10)

Emma Wakefield (11)

Unknown body found at New Scotland Yard (7)

Murder cases ending in acquittal
Total: 7

John King (1)

Michael Lewis (6)

Eliza Jane Schummacher (11)

Frances Wright (9)

Newborn twins of Dora Hart (12)

Newborn child of Florence Lovett (12)

Murder cases ending in conviction and death sentence
Total: 5

Elizabeth Bartlett (16)

Emily Bignall (3)

Sidney Pierrepoint (13)

Joseph Rumbold (14)

Margaret White (9)

Murder cases ending in verdict of guilty, but insane
Total: 7

Frank and Bertie Morris Aston (13)

Sarah Brown (9)

Mary Newman (9)

Frank Reynolds (13)

Mabel Spickernell (13)

Charlotte Whale (3)

Murder cases ending in manslaughter conviction
Total: 1
Clarence Henry Longman (13)

Murder–suicide
Total: 3
Susannah Barrell (9)
Major Thomas Hare (3)
Hannah Potzdamer (5)

Murder cases in which defendant was found unfit to stand trial
Total: 1
Percy Ostler (15)

Manslaughter cases ending in conviction.
Total: 3
Elizabeth Gibbs (2)
William Hall (5)
William Walker (4)

Manslaughter cases ending in acquittal
Total: 12
Annie Astell (4)
David Cavalier (2)
Jane Healey (9)
John Kellar (4)
James Langley (2)
Robert Marjoram (3)
Michael Pattern (5)

Emily Roberts (9)

Ann Rowley (2)

Mary Sandford (9)

John Shorting (4)

James Williamson (2)

Other cases (excluding large number of unknown victims of infanticide):

George Best, manslaughter charge dismissed by magistrate (4)

Henry Talbot, manslaughter charge dismissed by magistrate (4)

William Bate Curner, natural causes (6)

Jane Mulchay, manslaughter charge dropped before trial (13)

Newborn child of Annie Burbridge, murder charge dropped before trial (12)

Newborn child of Dinah Israel, manslaughter charge dismissed by Grand Jury (12)

Newborn child of Julia Magson, murder charged dropped before trial (12)

Newborn child of Catherine Morgan, manslaughter charge dropped before trial (12)

Newborn child of Ruth Newman, murder charge dismissed by Grand Jury (12)

BIBLIOGRAPHY

～ Newspapers and Journals ～

Birmingham Post
Daily News
Daily Telegraph
East London Advertiser
East London Observer
Illustrated London News
Illustrated Police News
Lloyd's Weekly Newspaper
Morning Post
Murray's Magazine
News of the World
Night and Day
Pall Mall Gazette
Penny Illustrated Paper
Punch
Reynolds's Weekly Newspaper
The *Standard*
The *Star*
The *Times*
Woman's World

~ Government and Judicial ~

Parliamentary Papers: 1893 Vol.71, p.981 – Return of persons
sentenced to death from 1/1/1884 to 31/12/1892

Judicial Statistics for 1888

Reports of the Commissioner of Police of the Metropolis for
the years 1887, 1888 and 1891

National Archives, CRIM 1/29/1 to 1/30/6, HO 144/10064,
ASSI 36/32

Fifty-first annual report of the registrar-general, England 1888

The Old Bailey proceedings online, 1674-1913 (www.oldbai-
leyonline.org), Tim Hichcock et al.

~ Guidebooks, Manuals ~

Dickens, C. Jr, *Dickens's Dictionary of London* (1888)

Pascoe, C.E., *London of To-day, An Illustrated Handbook for the
Season* (1888, 1889)

Panton, J.E., *From Kitchen to Garrett, Hints for Young Householders*
(1888)

~ Memoirs, Diaries, Letters, etc. ~

Anderson, Sir R., *The Lighter Side of My Official Life* (1910)

Arrow, C., *Rogues and Others* (1926)

Ashley, F.W., *My Sixty Years in the Law* (1936)

Asquith, M., *The Autobiography of Margot Asquith* (1962)

Berrett, J., *When I was at Scotland Yard* (1932)

Berry, J., *My Experiences as an Executioner* (1892)

Besant, A., *An Autobiography* (1939)

Bowen-Rowlands, E., *Seventy-Two Years at the Bar: A Memoir of
Sir Harry Bodkin Poland* (1924)

Bower, Sir J.W.N., *Fifty-Two Years a Policeman* (1926)

Buckle, G.E., *The Letters of Queen Victoria 1886-1901, 3rd series,
Vol. I* (1930)

Burns, J., *1888 Diary* (British Library Manuscripts add. 46310)

Carlin, F., *Reminiscences of an ex-Detective* (1927)

Cavanagh, T., *Scotland Yard Past and Present* (1893)

Bibliography

Cornish, G., *Cornish of the Yard* (1935)

Dew, W., *I Caught Crippen* (1938)

Divall, T., *Scoundrels and Scallywags, and Some Honest Men* (1929)

Fuller, R., *Recollections of a Detective* (1912)

Goldsmid, H.J.J., *Dottings of a Dosser* (1886)

Hawkins, Sir H., *The Reminiscences of Sir Henry Hawkins* (1905)

Lansdowne, A., *A Life's Reminiscences of Scotland Yard* (1893)

Leeson, B., *Lost London: Memoirs of an East End Detective* (1934)

Littlechild, J.G., *The Reminiscences of Chief Inspector Littlechild* (1894)

McKenny, H.G., *A City Road Diary, 1885–1888* (1978)

MacNaghten, M., *Days of my Years* (1914)

Moser, M. & Rideal, C.F., *Stories from Scotland Yard* (1890)

Neil, A., *Forty Years of Man-hunting* (1932)

Nevinson, M.W., *Life's Fitful Fever* (1926)

Rothschild, C. de, *Reminiscences* (1922)

Shaw, G.B., *The Diaries 1885–1897* (1986)

Shaw, G.B., *Collected Letters, Vol. I* (1985)

Sims, G.R., *How the Poor Live and Horrible London* (1889)

Smalley, G., *London Letters* (1890)

Smith, Sir H., *From Constable to Commissioner* (1910)

Stanley, H.M., *In Darkest Africa* (1890)

Sweeney, J., *At Scotland Yard* (1903)

Treves, Sir F., *The Elephant Man and Other Reminiscences* (1923)

Wells, H.G., *An Experiment in Autobiography* (1934)

Wensley, F.P., *Detective Days* (1931)

~ Secondary Sources ~

Allason, R., *The Branch: A History of the Metropolitan Police Special Branch 1883–1983* (1983)

Altick, R., *Victorian Studies in Scarlet* (1972)

Barker, T.C. & Robbins, M., *A History of London's Transport* (1975)

Begg, P., *Jack the Ripper: The Facts* (2009)

Bell, R.C., *The Ambulance: A History* (2009)

Bentley, D.J., *English Criminal Justice in the Nineteenth Century* (1998)

Booth, C., *Life and Labour of the People in London* (1889)

1888: The Year of the Ripper

Booth, W., *In Darkest England and the Way Out* (1890)

Bosanquet, H., *Social Work in London 1869–1912* (1971)

Browne, D.G, *The Rise of Scotland Yard* (1956)

Clark, R., *Capital Punishment in Britain* (2009)

Clarkson, C.T. & Richardson, J.H., *Police!* (1984 – originally published in 1889)

Colquhoun, K., *Mr Briggs' Hat: A Sensational Account of Britain's First Railway Murder* (2011)

Conan Doyle, A., *A Study in Scarlet, 1887* (2001)

Critchley, T.A., *A History of Police in England and Wales* (1978)

Curtis, Jr., L.P., *Jack the Ripper and the London Press* (2001)

Davidson, A., *Cecil Rhodes and his Time* (1984)

Emsley, C., *Crime and Society in England 1750–1900* (2005)

Evans, S., & Skinner, K., *Letters From Hell* (2001)

Fishman, W.J., *East End 1888* (1988)

Flanders, J., *The Invention of Murder* (2011)

Gainer, B., *The Alien Invasion* (1972)

Gray, D., *London's Shadows* (2010)

Greenwood, J., *The Seven Curses of London* (1984)

Greeves, I.S., *London Docks 1800–1900* (1980)

Hibbert, C. *et al.*, *The London Encyclopaedia* (2008)

Howell, M., *The True History of the Elephant Man* (1983)

Hunt, J.D., *Gandhi in London* (1978)

Kapp, Y., *Eleanor Marx: The Crowded Years, 1884–1898* (1976)

Lee, W., *A History of Police in England* (1901)

Lewis J.R., *The Victorian Bar* (1982)

Liebowitz, D., & Pearson, C., *The Last Expedition* (2005)

Logan, W., *The Great Social Evil* (1871)

McLaren, A., *A Prescription for Murder* (1993)

Marriott, J., *Beyond the Tower: A History of East London* (2011)

Mayhew, H., *London Labour and the London Poor* (1968)

Mearns, A., *The Bitter Cry of Outcast London* (1883)

Morrison, W.D., *Crime and its Causes* (1891)

Owen, D., *The Government of Victorian London 1855–1889* (1982)

Pope, W., *The Story of the Star 1888–1938* (1938)

Prothero, M., *The History of the Criminal Investigation Department at Scotland Yard* (1931)

Bibliography

Raw, L., *Striking A Light: The Bryant and May Matchwomen and their Place in History* (2011)

Roberts, A., *Salisbury, Victorian Titan* (2000)

Rose, L., *Massacre of the Innocents* (1986)

Ross, E., *Love and Toil: Motherhood in Outcast London* (1993)

Rule, F., *The Worst Street in London* (2008)

Rylands, L.G., *Crime, its Causes and its Remedy* (1889)

St Aubyn, G., *Queen Victoria: A Portrait* (1992)

Stephen, J.F., *A History of the Criminal Law in England* (1996)

Tomalin, C., *Charles Dickens: A Life* (2011)

Trow, M.J., *The Thames Torso Murders* (2011)

Walker, N., *Crime and Insanity in England* (1968)

Walkowitz, J.R., *City of Dreadful Delight* (1992)

Walkowitz, J.R., *Prostitution and Victorian Society* (1980)

White, A., *The Problems of a Great City* (1895)

White, J., *London in the 19th century* (2008)

Wiener, M.J., *Men of Blood: Violence, Manliness, and Criminal Justice in Victorian England* (2010)

Wilson, G.B., *Alcohol and the Nation: a Contribution to the Study of the Liquor Problem in the United Kingdom from 1800–1935* (1940)

NOTES

1. Weather conditions *The Times*, 2 January, and *Penny Illustrated Paper*, 7 January. Elizabeth Gibbs' case in the Proceedings of the Old Bailey online, reference t18880130-291.

2. The homicide statistics are taken from the Report of the Commissioner of Police of the Metropolis for the Year 1888 [Parliamentary Papers], Table 15, p.32. Alternatively the 'Fifty-first annual report of the Registrar General for the Year 1888', based on the final resolution of each case, gives a total of sixty-nine homicides for London (thirty male, thirty-nine female). The Judicial Statistics for the year ending 29 September 1888 gives a total of 150, with sixty-one murders (including thirty-one infanticides) and eighty-nine manslaughters for the Metropolitan Police District, and two murders and three manslaughters for the City of London.

3. Dalrymple quoted in Curtis, P.L., *Jack the Ripper and the London Press*, p.11. Cobb quote from the review of Marie Besnard in *A Second Identity* (1969).

4. Jubilee exclamations found in McKenny, H.G., *A City Road Diary*, p.64.

5. Quotations from the Queen's journal in Buckle, G. ed., Letters *of Queen Victoria*, 3rd series, Vol. I (1930), p.369. The number 1888 also has an ominous ring to it – written in Roman numerals it has thirteen letters, and it is the UN identifying number for chloroform, drug of choice for several murderers.

6. 'The Fastest Ship in the World', *Belfast Newsletter*, 4 January 1888; advert for the Orient Line, the *Standard*, 4 January. The cheapest one-way ticket cost £13 13s.

7. Two months later, on 29 October, the British would yield control of the waterway and agree to its neutrality under the Convention of Constantinople.

Notes

8. The International Meridian Conference in Washington DC had chosen the Royal Greenwich Observatory as the location of the Prime Meridian four years earlier in October 1884. For a contemporary account of travelling from London to Australia, see the Diary of John Rawes, *Journey from London to Adelaide*, transcribed at: www.rawes.co.uk/rawes/corres/co18.htm.

9. Details of Tilbury from Greeves, I., *London Docks*, p.13.

10. Gandhi's arrival told in Hunt, J.D., *Gandhi in London*, pp.2, 7, 8, 32; and Gandhi, M.K., *An Autobiography* (2001), pp.54, 61. Much of the story of John King is adapted from the transcript of the trial at the Old Bailey, Proceedings of the Old Bailey online, 22 October 1888, reference t18881022-963.

11. According to the census, John King was born in Co. Antrim, but he had married a Scottish woman, lived in Scotland and worked in Scotland, most likely at J. & J. White's chemical works in Shawfield. They produced 70 per cent of the UK's chromate products until closing in 1967. Much of the story of John King is adapted from the transcript of the trial at the Old Bailey, Proceedings of the Old Bailey online, 22 October 1888, reference t18881022-963.

12. Contemporary press reports used for this account include *Lloyd's Weekly Newspaper*, 16 & 23 September; *Reynolds's Newspaper*, 16 & 28 September; *Glasgow Herald*, 16 & 22 September and 23 & 27 October; *The Times* 17, 22 & 26 September and 4 & 27 October; *Leeds Mercury*, 26 September; *Morning Post*, 26 September & 27 October; *Illustrated Police News*, 3 November. McKill and King family history culled from UK censuses between 1871 and 1901; US Federal Census, 1930; and 1920 New York passenger list.

13. Pascoe, C.E., *London of To-Day, 1888*, p.15 and pp.20-5.

14. 'The Streets of London', *Woman's World*, 1888, Vol. I, p.481.

15. In 1888 Tower Bridge was under construction and former Prime Minister William Gladstone gave his backing for a Channel Tunnel between England and France.

16. Gloved hand quote from Richardson, J.H., *Police!*, p.247.

17. Piccadilly Circus and Eros in Hibbert-Page, C., *The London Encyclopaedia*, p.275, 639. 'Cheapest form of travelling' quote from *London of To-Day*, 1888, p.393. Heyday of the omnibus, Barker, T.C., *A History of London Transport*, Vol. I, p.241. London General Omnibus Company versus the Road Cars, Pope, *The Story of the Star*, p.6.

18. Dickens, C., *Dictionary of London* (1888), pp.97, 196. *London of To-Day,* 1888, p.303. Hibbert-Page, C., *London Encyclopaedia,* p.638. Queen Victoria quote from Mason, M., *Walk the Lines*, p.285.

19. Accident figures in Richardson, J.H., *Police!*, p.248.

20. Account of James Langley case gathered from the Proceedings of the Old Bailey online, reference t18880227-363, and reports in *The Times,* 14 February and 3 March; *Lloyd's Weekly Newspaper,* 5 February; *Morning Post,* 9 February.

21. Williamson case details from Proceedings of the Old Bailey online, reference number t18881022-972. Reports in *The Times,* 25 September and 15 October.

22. Dickens, C. *Dictionary of London* (1888), p.233.

23. Cabs were regulated by the public carriage department at Scotland Yard. There were 2,000 applications for licences every year and some drivers were in their eighties. To get a licence you had to provide two certificates of character, be able to read and write, and pass the nineteenth-century equivalent of the Knowledge. From Richardson, J.H., *Police!*, p.250-2.

24. David Cavalier case culled from the Old Bailey Proceedings, reference t18880917-833; *The Times,* 21 September; *Lloyd's Weekly Newspaper,* 23 September.

25. The Gibbs case uses details from the Proceedings of the Old Bailey online, reference t18880130-291, and reports in *The Times* 5–6 January; the *Standard,* 5 January, Censuses for 1861 to 1901. Bayfordbury Mansion was used by Dr Barnardo Homes during the Second World War.

26. Fatal bicycle accident reported in the *Morning Post,* 8 February.

27. Nott-Bower, *Fifty-two Years a Policeman,* p.311; Bell, R., *The Ambulance,* pp.23, 47.

28. Panton, J.E., *From Kitchen to Garrett* (1888), pp.2-3.

29. Details of the Hare murder case from *The Times* report 28–29 August; the *Standard,* 28 August; the *Morning Post,* 29 August; *Reynolds's Newspaper,* 2 September.

30. Davidson, *Cecil Rhodes and his Time,* p.62. In 1888, Rhodes was negotiating for mining rights from the Matabele tribe and meeting the Irish MP Charles Stewart Parnell to discuss a plan for Home Rule. Two years later, he took office as Prime Minister of the Cape colony. Rotberg, R., *The Founder,* p.230-231; Robb, G., *Rimbaud,* p.390.

31. Although Major Hare's personal estate on his death was valued at £41, when his wife died five years later she left more than £1,200. In 1891, aged sixty-three, she was living with her two youngest sons and two servants in Parklands, Surbiton Hill.

32. Shenley is home to Arsenal FC's training ground. The village is now covered by the Hertfordshire police rather than the Met.

33. Details of the Bignall case are taken from the depositions at the National Archives, ASSI 36/32, and newspaper reports in *Lloyd's Weekly Newspaper,* 11 March; *Reynolds's Newspaper,* 11 & 18 March; the *Morning Post,* 13 March;

The Times, 1 August; the *Bristol Mercury and Daily Post*, 4 August; *Daily News*, 17 August.

34. Pears soap details from 'Ancient Pompeii in Modern London', *Ipswich Journal*, 2 July; *Lloyd's Weekly Newspaper*, 8 January.

35. Procter case details from Proceedings of the Old Bailey online, reference t18880528-556, and reports in the *Birmingham Daily Post*, 19 April; *Lloyd's Weekly Newspaper*, 22 April and 3 June; *The Times*, 24 & 30 April and 1 June; *Lancaster Gazette*, 25 April.

36. Marjoram case from Proceedings of the Old Bailey online, reference t18880528-586, and reports in *The Times*, 15 May; *Lloyd's Weekly Newspaper*, 20 May and 3 June.

37. *East London Advertiser*, 6 October. Details on Watney market from: www.stgite.org.uk/media/watneymarket.html.

38. Talbot case details from reports in *The Times*, 14 July; *Daily News*, 14 July; *Lloyd's Weekly Newspaper*, 15 July; the *Standard*, 21 July.

39. Hibbert-Page, C., *London Encyclopaedia*, p.191; Dickens, C., *Dictionary of London* (1888), p.82.

40. Reports of Best case in *The Times*, 28–29 September and 2 & 6 October; *Daily News*, 6 October; *Illustrated Police News*, 6 October; *Lloyd's Weekly Newspaper*, 7 October; *Reynolds's Newspaper*, 7 October.

41. Report of the Commissioner of Police of the Metropolis for the year 1888, p.27. In 2001 the Metropolitan Police made more than 20,000 arrests for drunk and disorderly behaviour. The introduction of on-the-spot fines in 2004 has reduced this figure to around 5,000 a year.

42. Details of the Kellar case in Proceedings of the Old Bailey online, reference t18890107-137 and reports in *Morning Post*, 4 & 10 January; the *Standard*, 4 January; *Lloyd's Weekly Newspaper*, 6 & 13 January.

43. Details of the Walker case in Proceedings of the Old Bailey online, reference t18880730-773, and reports in *Lloyd's Weekly Newspaper*, 8 July; *Reynolds's Newspaper*, 8 July; and *The Times*, 20 July. Agency copy carried in the *York Herald*, 6 August, focused more on the Old Bailey judge's remarks than the depositions taken by the coroner, which were 'illegible' and 'might as well be written in Egyptian'.

44. Callaghan statement in Evans, S.P. & Skinner, K., *Letters From Hell*, p.161. Later research suggests Bell Smith left for New York several days before the murder of Mary Kelly (*see* http://www.jtrforums.com/archive/index.php/t-2921.html).

45. Wilson, G., *Alcohol and the Nation*, p.331.

46. Details of the Shorting case in Proceedings of the Old Bailey online, reference t18880702-684, and reports in the *York Herald*, 30 May; *The Times*, 30 May and 6–7 June; *Reynolds's Newspaper*, 10 June; *Morning Post*, 5 July. In another coincidence, Elizabeth Fisher, the sister of 'Ripper' victim Catherine Eddowes, lived near the Hatcliffe Arms at No. 33 Hatcliffe Street.

47. White, J., *London in the 19th Century*, p283; Sims, G., *How the Poor Live*, p.79; *The Autobiography of Margot Asquith*, p.43.

48. Astell case in Proceedings of the Old Bailey online, reference t18880528-546, and reports in *Lloyd's Weekly Newspaper*, 29 April; *Morning Post*, 9 & 16 May; *Reynolds's Newspaper* 13 & 20 May; *The Times*, 16 May; and the *Pall Mall Gazette*, 31 May. If the source of the quarrel between the two women emerged at the inquest it was not revealed in the newspapers. The *Standard* said that the evidence of the husband and a friend of Mrs Astell 'made the origin of the quarrel perfectly clear'.

49. Besant's article 'White Slavery in London' was published in *The Link* magazine, Issue 21 (23 June 1888). Report on the end of the strike in *Reynolds's Newspaper*, 22 July 1888. Further details from Raw, L., *Striking a Light*, pp.129–53, 231, and Pelling, H., *A History of British Trade Unionism*, p.97.

50. Stanley, H.M., *In Darkest Africa*, p.247; Liebowitz, D., *The Last Expedition*, pp.117, 159, 177. Stanley was equipped with a prototype of the world's first self-powered machine gun, invented by Hiram Maxim in 1884 and manufactured in Hatton Garden, London.

51. Savages quote by Julian Huxley in 1888, taken from Fishman, W.J., *East End 1888*. Lord's daughter anecdote in Rideal, C.F. & Moser, M., *Stories from Scotland Yard*. The princess' visit to Merrick is told in Howell, M. & Ford, P., *The True History of the Elephant Man*, pp.151–5. Merrick had previously been displayed at a shop in Whitechapel Road.

52. Sims, G., *How the Poor Live*, p.3; Goldsmid, H.J.J., *Dottings of a Dosser*, p.9; Kapp, Y., *Eleanor Marx*, Vol. II, p.263.

53. Furore for social facts quote from *Tempted London*, p.215; Booth's poverty line in Fishman, W.J., *East End 1888*, p.4.

54. *Illustrated London News*, 22 September 1888, p.352; *East London Observer*, 15 September 1888, quoted in Curtis Jr., P., *Jack the Ripper and the London Press*, p.130.

55. Ex-Detective Inspector John Sweeney wrote in his 1904 memoir, *At Scotland Yard*, about his personal experience of the 'native population' being driven out by the influx of foreigners, pp.300, 313. See Fishman, W.J., *East End 1888*, for a more detailed picture of Jewish immigration.

Notes

56. Report on the Lords Sweating Committee, *Reynolds's Newspaper*, 18 November. Report from the Select Committee on emigration and immigration (foreigners), 1888, p.40; Gainer, B., *Alien Invasion*, p.60; White, J., *Problems of a Great City*, p.144.

57. Report of the select committee on immigration and emigration (foreigners) pp.40-42; Booth, *London Labour*, Vol. I, part 3, pp.543, 550.

58. Details of boot finishing from report on House of Lords committee on sweating and *Reynolds's Newspaper*, 18 November. Scene at soup kitchen from Israel Zangwill's 1892 novel *Children of the Ghetto*, p.11.

59. Potzdamer story found in *Lloyd's Weekly Newspaper*, 5 February; *Aberdeen Weekly Journal*, 4 February; *The Times*, 4 February; *Morning Post*, 2 & 4 February. The Jewish witnesses at the inquest required an interpreter. To put Potzdamer in perspective, some of these papers also carried a report of a chemist who poisoned his wife, six children and himself in Salford.

60. Quote on the Mint by Thomas Miller in *Godfrey Malvern*, p.226, quoted in White, J., *London in the 19th Century*, p.9; Fuller, R., *Recollections of a Detective*, p.34; Goldsmid, H.J., *Dottings of a Dosser*, p.63; Divall, T., *Scoundrels and Scallywags*, p.31.

61. Statistics on Post Office, http://postalheritage.org.uk/page/statistic; Dickens, C., *Dictionary of London* (1888), p.200.

62. Hall case in Proceedings of the Old Bailey online, reference t18890107-178, and reports in *The Times*, 12 December; *Lloyd's Weekly Newspaper*, 16 December and 13 January; *Morning Post* 22 December and 10 January, 1889.

63. *Household Words*, Vol. II (1850), p.463; White, J., *London in the 19th Century*, pp.85, 88, 106, 116.

64. Flanders, J., *The Invention of Murder*, p.77; Report of the Commissioner of Police for the Metropolis for the year 1888, p.3.

65. Dew, W., *I Caught Crippen*, pp.1, 85; Leeson, B., *Lost London*, pp.17, 30; Wensley F.P., *Detective Days*, xii, pp.1-2, 8, 13; Sweeney, J., *At Scotland Yard*, pp.1, 13; Divall, T., *Scoundrels and Scallywags*, pp.11,13; Fuller, R., *Recollections of a Detective*, p.23; Carlin, F., *Reminiscences of an ex-Detective*, p.18; Neil, A., *Forty Years of Man-Hunting*, pp.51, 277; Cavanagh, T., *Scotland Yard Past and Present*, pp.2, 24. The Report of the Commissioner of Police for the Metropolis, 1888, states that 2,291 suspects were taken into custody for assaults on police, with 2,230 summarily convicted or held to bail, thirty-three discharged by magistrates and twenty-eight committed for trial (of which twenty-one were convicted and seven acquitted).

66. Rothenstein, W., *Men and Memories* (1931), p.167. The correspondence of James McNeill Whistler: www.whistler.arts.gla.ac.uk. In June 1888 Whistler resigned from the Society of British Artists after a feud with other members.

67. Lewis case details from Proceedings of the Old Bailey online, reference t18880702-656, and reports in the *Morning Post*, 2 June; the *Standard*, 2 & 5 June; *Lloyd's Weekly Newspaper*, 3 June; *The Times* 5 & 23 June and 7 July; *Reynolds's Newspaper*, 10 June. According to Richardson, J.H., *Police!*, p.101, widows of constables killed on duty received a pension of £15. According to the Report of the Commissioner of Police for the year 1888 there were 547 constables assigned to B Division.

68. Smalley G.W., *London Letters*, Vol. II, pp. 369-376.

69. Goldsmid, H.J., *Dottings of a Dosser*, pp.136-7.

70. Bosanquet, B., *Social Work in London*, p.327. The 'Classes against the Masses' slogan is referred to in McKenzie N. & J. ed., *The Diary of Beatrice Webb*, p.149.

71. Proceedings of the Old Bailey online, trial of Burns and Cunninghame-Graham, reference t18880109-223.

72. Browne D.G., *The Rise of Scotland Yard*, p.204; *The Story of the Star*, pp.9-19. The figure of 10,000 is generally accepted, (*see East End 1888*, p.266), while the figure of 150,000 was given in the *Reynolds's Newspaper*, 8 January, in a report of the funeral of one of the marchers.

73. Besant, *An Autobiography*, p.423. *Pall Mall Gazette*, 16 November 1887: 'The Tory Terror. Notes from Trafalgar Square.' Other accounts of the riots can be found in the Proceedings of the Old Bailey online, Burns case reference t18880109-223. The police claimed that seventy-seven constables were injured. The figures of three dead, 200 injured is from *East End 1888*, p.266

74. *Reynolds's Newspaper*, 8 January; *Morning Post*, 9 & 17 January 1888; *Pall Mall Gazette*, 10 December 1887, refers to another fatality, John Dimmick, who was hit over the head and died after developing pneumonia.

75. *East End 1888*, p.266; *Reynolds's Newspaper*, 11 March 1888; *Birmingham Daily Post*, 7 May; *Morning Post*, 16 July; *The Times*, 12 November and 13 December 1888.

76. Allason, R., *The Branch*, p.9; Prothero, W., *The History of the CID*, p.128. *The Rise of Scotland Yard*, p.209; *The Times*, 13 November.

77. Anderson, R., *The Lighter Side*, p.133.

78. Gray, D., *London's Shadows*, p.225; *The Times* editorial calling for use of bloodhounds, 1 October. Warren's statement, the Cobbe letter and reports on use of bloodhounds also in *The Times*, 10 October 1888.

79. 'The Police of the Metropolis' in *Murray's Magazine*, November 1888.

80. 'The Metropolitan Police and its management', a reply to Sir Charles Warren's article in *Murray's Magazine*, by a PC, 1888.

81. *The Rise of Scotland Yard*, p.209; *The Times*, 13 November.

Notes

82. Report of the Commissioner of Police of the Metropolis for the year 1888.

83. The *Illustrated Police News*, 17 November, published the first in a series on unsolved cases, beginning with the 1838 murder of Eliza Grimwood.

84. *The Times* reports, 12 September and 3, 6, 8 & 13 October 1888; *Daily News*, 9 October 1888; Trow, M.J., *The Thames Torso Murders*, pp.45-55. There are also articles on all the cases discussed at the Casebook: Jack the Ripper, www.casebook.org. The 'narrow escape of detectives' was reported in the *Birmingham Daily Post*, 4 October.

85. Shadwell drowning case of George Montel, *Lloyd's Weekly Newspaper*, 3 June 1888. Cooper death from the *Standard*, 30 August 1888.

86. Thames body figures for 1882 from *Thames Torso Murders*, p.19. Missing person's numbers from *Stories from Scotland Yard*, p.86. *The Times* reports, 12 September and 8 October.

87. *Evening Standard*, 29 September. Ripper letter, 5 October, quoted in Begg, P., *The Facts*, p.200; *Police!*, p.134.

88. Conan Doyle, A., *A Study in Scarlet*, pp.12, 15, 18. The short story 'Scandal in Bohemia' is in *The Adventures of Sherlock Holmes*. It was unusual for Doyle to give a full date.

89. French case details from *Daily News*, 24, 26 & 30 July 1888; *Manchester Times*, 28 July; *Lloyd's Weekly Newspaper*, 29 July; *The Times*, 31 July; *Morning Post*, 31 July and 20 August; the *Standard*, 9 August; *Huddersfield Daily Chronicle*, 19 September. The 'Walthamstow Mystery' case was illustrated in the *Illustrated Police News*, 28 July and 4 August.

90. The Smith family are shown living at No.16 Hemsworth Street in the 1871 census and at No.33 in the 1881 census. Albert was born in Suffolk and Ann in Wales. They had at least eleven children. Reports on the case in *The Times* 26, 28 & 30 April and 1, 2, 7 & 9 May; *Daily News*, 28 & 30 April; the *Standard*, 28 April; *Lloyd's Weekly Newspaper*, 29 April and 13 May; *Reynolds's Newspaper*, 6 May; *Penny Illustrated Paper*, 5 May; *Illustrated Police News*, 5 May. The initial description of the case as an 'outrage and murder' in the East End may have been an over-enthusiastic attempt to shock readers just three weeks after the prostitute Emma Smith was sexually assaulted and murdered in Whitechapel. Coincidentally, the 'Ripper' victim Annie Chapman was born Annie Eliza Smith.

91. The *Morning Post*, 29 October; *Birmingham Daily Post*, 29 October 1888; *Lloyd's Weekly Newspaper*, 9 August 1891.

92. *Invention of Murder*, p.166. Report of the Commissioner of Police of the Metropolis for the year 1888, p.32.

93. Sidney Herbert sent Florence Nightingale out to the Crimea during the war and supported her movement for reform. In 1888 'the Lady with the Lamp' was sixty-eight years old and still campaigning from her home at No.10 South Street off Park Lane. Nightingale died in 1910. Details of the Clark case from *The Times*, 25 & 28 January; *Morning Post*, 27 January; *Daily News*, 28 January; *Bristol Mercury*, 28 January; the *Standard*, 28 January; *Lloyd's Weekly Newspaper*, 29 January; *Reynolds's Newspaper*, 29 January and 5 February; *Penny Illustrated Paper*, 4 February. Some accounts give her first name as Louisa and her surname as Clarke, but her death certificate is in the name of Lucy Clark aged forty-nine.

94. Canonbury in Hibbert *et al.*, *London Encyclopaedia*, p.128. Details of the Frances Wright case in Proceedings of the Old Bailey online, reference t18881022-977; and newspaper reports from *The Times*, 17, 18, 19 & 24 May and 21, 22 & 29 September and 6,13, & 20 October; the *Standard*, 23 May, and 13 November; *Lloyd's Weekly Newspaper*, 23 September; *Reynolds's Newspaper*, 14 October; *Penny Illustrated Paper*, 3 November. Details of life of Charles Cole Wright and wife Frances from censuses and birth, marriage and death records.

95. Bright case in *The Times*, 22 May 1888, and Proceedings of the Old Bailey online, reference t18880917-832. Earlier in the year, Maria Bright had given evidence in the trial of Thomas Callan and Michael Harkins, two Irish terrorists accused of plotting to assassinate Queen Victoria during the 1887 Jubilee celebration. The statistic of 26 per cent is quoted in *Invention of Murder*, p.166. Wiener M., *Men of Blood*, p.3-4; Emsley, C., *Crime and Society in England*, p.102; Wright, T., *The Great Unwashed*, p.131-4. Nevinson, M., *Life's Fitful Fever*, p.91.

96. Newman case in Proceedings of the Old Bailey online, reference t18880702-635.

97. Roberts case in Proceedings of the Old Bailey online, reference t18881022-954, and reports in *Lloyd's Weekly Newspaper*, 21 October; the *Standard*, 22 & 24 October; *The Times*, 22 October; Paull Ripley, M.A., *Vermont Hall*.

98. Dickens quote from *Our Mutual Friend* in Hibbert, *London Encyclopaedia*, p.703. Description of Paradise Street from Booth's Poverty Map and Steele, J. ed., *The Streets of London, South East*, p.129. Donne Place no longer exists, having been replaced by the Millpond Estate. Healey case in Proceedings of the Old Bailey online, reference t18881022-999, and reports in *Morning Post*, 28 August and 5 September; *Lloyd's Weekly Newspaper*, 2 and 16 September; *Reynolds's Newspaper*, 2 September; *Daily News*, 20 September.

99. Discussion of 'good' and 'bad' wives, the 'right of chastisement' and increase in convictions for murder, *Men of Blood*, p. 207.

Notes

100. White case in Proceedings of the Old Bailey online, reference t18880423-481, and reports in the *Standard*, 5 and 7 March; *Penny Illustrated Paper*, 10 March, featuring the 'nagging wives' summary; *Lloyd's Weekly Newspaper*, 11 March; *The Times*, 2 May; *Daily News*, 3 May.

101. Barrell case in the *Standard*, 4 July; and *Lloyd's Weekly Newspaper*, 8 July 1888.

102. Case details in Proceedings of the Old Bailey online, reference t18880730-783.

103. Reports in *The Times*, 20 & 21 June and 4 August; *Lloyd's Weekly Newspaper*, 24 June and 5 August; *Morning Post*, 4 August. Mary Sandford was said to be the daughter of a Buckinghamshire farmer, although both her parents were dead. In the 1881 census William S. Jeffery, aged forty-two, architect, is listed as living at No.33 Rollo Street with Mary Jeffery, aged thirty-nine. A retired architect by the name of William Septimus Jeffery died in 1896.

104. Description of Regency Street area of Wesminster in Booth, C., *London Labour*, Vol. II, p.4. Brown case in Proceedings of the Old Bailey online, reference t18881022-955; and reports in *The Times*, 1,2,4,10 & 26 October 1888; *Reynolds's Newspaper*, 14 October; *Birmingham Daily Post*, 4 October.

105. Morrison, W.D., *Crime and its Causes*, p.154. *Crime and Society*, pp.98, 103; *Alcohol and the Nation*, p.308; and *Men of Blood*, p.290.

106. 'Incomplete beings' from Pauline Tarnovsky, 'Anthropological Study of Prostitutes and Female Thieves' (1889), quoted in Rafter, N. ed., *The Origins of Criminology*, p.179.

107. Logan, W., *The Great Social Evil*, pp.6, 96, 179; Greenwood, J., *Seven Curses of London*, p.272. Walkowitz, J., *City of Dreadful Delight*, p.23; *Crime and Society in England*, p.150.

108. Police estimate given in Vicinus, M. ed., *Women in the Victorian Age*, p.77. Return of number of prostitutes apprehended from Report of the Commissioner of Police of the Metropolis for the Year 1888, p.33; *London Labour and the London Poor*, Vol. III, pp.215-260.

109. Argyll Rooms in *Scotland Yard Past and Present*, p.198; *Crime and Society*, pp.96-8. Charrington in *East End 1888*, p.249; and *London's Shadows*, pp.153-5.

110. The Elizabeth Cass case in proceedings of the Old Bailey online, reference t18871024-1058. Statistics for arrests of prostitutes from Report of the Commissioner of the Police for the Metropolis 1888, p.33.

111. Common lodging houses in Rule, F., *The Worst Street in London*, pp.50,78. Report of the Commissioner of Police for the Metropolis for the year 1888, p.6.

112. Smith case in *The Facts*, pp.28-31; Casebook: Jack the Ripper, www.casebook.org/victims/emmasmit.html; *The Times*, 9 April; *Belfast Newsletter*, 9 April.

113. *I Caught Crippen*, pp.91-5; MacNaghten, M., *Days of My Years*, p.57; Nott-Bower, J.W., *Fifty-two years a Policeman*, p148.

114. Casebook: Jack the Ripper; *The Facts*, pp.25-8.

115. The coroner at the Emma Smith inquest, Wynne E. Baxter, similarly declared in that case that 'it was impossible to imagine a more brutal and dastardly assault'. Tabram murder in *The Facts*, pp.32-8, and Casebook: Jack the Ripper. Reports in *The Times*, 8, 10 & 24 August. Interestingly, but most likely irrelevantly, a Henry Tabram, said to be a costermonger from Islington, was charged with using threatening and menacing language to a Martha Tabram in October 1869 (*Lloyd's Weekly Newspaper*, 10 October 1869). This Martha Tabram was said to have a family of six children. The complaint was dismissed.

116. Polly Nichols details from *The Facts*, pp.39-53, and Casebook: Jack the Ripper, www.casebook.org/victims/polly.html; *Dottings of a Dosser*, p.26. Also reports in *The Times*, 31 August and 1,3, 4 & 18, 24 (description of clothing) September.

117. *The Facts*, pp.65-85; Casebook: Jack the Ripper, www.casebook.org/victims/chapman.html. Baxter's summing up quoted in *The Times*, 27 September.

118. A theatrical version of Jekyll and Hyde was staged in London in 1888 and starred the American actor Richard Mansfield but was closed early because of the Ripper murders.

119. Hughes, M., *A London Family*, p.362; Mackenzie, C., *My Life and Times*, *Octave One*, pp.164-5. Account of noisy crowds shouting 'Down with the Jews' in *Lloyd's Weekly Newspaper*, 9 September.

120. *The Times*, 10 & 27 September; Perry Curtis Jr, *Jack the Ripper and the London Press*, p122-39; Dew, *I Caught Crippen*, p.107; MacNaghten, *Days of My Years*, p55; *Diary of John Burns*, 1888; British Library manuscripts add. 46310.

121. Stride details from *The Facts*, pp.136-64; Casebook: www.casebook.org/victims/stride.html ; *Night and Day*, Issue 129, November 1888, p.120.

122. The writing was rubbed off on the orders of Sir Charles Warren for fear it would incite further anti-Semitic feeling.

123. A more famous ear-clipping took place on 23 December 1888, when Van Gogh took a razor to himself at his cottage in Arles. He gave the severed ear to a girl named Rachel at a local brothel. *See* Gayford, M.,

The Yellow House, p.285. Details on Eddowes case from *The Facts*, pp.165-83 and Casebook: Jack The Ripper, www.casebook.org/victims/eddowes.html; *The Times*, 1 October 1888.

124. *The Facts*, pp.267-313; *I Caught Crippen*, p.86. Lyrics of Kelly's song from Casebook: Jack the Ripper, www.casebook.org/victims/mary_jane_kelly. violets.html; *Jack the Ripper and the London Press*, p.204; Buckle, G. ed., *Letters of Queen Victoria*, 3rd series, Vol. I, pp.447-9.

125. Barnado quoted from *Night and Day*, Issue 129, November 1888, p.101. Details of lodging house in Flower and Dean Street from *Night and Day* pp.124,141 in Issue 130, December 1888. Booth's request was reported in *The Times*, 11 December 1888. The Home Secretary announced in Parliament the government could not assist eight days later. Criticism of memorial in letter to *The Times* from J. Llewelyn Davies, of Christ Church, Lisson Grove, 25 December. Booth's plan outlined in Booth, W., *In Darkest England*.

126. Letter to Editor, *The Times*, 17 October from Brooke Lambert, Chairman, The Vicarage, Greenwich. 'Surgical genius' mentioned in letter to *The Times* from E. Fairfield of South Eaton-place on 1 October 1888. Reference to George Bernard Shaw's letter to the *Star*, 24 September; Weintraub S. ed., *George Bernard Shaw, The Diaries*, Vol. I. *The Graphic*, 6 October 1888, p.358. James J. Cooke's letter printed in *War Cry*, 1 December 1888, under heading 'The Latest Whitechapel Murder'.

127. Mylett case from reports in *The Times*, 22,24 & 26 December 1888 and 10 January 1889; *Daily News*, 22 December; the *Standard*, 26 & 28 December 1888 and 3 January 1889; the *Star*, 24 & 27 December; *Birmingham Daily Post*, 27 December; *Lloyd's Weekly Newspaper*, 20 December 1888 and 13 January 1889. As in previous cases, the details given in newspaper reports are often contradictory. Alice Graves' case from *The Times*, 28 December 1887, and *Morning Post*, 4 January 1888. See also Casebook: Jack the Ripper: www. casebook.org/victims/mylett.html; and research into Mylett history at http://forum.casebook.org/showthread.php?t=1071; *The Facts*, p.314. Dew quote in *I Caught Crippen*, p.158. Anderson in *The Lighter Side of My Official Life*, p.136.

128. Rose, L., *Massacre of the Innocents*, p.86; McLaren, Dr T., *Prescription for Murder*, pp.78-9, 83.

129. Gorman case in *The Times*, 28 March; *Lloyd's Weekly Newspaper*, 1 April 1888.

130. Emma Wakefield was the youngest of nineteen children. On her death only two remained alive. She earned 9s a week at Mr Homan's factory at No.93

Charrington Street. Reports in *Reynolds's Newspaper*, 7 October; *Lloyd's Weekly Newspaper*, 14 October; the *Star*, 10 October. Westcott was a freemason and founding member of 'The Esoeric Order of the Golden Dawn' in 1888.

131. Schummacher case in Proceedings of the Old Bailey online, reference t18880917-864, and reports in *Birmingham Daily Post*, 3 July and 25 September; the *Standard*, 3-4 July and 17 & 23 August; *Lloyd's Weekly Newspaper*, 8 July; *Morning Post*, 18 July, 17 August and 25 September; *The Times*, 18 July, 17 August and 25 & 26 September; *Daily Telegraph*, 25 September; *Reynolds's Newspaper*, 30 September. Depositions in case and dying declaration at National Archives, CRIM 1/30/6. James Gloster's role in Matabele Gold Fields Limited in *Freeman's Journal*, 23 January 1895. In 1881 Schummacher was living in Charlwood Street with her one-year-old son. He died the following year.

132. Statistics from fifty-first annual report of the Registrar-General of Births, Deaths and Marriages, 1888. Out of a total of sixty-nine homicides in London, thirty-two victims were aged between zero and three months. It has also been calculated that between 1863 and 1887 more than 60 per cent of all homicide victims were less than twelve months old; *Massacre of the Innocents*, p.7.

133. Irish exhibition details in *The Times*, 4 June 1888. Ruth Newman case from depositions in the National Archives, CRIM 1/30/3; the Proceedings of the Old Bailey online, reference t18880917-823, and reports in *The Times*, 17 & 23 August and 20 September; *Morning Post*, 18 August; the *Standard*, 18 & 23 August; *Bury and Norwich Post*, 21 August. A report in the *Reynolds's Newspaper* for 1 January 1888, reveals that another dead baby boy was found under the seat of a third-class carriage at Mansion House station on Friday, 23 December 1887. The police were unable to track down the mother and the jury returned an open verdict. In March 1888, twin baby girls were found in a basket under the seat of a third-class carriage at New Cross station. They had been left on the train in Brighton by eighteen-year-old waitress Sabina Tilley, who claimed they had suffocated during breastfeeding. She was found not guilty at the Sussex Assizes.

134. Wheatsheaf Alley case in *Illustrated Police News*, 12 May 1888. Wapping case in *Illustrated Police News*, 2 June. Spring Gardens case in *The Times*, 9 July. Limehouse case in *Lloyd's Weekly Newspaper*, 29 July.

135. Estimated suspicious infant deaths from *Invention of Murder*, p.224. It was reported in one newspaper that 200 children a year died by accidental suffocation in Central Middlesex, during an inquiry into the death of a five-month-old girl at her home in Drury Lane after sleeping in the same narrow

Notes

bed as her mother and father. Woolwich mutilation case in *Pall Mall Gazette*, 13 November 1888; and *Lloyd's Weekly Newspaper*, 18 November; Blanchard case in *The Times*, 30 May 1888, and Proceedings of the Old Bailey online, reference t18880702-636. Robson case in *Illustrated Police News*, 26 May 1888; *The Times*, 23 June 1888.

136. Morgan case in Proceedings of the Old Bailey online, reference t18880730-766, and reports in *The Times*, 28 July and 4,8, & 10 August; *Lloyd's Weekly Newspaper*, 29 July; *Western Mail*, 6 August.

137. Burbridge case in Proceedings of the Old Bailey online, reference t18880917-910. Reports in *Reynolds's Newspaper*, 8 July; *The Times*, 2 August and 21 September. Depositions in National Archives, CRIM 1/30/5.

138. It was part of a distinctive red-brick terrace designed by Ernest George and completed in 1887. Number 104F was later occupied by the Irish MP Wilfrid Scawen Blunt in 1892 and the Conservative MP George Wyndham in 1898. The young Winston Churchill lived at No. 105 in 1902.

139. Magson case in *The Times*, 31 July and 9 August 1888. Depositions at Marlborough Street Police Court in National Archives, CRIM 1/30/2.

140. Lambert case in *The Times*, 16 May 1888; and the *Standard*, 16 May; and Proceedings of the Old Bailey online, reference t18880702-642. Home Office baby case in *The Times*, 8 and 22 November 1884.

141. Hart case in Proceedings of the Old Bailey online, reference t18880423-454 and reports in *Reynolds's Newspaper*, 12 February 1888; *Lloyd's Weekly Newspaper*, 12 February, 18 March and 6 May; *Daily News*, 30 March; *The Times*, 27 & 29 April.

142. Skidmore Street, off White Horse Lane near Stepney Green, no longer exists. Lovett case in Proceedings of the Old Bailey online, reference t18880227-332. Reports in *The Times*, 4 & 29 February. Depositions at inquest in national Archives, CRIM 1/29/1.

143. Israel case in Proceedings of the Old Bailey online, reference t18881119-22; and reports in the *Birmingham Daily Post*, 31 October 1888; *Illustrated Police News*, 3 November; *Lloyd's Weekly Newspaper*, 11 November.

144. NSPCC, *A History of the NSPCC* (2000).

145. In 1891 Longman was in the convict prison at Gillingham, aged twenty. Details of the case from Proceedings of the Old Bailey online, reference t18891118-53. Depositions in National Archives, CRIM 1/32/4. Reports in *Lloyd's Weekly Newspaper*, 22 April 1888; *Daily News*, 23 April 1888 and 25 November 1889; *The Times*, 18 October 1889 and 23 & 25 November 1889; *Morning Post*, 23 November 1889.

146. Wells, H.G., *An Experiment in Autobiography*, p.228.

147. *Reynolds's Newspaper* case in Proceedings of the Old Bailey online, reference t18880917-824, and reports in the *Morning Post*, 11 August; and *The Times*, 20 September.

148. Mulchay (also spelt Mulcahy in some reports) case details from Proceedings of the Old Bailey online, refence t18881210-98 and reports in the *Morning Post*, 21 November 1888; *Reynolds's Newspaper*, 25 November; the *Standard*, 28 November. Dickens at Marylebone Workhouse, Tomalin, C., *Charles Dickens*, xxxix-xlvi; Dickens, C., 'A Walk in a Workhouse', *Household Words*, 25 May 1850. See also details of workhouse at http://www.workhouses.org. uk/StMarylebone.

149. Spickernell case in Proceedings of the Old Bailey online, reference t18890204-214, and reports in the *Daily News*, 31 December 1888; *The Times*, 31 December 1888 and 2 January 1889; the *Standard*, 2 January 1889; *Morning Post*, 14 January. For more on the Submarine Telegraph Co. see http:// atlantic-cable.com/stamps/Cableships/indexstc.htm.

150. Aston case in Proceedings of the Old Bailey online, reference t18880319-407, and reports in the *Morning Post*, 22 February 1888; the *Standard*, 22 February and 21 March; *The Times*, 22 & 28 February; *Lloyd's Weekly Newspaper*, 4 March.

151. Pierrepoint was still in prison in 1893, according to the 'Return of persons sentenced to death for the crime of murder in England and Wales', Parliamentary Papers, 25 April 1893. Details of case in Proceedings of the Old Bailey online, reference t18880702-691, and reports in *The Times*, 28 & 31 May and 6 July, 1888. Neate Street was the home to a ginger beer, ale and mineral water factory belonging to the R. White firm.

152. Rumbold case details from Proceedings of the Old Bailey online, reference t18880730-759. The 1881 census suggests that Rumbold was born in January 1867 and lived in East Street, Marylebone, with his mother and two brothers. His mother Susan, a widower, died in 1886.

153. Letter to *The Times* from 'Regents Park', 29 May, and letter from Romanes to *The Times* on 31 May 1888. This initiated a debate about whether the park gates should be locked. There were also calls for 'an inquiry into the arrangements of the park generally, to be followed by the passing of an act of Parliament'. *See* letters from John Lloyd and W.R.W. on 2 June. For discussion of park in Parliament *see The Times*, 8 & 13 June 1888.

154. Report of further feuding in *The Times*, 31 July 1888.

155. *Lloyd's Weekly Newspaper*, 5 August 1888.

156. Galletly was still serving his sentence in 1893, according to the 'Return of persons sentenced to death for the crime of murder in England and Wales', 1893, Parliamentary Papers. He is listed in the Census of 1891 as being a twenty-year-old labourer at Portland Prison. The execution date was reported by *Lloyd's Weekly Newspaper*, 12 August. Galletly was reported to have behaved well since his detention at Newgate Prison and was being visited twice a day by the chaplain. 'He asserts that the temptation to use the knife was quite sudden, and he committed the act without thinking of the consequences.' Report of reprieve in *North Eastern Daily Gazette*, 15 August 1888.

157. *The Times*, 4 August 1888; Sentences of Cole and others in the *Standard*, 6 August 1888.

158. *The Times* editorial, 3 August 1888.

159. Report on gangs in *Pall Mall Gazette*, 13 October 1888.

160. Lawyers ridiculed the Queen for failing to understand the concept of *mens rea. See* Walker, *Crime and Insanity*, pp.188-190; St Aubyn, *Queen Victoria*, pp.421-2.

161. Clark, R., *Capital Punishment in Britain*, p.258.

162. Mr Justice Hawkins quoted in *The Times*, 5 July 1888. Evidence in Charles Latham trial from Proceedings of the Old Bailey online, reference t18880702-635.

163. Quotes from Proceedings of the Old Bailey online reports on the cases of Emma Aston, Charles Latham, Mary Ann Reynolds, John Brown and Julia Spickernell.

164. Depositions to Greenwich Police Court and coroner's inquest at National Archives, CRIM 1/29/1. Reports in the *Morning Post*, 14 January; *Birmingham Post*, 14 January; *Lloyd's Weekly Newspaper*, 15 January; the *Standard*, 20 January and 2 February 1888; *York Herald*, 4 February.

165. It has since been suggested that Kelly is a candidate for Jack the Ripper because of his mental illness, apparent dislike for prostitutes, history of violence towards women and his claim to have visited the East End after his escape in 1888. Further details in Tully, J., *The Secret of Prisoner 1167;* and papers relating to Kelly held at the National Archives, HO 144/10064.

166. Description of procedure and execution taken from Berry, J., *My Experiences as an Executioner*, pp.12, 30-2, 38-46; and reports of *The Times*, 14 November 1888; and *Lloyd's Weekly Newspaper*, 18 November 1888.

167. Details of the Bartlett case from Proceedings of the Old Bailey online, reference t18881022-953.

168. Before 1837 the monarch was more directly involved in deciding the fate of condemned men and sat with the Privy Council, known as the 'hanging cabinet', to consider the recommendations of the Recorder of London. Queen Victoria was happy to delegate the decision to the Home Secretary, *Capital Punishment in Britain*, p.246. Newspaper coverage of verdict in *The Times*, 25 October 1888, and *Morning Post*, 26 October. Reports on execution date in *Lloyd's Weekly Newspaper* and *Reynolds's Newspaper*, 11 November.

169. The death sentence was also being passed on Newgate Prison itself. Less than a month later the Corporation announced that the City Lands Committee had unanimously agreed to demolish both the gaol and the Central Criminal Court. The plan was to replace it with a 'grand new sessions house, suitable for modern requirements, as well as a fine row of shops', according to *The Times*, 11 December 1888. The new Central Criminal Court opened in 1907.

170. *The Times*, 1 January 1889.

171. Walkowitz, J.R., *City of Dreadful Delight*, p.191. Quote of 'a series of unique atrocities' from *Liverpool Mercury*, 29 December 1888.

172. *Liverpool Mercury*, 29 December 1888.

173. The modernist poet T.S. Eliot and John Logie Baird, the inventor of the television, were both born in 1888.

174. Salisbury pledge to Queen Victoria on two power standard in Porter, R., *London: A Social History*, p.539.

175. In 1888 the state of New York agreed to replace hanging with electrocution.

176. *The Story of the Star*, pp.7, 19.

177. Cornish, G.W., *Cornish of the Yard*, p.1.